Integrating LibGuides into Library Websites

LIBRARY INFORMATION TECHNOLOGY ASSOCIATION (LITA) GUIDES

Marta Mestrovic Deyrup, PhD
Acquisitions Editor, Library Information and Technology Association,
a division of the American Library Association

The Library Information Technology Association (LITA) Guides provide information and guidance on topics related to cutting-edge technology for library and IT specialists.

Written by top professionals in the field of technology, the guides are sought after by librarians wishing to learn a new skill or to become current in today's best practices.

Each book in the series has been overseen editorially since conception by LITA and reviewed by LITA members with special expertise in the specialty area of the book.

Established in 1966, the Library and Information Technology Association is the division of the American Library Association (ALA) that provides its members and the library and information science community as a whole with a forum for discussion, an environment for learning, and a program for actions on the design, development, and implementation of automated and technological systems in the library and information science field.

Approximately 25 LITA Guides were published by Neal-Schuman and ALA between 2007 and 2015. Rowman & Littlefield took over publication of the series beginning in late 2015. Books in the series published by Rowman & Littlefield are

Digitizing Flat Media: Principles and Practices
The Librarian's Introduction to Programming Languages
Library Service Design: A LITA Guide to Holistic Assessment, Insight, and Improvement
Data Visualization: A Guide to Visual Storytelling for Librarians
Mobile Technologies in Libraries: A LITA Guide
Innovative LibGuides Applications
Integrating LibGuides into Library Websites

Integrating LibGuides into Library Websites

Edited by
Aaron W. Dobbs
Ryan L. Sittler

ROWMAN & LITTLEFIELD
Lanham • Boulder • New York • London

Published by Rowman & Littlefield
A wholly owned subsidiary of The Rowman & Littlefield Publishing Group, Inc.
4501 Forbes Boulevard, Suite 200, Lanham, Maryland 20706
www.rowman.com

Unit A, Whitacre Mews, 26-34 Stannary Street, London SE11 4AB

British Library Cataloguing in Publication Information Available

Library of Congress Cataloging-in-Publication Data Available

ISBN 978-1-4422-7032-9 (cloth : alk. paper)
ISBN 978-1-4422-7033-6 (pbk. : alk. paper)
ISBN 978-1-4422-7034-3 (ebook)

∞™ The paper used in this publication meets the minimum requirements of American
National Standard for Information Sciences—Permanence of Paper for Printed Library
Materials, ANSI/NISO Z39.48-1992.

Printed in the United States of America

To our (now retired) Third Amigo, Doug Cook. Thank you for shielding us from the plethora of stinging nettles (editorial minutiae) with grace and humor and playing Lucky Day to our Dusty Bottoms and Ned Nederlander.

Contents

Part III. Designing and Developing Effective LibGuides

Part IV. Pedagogy and Instruction with LibGuides

List of Figures and Tables

FIGURES

TABLES

Foreword

As a trainer and technical support specialist for Springshare, I spent five years exploring how to do things within LibGuides. Returning to academia reminded me that "how" isn't the end-all and be-all. I'm grateful for the chance to write this foreword, as reading *Integrating LibGuides into Library Websites* has provided me (and will provide you) with numerous opportunities to ask why we use LibGuides and what we put in them—and to delve into how other libraries have answered these questions.

This book's strength comes from its focus on content. You'll learn how to come up with, and then apply, a content strategy while using LibGuides. You'll learn how best to set up your navigation and formatting to support that content. You'll learn how to make sure your LibGuides are accessible—because accessible design benefits us all.

You'll learn how to design and present learning activities in various ways—because everyone learns differently (a concept known as Universal Design for Learning). And this book doesn't just focus on the "big concepts" behind LibGuides; you'll find chapters that focus on the practical skills needed to administer, create, and maintain your LibGuides effectively.

This book is an important part of the LibGuides literature. I look forward to seeing the discussions it inspires and how it changes our use of LibGuides for the better.

Laura J. Harris, M.S.I.
Online Learning Librarian
State University of New York, Oswego

Preface

LibGuides started out in 2006 and has since grown into a suite of products called LibApps that now encompass a variety of services and functions. The current products offered by Springshare include LibGuides, LibAnswers, LibAnalytics, LibCal, LibSurveys, LibStaffer, and LibInsight, and new products are being developed all the time—including a product called LibWizard, which allows users to develop tutorials on the fly. Unfortunately, at the time of writing, LibWizard was not available and is not addressed in this book. However, we are excited by the fact that Springshare keeps adding functionality to their popular platform—and surely hope to include LibWizard in future publications.

One of the things that makes LibGuides great is that the user community features a variety of libraries—school, public, academic, and special. Drawing on this vast array of institutions, and the people who work at them, we are able to gain insight into how various constituencies are integrating LibGuides into their websites and how to improve our own usage. In fact, no surprise, that's how we came up with the title of this book: *Integrating LibGuides into Library Websites*. To this end, we need to mention that the audience for this book is—by design—quite broad. New LibGuides users, experienced admins, folks who haven't migrated to version 2, and even those just *considering* buying into the LibGuides package can benefit from this book. We hope everyone who reads it will find a way to level up their library web presence.

We also need to mention that we received a ton of great proposals for chapters in this book, and the final content was selected based on a variety of factors that include, but are not limited to, content, how individual chapters fit with each other, reducing information duplication (as much as is feasible), and other intangibles. Writing style varies from chapter to chapter because we felt it best to let LibGuides/LibApps users speak in their own voice and share their experiences as they see fit. The book is divided into four broad sections: Introduction and Overview of LibGuides and LibApps, Administering and Maintaining LibGuides, Designing and Developing Effective LibGuides, and Pedagogy and Instruction with LibGuides. So go on, take a look, and we hope you find something you can implement at your library. If you have questions about anything, please contact the authors of each chapter. Some have chosen to provide contact information—if they have not and you are unable to find them, please contact the editors and we will put you in touch. Please, enjoy this book. An overview of each section follows.

INTRODUCTION AND OVERVIEW OF LIBGUIDES AND LIBAPPS

You've heard a lot about the new LibGuides, but maybe you're not sure how to leverage the functionality of the new version or whether you should integrate the various pieces of LibApps. This section introduces ideas and options for both newer users and administrators.

ADMINISTERING AND MAINTAINING LIBGUIDES

You've heard a lot about responsive or mobile-first design, but maybe you're not sure how to leverage or integrate the administrative pieces/parts of LibGuides. This section covers the stuff LibGuides administrators and web designers should understand before breaking (and fixing) their LibGuides sites. Support your content creators and users with a solid understanding of LibGuides administration.

DESIGNING AND DEVELOPING EFFECTIVE LIBGUIDES

You've heard a lot about accessibility and usability, but maybe you're looking for both theoretical and concrete ideas to implement to improve your LibGuides content. This section focuses on usability and accessibility recommendations for LibGuides authors and content creators. Level up your LibGuides content with improved accessibility and usability.

PEDAGOGY AND INSTRUCTION WITH LIBGUIDES

You've heard about pedagogy and probably have a clue about teaching, but maybe you're looking for ideas on how to better leverage LibGuides in your teaching. This final section highlights tips and best practices for building effective pedagogy into LibGuides. It's great to have a useful, accessible site as a starting point. Take your LibGuides to the next level using sound pedagogical design and practices.

Chapter 1—"Good Foundations: Setting Up Your LibGuides System for Easy Long-Term Maintenance" by Emily Marie King

LibGuides offers a lot of flexibility and is easy to use which can complicate site maintenance over time. The author discusses defining content strategy even before touching the administrator controls, the initial setup of your LibGuides system, and setting up content workflows.

Chapter 2—"Manager, Librarian, and Web Developer: How a Multidisciplinary Team Reimagined LibApps" by Stefanie Metko, Lauren Pressley, and Jonathan Bradley

LibApps are a set of interrelated systems that can be easily incorporated into a holistic site structure. The authors discuss integrating LibGuides, LibChat, LibCal, LibSurveys, and custom code to provide students and the libraries at Virginia Tech with an integrated user experience.

Chapter 3—"Making the Case for Migration: Enhanced Functionality with LibGuides Version 2 CMS and the A–Z Database List" by Christine Tobias

LibGuides is more than keeping up with user expectations. The author describes preparing for migration to a new system, planning content review and updates pre-implementation, updating for new content, and maximizing functionality.

Chapter 4—"Using LibGuides CMS and Customized Templates to Create and Maintain Your Library Website" by Brighid M. Gonzales

LibGuides functionality is built on the Bootstrap framework. The author provides an overview of Bootstrap and discusses options for building custom templates at the Bootstrap level, adjusting responsive screen-width breakpoints, and modifying page layout and display with CSS.

Chapter 5—"LibGuides Administration" by Paul Thompson

LibGuides administration is fairly straightforward and can benefit from a thorough understanding of the options available. The author steps through each of the administrative options and offers ideas for layout development, CSS and JavaScript troubleshooting using browser development tools, and leveraging LibGuides asset statistics, widgets, and APIs for additional functionality.

Chapter 6—"LibGuides Administration: Roadmap to Engaging Content" by Jennifer W. Bazeley, Jennifer J. Natale, and Elizabeth Sullivan

LibGuides administration can benefit from active content administration, content standards, and user training. The authors discuss organizing and implementing an active content management team and using LibGuides as a resource to train content creators.

Chapter 7—"Content Wrangling for LibGuides Administrators" by Aida Marissa Smith

LibGuides content can easily spiral out of control without a content management strategy. The author discusses processes for building support for an overarching strategy, defining content guidelines, and adopting content maintenance schedules and guidelines.

Chapter 8—"Making User-Friendly Guides: Navigation and Content Considerations" by Joshua Welker

LibGuides design should be informed by information architecture principles and accommodate the mental models of the beginning researcher and expert researchers. The author discusses the usability of various navigation options, makes content usability recommendations, and highlights design challenges affecting content display at various screen sizes.

Chapter 9—"To the Left, to the Left: Implementing and Using Side Navigation and Tabbed Boxes in LibGuides" by Jaleh Fazelian and Melissa Vetter

LibGuides version 2 offers two default templates, the tabbed navigation used in LibGuides version 1 and left-side navigation. Based on focus group feedback, the authors describe a process for transitioning LibGuides from tabbed navigation to side navigation.

Chapter 10—"Making LibGuides Accessible to All" by Danielle Skaggs

LibGuides should be intentionally designed for accessible navigation by people with visual, mobility, and hearing disabilities with screen readers and keyboard navigation and validated by accessibility tools. The author provides accessibility recommendations for the LibGuides administrator and the LibGuides content author.

Chapter 11—"LibGuides: Creating Accessible User Experiences" by Melissa Fortson Green

LibGuides content should be designed to be accessible for users with accessibility needs. The author shares accessibility design challenges and solutions, along with specific considerations for each LibGuides content type, methods for testing usability, and recommendations for administrators.

Chapter 12—"Infusing Pedagogy into LibGuides" by Elizabeth German and Stephanie Graves

LibGuides have become a pervasive instruction tool and need to be designed with good pedagogy in mind. The authors discuss incorporating learning outcomes, lesson plans, and differentiated instruction in LibGuides design.

Chapter 13—"Access and Universal Design for Learning in LibGuides 2.0" by Kimberly Shotick

LibGuides can be designed to be an accessible learning environment using the principles of Universal Design for Learning. The author highlights existing best practices for meeting web standards and offers recommendations for incorporating these into LibGuides.

Chapter 14—"LibGuides Two Ways: Teaching Information Literacy In and Out of the Classroom" by Lucinda Rush

LibGuides are used as instructional tools both in formal settings and informally at a user's point of need. The author describes development of research fundamentals LibGuides which incorporate information literacy and formative assessment.

Chapter 15—"Redesigning LibGuides as Online Learning Modules" by Melissa Gomis

LibGuides can be used as effective teaching tools for technology, providing general overviews of common research and learning tasks. The author discusses supporting a flipped classroom model for open workshops in LibGuides.

One final note, you may wish to also look at this book's sister publication, *Innovative LibGuides Applications: Real-World Examples*, if you want to see some unique ways in which other libraries are using LibGuides/LibApps.

Acknowledgments

Your intrepid editors congratulate the Springshare team for the rollout and continuous improvements of the LibApps suite of LibGuides-related services. All Springshare images have been used with Springshare's permission. No Springshare products were permanently harmed in quests for local expression.

Thanks go to the LITA managing editor, Marta Deyrup, and our Rowman & Littlefield editor, Charles Harmon, for helping us behind the scenes throughout the process. We'd also like to thank each of our chapter authors for their amazing work and expertise. This book would not have happened without their experiences and expertise. We trust that the examples, references, suggested practices, and additional resource lists provided in these chapters will help you in your quest to build accessible, useable, and useful research guides for your libraries and for your users.

We also need to thank Laura Harris of SUNY Oswego for both helping with fact-checking and writing the foreword for this book. Dr. Doug Cook also needs to be recognized—he is enjoying a well-deserved retirement, and though he didn't help directly with this book, his past guidance and his spirit were present with us every step of the way. Finally, Aaron would like to thank his wife, Julie, and daughters, Natasha and Alena, and his whole work gang for their generosity, patience, and fortitude. And Ryan would like to thank his wife, Heatherlee, for her love and patience throughout this process.

I

INTRODUCTION AND OVERVIEW OF LIBGUIDES AND LIBAPPS

1

Good Foundations

Setting Up Your LibGuides System for Easy Long-Term Maintenance

Emily Marie King, MSLS, College of Southern Nevada

LibGuides, like many content management systems, is a powerful platform that helps libraries quickly create and organize online content. This ease of creation is a double-edged sword for many libraries. Content in your LibGuides system can easily become unmanageable without appropriate guidelines and review processes. It is essential to develop a solid infrastructure for efficiently managing the content over time if you are to prevent this. If you are reading this book, you are probably already committed to taking the time necessary to overcome this challenge.

This chapter will describe the steps you can take while setting up your LibGuides system to ensure that long-term maintenance is just as easy as creating an individual LibGuide from scratch. Since this chapter is focused on the LibGuides system setup, it will be most relevant for your institution's LibGuides system administrator, but the ideas covered will be of interest to anyone contributing content to your system. Additionally, while this chapter is focused on administrators who are initially setting up their LibGuides systems, these steps can be applied at any time to create a more robust and manageable platform.

Even though the terms *library website* and *library web presence* seem to refer to the same thing, they encompass two distinct concepts that are important to keep in mind as you read the chapter. The *library website* refers to the library home page and any informational pages that the library maintains. The *library web presence*, on the other hand, refers to the library website, the library catalog, the library databases, and any library presence within the campus learning management system or other online campus portal. Typically the library website is the part of the library web presence that the library can exercise the most control over, but the entire library web presence is how our users experience the online library. Similarly, the term *content creator* applies to anyone who creates original text or selects links or images that will appear on a LibGuide page. Typically content creators are public service librarians, but with the wide range of content that you can adapt for LibGuides, content creators can be anyone on your library staff or even patrons who are adding content to your LibGuides system.

CONTENT STRATEGY PLANNING

The content strategy step is the most important part of the set-up process. It is here that you will make all the decisions about how your LibGuides system is going to work, how it is going to fit in with the rest of your library web presence, and define why users will visit any of the pages in your LibGuides system. The content strategy step is basically a list of decisions that you need to make up front. When working in a large institution, you should include major stakeholders in this part of the process, as much as possible, to ensure you get their perspective on the needs of your LibGuides system.

Unfortunately, this is also often overlooked because it is entirely nontechnical. Strictly speaking, you can have live content without completing this step. If you skip content strategy, you will be making things harder for your patrons when they try to use and navigate your content. Lack of content planning makes the creation of LibGuides more time-consuming because creators will have to make decisions on the fly, on a guide-by-guide basis, that could have been addressed previously. This usually leads to inconsistent content and policies or lots of extra work reviewing and updating individual guides. Skipping the planning step is the equivalent to setting up a library and figuring out how to organize the books one by one as you get them out of the box.

LibGuides System Purpose

The first decision you will make is what role LibGuides are going to have in your library web presence. Think of this as the mission statement for your LibGuides system. This role will vary widely between institutions. Browsing through the forum pages on the Springshare Lounge (http://springsharelounge.com/group/libguides-2), you will find institutions using LibGuides as a companion to library instruction sessions, as curated guides to specific subjects, as overviews of special collections, or even as their complete library website. The best definitions of purpose are simple and specific, but also broad enough to encompass everything that you need your LibGuides system to do. For example, if you work in an institution where students need a place in the library web presence to learn about the research process and to find library databases and other specific information for research assignments, a good purpose statement for the LibGuides system would be *LibGuides are instructional web pages that teach students how to navigate the research process and informational web pages that direct students to the best resources for their assignments.*

LibGuides System Goals

When you define the purpose of your LibGuides system it will, by necessity, be overarching. The next step is to break down your purpose into smaller, concrete Lib-Guides system goals. The more specific and task orientated you can make these goals, the easier it will be set up your system. Also, it will be easier for your patrons to use the site once it is live. These goals should be functional and not specific to a subject or content area. A good rule for these goals is that stakeholders outside of the library (for instance, a student or faculty member you may be working with) should be able to read the goal and understand it. Another thing to keep in mind as you create these goals is that you do not want to have goals that overlap. An individual LibGuide should only fit one goal. We will eventually be mapping these goals into groups in the LibGuides system, and each guide will only be able to be part of one group.

Let's look at the purpose we defined earlier in order to help in creating goals: Lib-Guides are instructional web pages that teach students how to navigate the research process and informational web pages that direct students to the best resources for their assignments. Now we'll break this statement into discrete goals. Appropriate goals for this purpose might include the following: provide tutorials on how to do common research tasks, highlight specific resources students will need for specific classes, highlight the best resources for getting started in popular subject areas, or provide a list of all library databases that relate to a specific subject area. Depending on your purpose statement, you might also consider some of these other common goals for LibGuides: provide profile information and subject expertise for individual librarians, provide information about a specialized collection held at the library, provide directions on how to navigate a specific library database, provide information about library events, provide a home page for the library, or provide information about grant programs available through the library. This is by no means an exhaustive list, but it can help you to start thinking about goal articulation.

Integration

Users must be able to locate your guides if they are to be successful. While it is tempting to just put a link to LibGuides on your home page and then let patrons find it themselves, it will be far more effective to strategically integrate the content with your library web presence. To do this, take each of your goals and ask these questions:

- Who does this content serve?
- How are users interacting with the library now?
- Where can we place this content so users can find it?

Many libraries will not have concrete data to answer these questions, but fortunately, data is not strictly necessary. The purpose of these questions is to put yourself in the shoes of the patrons that have information needs that your LibGuides solve.

If we wanted to do this exercise with one of the goals we defined before, it might look like this:

Goal: Provide tutorials on how to do common research tasks.

- Who does this content serve?
  This content is designed to serve two groups: the students who need to learn how to do research tasks and instructors who are teaching students how to do research.
- How are these users interacting with the library now?
  The students who don't already know how to do research are not likely to be familiar with the library web presence and are likely being directed to this content because of a course assignment that requires research or because an instructor has sent them here as part of an assignment. The instructors looking for this content are most likely familiar with the research process and the library website from their previous experiences doing research.
- Where can we place this content so these users can find it?
  For the students, having this content in their learning management course would be the most direct way to access it. If that is not possible, a link in the main navigation or the home page that matches the wording they are likely to hear from their instructor is probably the best way to connect them to this content. For the instructors, since they have most likely used the library website before, it would probably be most helpful to have links to library tools for instructors or library tutorials on the library home page or main navigation.

These questions put you in the shoes of your potential users who will use the content in your library web presence. Once you have defined the purpose, goals, and ideas about how your LibGuides content will be used and accessed, you are ready to start programming the system.

LIBGUIDES SYSTEM SETUP

This step of the process is the technical part. Here you will map the settings and goals, which you have already defined for your library, into the LibGuides system. This is mostly handled by your LibGuides administrator. If you do not have administrator access, you will be restricted to the default LibGuides settings or the LibGuides system settings the administrator has set up for you.

Most settings have three levels: system settings, group-level settings, and guide-level settings. Guide level will override group level and group level will override system level. If a setting is not set at the group or guide level, then that setting will be automatically inherited from the higher level. Please note that LibGuides is an evolving system, and your LibGuides system might have additional options that are not mentioned here.

LibGuides System-Level Settings

The system level includes all the global settings that apply to everything within LibGuides. This is the best place to set the default styles of your LibGuides system to ensure a consistent look and assign names to things that will be used system-wide. To start this customization, go to the Admin menu in your LibGuides system and select System Settings. These will let you define basic information about your library that LibGuides will use like the URL of your library home page and/or your library's EZproxy prefix. All the settings that you can update are clickable, and you will likely need to change most of these before you go "live." This is a general overview of the settings you have to check as part of your system setup. You will find more detailed information about how to choose the best settings for your system and do specific customizations in the next section of this book.

Next go to the Admin menu again and select Look & Feel. The screen you will be looking at is Header / Footer / Tabs / Boxes. Open the page header box. If you have an image that you want as your header upload it to the Page Header section. If you are planning to create a custom header and footer just leave this section alone for now. You have the option of adding two different banner images, one for all the guide pages in your LibGuides system and one for all the other pages that the system will automatically generate for you.

Next go the Tabs & Boxes Options part of the page and set the colors that you want for your boxes and tabs. If you are trying to match institutional branding, your public relations office or marketing office can usually give you the exact hexadecimal colors to match your school colors. Using your institution's predefined hexadecimal colors is preferable to trying to pick colors that look similar because your computer screens often have slight differences in the way they display colors. If you want color ideas, variations, or shades, there are many online sites that will show you color palettes and browser extensions that will assist you in getting hexadecimal color codes. Even if you plan to change the style of your page with CSS, it is best to set up your colors here first because changes will be propagated through the system without any need for extra coding. They will also be automatically applied to any new features that Springshare adds to your system.

After you have finished customizing your colors, go into the Language Options tab. Here you can adjust any text automatically generated by the LibGuides system to match the terminology that your library uses. For example, the system automatically generates a list of subject specialties on your librarians' profile pages with a heading of My Subject Specialties. If you want the heading for that section to be My Subject Areas instead because that is the terminology you use at your library, you would just go into the Custom Value box and type in "My Subject Areas." It will update this language anywhere that has a list of the librarian's subject specialties listed.

You may want to stop your look and feel customization here. If you are not comfortable with editing HTML or CSS, everything beyond this point requires a solid understanding of both. Additionally, if you do feel comfortable with HTML and CSS, but you have customized your site to your liking with the tools we have already used, you want to stop here as well. Long-term maintenance of your LibGuides system will always be easier if you limit the number of features you are incorporating. Nonetheless, many institutions choose to further customize their systems.

Adding Custom Headers, Footers, and CSS Styles

The most common reason for custom HTML and CSS in LibGuides is to change the header or footer. The header and footer will wrap your content in code that will make your pages look like the others from your institution. This is usually done when there is a common header and footer running through your institutional site.

If your library website is already responsive, start by copying all the HTML code that makes up your library header and footer into a plain text document. This will be the code that is the same on all your pages. Make sure that you note each piece of the code you change and why. This way, anyone going back to it will be aware of the potential conflicts. If your main library website is not responsive, you will need to create a new header and footer specific to LibGuides.

Once you have made these updates to the code you are ready to add them into the LibGuides system. Go to the Admin menu and select Look & Feel; then in the Headers / Footers / Boxes / Tabs tab, select Page Header. Paste and save your HTML code into this box. Do the same with the footer code in the Page Footer section. The header code will now appear just after the <body> tag pages and the footer code will now appear just before the </body> tag.

Because we have not added the CSS, your pages will probably look a bit funny, but we will fix that now. LibGuides already has three different sets of stylesheets added. The first stylesheets that are loaded are the stylesheets from the Bootstrap CSS library (http://getbootstrap.com/). This library is responsible for most of the responsive classes that control the layout, tabs and pill navigation, and look of forms. The second stylesheet library that is pulled in is the Font Awesome Icon library. This CSS library lets you create scalable icons by adding classes into your HTML. You can view the library of icons and get more information about it at http://fontawesome. io/. Lastly, you have the LibGuides common CSS files. These are the stylesheets that control the LibGuides specific classes. Most of the classes that are defined in these stylesheet include "-lg-" in the class or ID name for a component on an individual LibGuide or "-lib-" in the class or ID name for page automatically generated to make them easier to recognize in your code.

Just like with your header and footer HTML, you probably want to go to your main library website and copy the CSS files into a plain text document. Remove any CSS rules that do not apply to the header and footer HTML code that you have added. After these rules, add any additional CSS to customize the look of LibGuides to your needs that are not covered in your library's existing CSS rule. Common updates are changing the font, changing spacing, and hiding elements that you don't want in your LibGuides system. Almost every CSS element that can be modified is in either the Bootstrap or LibGuides stylesheets, so make sure that you reference those stylesheets to understand how to override in your CSS rules. Be mindful that CSS element IDs may be named differently on the main LibGuides page compared to an individual subpage. For example, the ID for the name of the LibGuide is s-lib-public-header and the ID for the name of the page on each sub-page is s-lg-guide-header. If you want to change the size, font, or color of these texts, you need to write the rule to include both IDs. Specific customizations you may want to make are covered in other sections of this book.

Once you have your CSS rules written, you will go to the Admin menu again, select Look & Feel, and select the Custom JS/CSS. Anything added in this section will be added to the <head> section of all the pages in your LibGuides system. This code will load after all the other stylesheets, so it will override styles LibGuides calls by default. If you only have a few CSS rules, it is best to add them to this section using <style> tags. If you have many rules, you should save your CSS rules into a separate CSS document and use the link tag to pull it into the document here. This will require external server space as LibGuides does not have an option to upload a CSS document.

Using Templates

The last system-level setting that you have the option to configure is the page layout. Go to the Admin menu and select Look & Feel, then go to the Page Layout. When you click the tab you will see a list of the type of pages that have different layouts. Select a page you would like to edit. Once a page is selected, you will see layout options that you have for that page. You can choose whether you want a side navigation menu or a tabbed navigation menu for each LibGuide. For the LibGuides home page layout, you can choose which widgets you want to appear. All the pages have an option to apply a custom template. The basic LibGuides package from Springshare allows you to create one custom template for each type of page. The LibGuides CMS package allows you to create unlimited custom templates.

Custom templates let you change the HTML template that a page uses to generate content. These are one of the most powerful customization tools in the LibGuides system, but you should proceed with caution. When you create a custom template you are changing the base HTML that the pages will use to create your content. Accidently deleting essential HTML code in a template can throw the entire page off. It is best to only do small tweaks to the HTML templates and limit your changes to things you cannot accomplish through the other customization tools. Make sure you document any changes that you make to the template, so when Springshare makes changes to the default LibGuides system, you can check your template to make sure there are no conflicts.

Go to the Admin menu to create a custom template and select Look & Feel, then go to the Page Layout tab. Select one of the standard pages you would like to edit and then select Customize Templates. Because these templates are designed to be tweaks of the default template, you should start by selecting the template that most closely matches what you want do. You will see HTML and LibGuides Keywords that represent content that will be pulled out of the LibGuides Database to create the page (for a list of keywords with explanations about the data they retrieve, view the LibGuides documentation here—http://support.springshare.com/libguides/guidetemplates/customizeguidetemplates).

If you want to change the layout, you will need to use the grid layout classes provided by the Bootstrap library instead of creating your own layout styles. More information about using the Bootstrap layout grid can be found later in this book and in the Bootstrap documentation (http://getbootstrap.com/css/#grid). When you complete your layout changes, select "Save as New Template." After you have saved your custom template, you can apply it to that page type under the layout options header.

LibGuides System Level Content

LibGuides has a great deal of content that you can set up at the system level. Just like having the look and feel of the LibGuides system set at a system level to give your users a consistent experience, setting all the content you can at a system level will also ensure that you have a consistent patron experience. Common images like library logos, pictures of library events, library spaces, and library staff are things that content creators may need. You can create a shared library of these images that all content creators will have access to so that they are always using the most current ones. To add images to your shared library go to the Content menu, then select Image Manager. In the image manager you will have a personal library and a shared library. Add any common images into the shared library to make them available to your content creators. If you have other Springshare products, images in the shared library will also be available to use in them.

Databases are the next piece of content that you will want to set up at a system level. To add databases you will go to Content menu, then select Assets. Then select the tab for A–Z Databases List. You can either add databases one by one or import databases from SerialsSolutions or an Excel XML spreadsheet. There are two main reasons to add your databases here instead of just adding a link to them from a guide. First, by adding databases to this asset list, you are providing one location in LibGuides that has the information for each individual database. If anything changes with a database—like when there is a new URL or a name change, or if you decide that you are no longer going to subscribe to it—you can just change the information in this record, and it will automatically update the information everywhere in your system. The second reason is that by adding database assets here you automatically add them to a dynamically generated A–Z Database List.

When you set up your databases, you will notice that there is a subject association option for each one. This is another system level content setting that you will want to activate. Like the automatically generated A–Z Database List, LibGuides also creates an automatic page with all content that is associated with a particular subject (e.g., databases, guides, and librarians). These subjects can also be used for the LibGuides API and widgets if content creators want to add widgets to guides that have an automatically updating list of databases.

While not required, you may want to create common assets and boxes that will be used on multiple guides. Things like your catalog search, library hours, citing help, and other general descriptions about your library and services are good candidates for this type of content. The easiest way to do this is by creating a private guide that content creators will be able to copy. Similar to the databases, this will make it easier for content creators to add these to their guides and it will allow you to update all the guides at once if needed.

Guide Types and Group-Level Settings

The guide types and group-level settings will allow you to divide your content into logical areas. Having your goals in hand will help you focus your decisions on the strategic goals that you have for LibGuides implementation at your institution. First, we will look at the automatic pages set up by your LibGuides system. They are the home page, search results page, automatically created subject pages (those generated based on subject associations added to librarians, databases, and guides), librarian profile pages, and list of databases pages. Take each of the goals that you have for your system and see if one of these automatically generated pages will meet them. Let's look at the goals that we defined in the first part of this chapter:

1. Provide tutorials on how to do common research tasks.
2. Highlight specific resources students will need for specific classes.
3. Highlight the best resources for getting started in popular subject areas.
4. Provide a list of all library databases that relate to a specific subject area.

Our first and second goals do not lend themselves to the pages that are automatically created by the LibGuides system. The system does not use course information or common research task information to generate these pages, so they would be hard to map to those pages. However, the third and fourth goals might be solved by the subject pages because both goals relate to subject areas. Let's think about the typical content you will have on these pages. For the third goal we are likely to include the library databases that are best for the subject area: books, journals, and maybe even specific articles that are of interest to that subject area. We also might want to bring in materials from outside the library that are relevant for that subject area, local events, or school clubs.

If we look at the way those subject pages pull and display data, it is quickly apparent that this page might not work for goal 3 because the page cannot automatically generate all the different types of content we are hoping to add; plus we don't want an exhaustive list of *all* the databases, just the best. We also want to give context to the content we do select, so the automatically generated subject pages are not going to work for this goal. Luckily, for our fourth goal, an exhaustive list by subject area is exactly what we need, so we can map that purpose to the automatically generated subject pages. At this point, if you are using the custom template, you might want to make additional tweaks to it to adapt this page to meet the purpose that you have defined.

Since these pages are automatically generated, you will need a plan for all of them even if they don't map to your LibGuides system goals. This is because they will be searchable on the web. Take each page and think about how it would best represent the library if someone googled and found that page in their search results. Create a goal for each group of pages—even if it is a goal that does not directly relate to your LibGuides system's purpose and it is not something that you will actively integrate into your library web presence. After you have defined your goals, look at some example pages to make sure that the goals map to what people find when viewing that page. If needed, go back and update any system settings and page templates to match the purposes that you have defined.

The last type of page is the one on which you are going to have most of your content in LibGuides: the guide page. This is the page type that LibGuides was built for and where all your content creators will be adding their material. LibGuides lets you set guide types for each guide so you can separate them into logical groupings. The default types are general purpose, course guides, subject guides, topic guides, internal guides, and template guides. While these do not come with any styling or coding options, you can use the API and widget tools in LibGuides to pull out all guides of a particular type and add them into a landing page in your main library website (or in any of your LibGuides subpages).

Looking at the goals we have for our LibGuides system, the first three goals can all be accomplished with the creation of custom guides. By giving each of these groups a different guide type, you can point to guides of a particular type from the appropriate places in your library web presence. To ensure that everyone is applying the guide types consistently, make sure you have a clear definition for each of the types so content creators can easily distinguish what type of guide they are creating. When establishing these groups, keep in mind that a guide can only be assigned to one type of guide. If you find that you have a lot of overlap between your type groups, consider using subjects instead.

If you have a LibGuides CMS system, you can go beyond just coming up with definitions about when different guide types should be applied and leverage the widgets and APIs for them. You can also have groups for each of your LibGuides system goals. Each group gets a group home page, and you can create a custom header and footer, custom CSS and JS, custom language options, and custom templates that can be applied just to this group. This is a helpful feature if you want to have group pages as a landing page for your different LibGuides types or if different default layouts are needed for the different types of guides.

Let's go back to our example to see how it will work in practice. We have instructional guides for common research tasks, research guides for specific classes and class projects, and getting started guides for popular subject areas. We will create a new group for each. For the instructional group you will select a template (or create a new custom template) that is conducive to several screens of content viewed in a row because when a patron views them, they should view it all and it should be viewed in a specific order. For the course and subject guides group, a layout that allows users to drill down to a specific section is going to be most relevant for their needs. This means creating a template with an easy and intuitive navigation menu. For the course pages group, you might want to update the CSS rules to create a streamlined look and feel that will be less distracting when pages are loaded into the learning management system (where students are most likely access the content). You can add additional custom CSS that only applies to this group with the group function.

One last note about customizing at the group level: if you are going to create CSS styles for each of your groups and you have access to external server space, you should create a separate style sheet for each group and only include the CSS rules specific to that group. This will prevent potential code conflicts and make it easier to update later. Additionally, add rules that will apply to multiple groups at the LibGuides system level. This will reduce the amount of places that you have to update code if you want to make stylistic changes in the future.

WORKFLOWS

Your LibGuides system is now almost ready to go. The last piece that you need is to add the actual content. You will need to have some workflow policies in place to ensure that the content your creators add has the same consistency you have applied to your setup.

The first workflow that you should set up is for guide creation. The first piece of this policy will be how to do decide if and when a guide should be created. The earlier steps will have already created criteria that you can use to evaluate whether a particular idea should be a guide. Ask yourself, your review committee, or the content creator who had the idea whether this guide fits in with one of the defined LibGuides system goals. You might also want to add some additional criteria outside of the LibGuides system goals that could be relevant to the creation of the guide, such as Do we have someone with the subject expertise to create this guide? Does the staff have the time to devote to the creation of this guide? How important is the guide to our library's strategic goals? Is the scope of this guide too narrow or too broad? The questions will vary greatly based on your specific needs and resources.

As your library evolves, you may find that you want to add new types of content to your LibGuides system that do not fit into your original goals. You should not dismiss these ideas out of hand. Instead, you should plan for how these types of ideas will be addressed. If you decide you want to incorporate a new type of content into your system, you should create a new goal for it. For each new goal, you will have to go through the same steps that we did with our initial goals, so they will involve a larger time commitment than just a new guide. You will need to identify the goal, ask the integration questions, identify a location within your LibGuides system (an automatically generated page, a guide with a particular guide type, or a new group), and set up new workflows. Because of the time involved with setting up a new goal, you should have a defined review process that determines if the new goal is something that you can integrate into your LibGuides system.

Once you identify whether a guide should or should not be created, you need a workflow for the actual creation process. Define the specific content that you want in particular types of guides and where that content might go. For example, you might want a library welcome message and guide explanation on all of your guides. You might want to make sure there is a librarian profile or the library contact information on each guide. You will need to define what information you want for links. You need to define how you want content creators to refer to the library or specific departments within the library. If you have library or institutional style guides, this is a good place to include them. These are all pieces that are not automated, but still need to be consistent across the LibGuides system.

The last step in the creation workflow is to decide how guides will be made available to the public. You need to define clear criteria that have to be met before a guide becomes publicly available. LibGuides has a review process available if a review by a person or committee is necessary; administrators will automatically be notified so that they can review and approve the content. If you decide to turn on the review process, you will want to select reviewers and set a realistic review timeline so that content creators will know when their guide might be available to the public.

Once a guide is created it will not stay fresh and new forever. Links go bad, resources and services get updated, and new resources become available. The next workflow that you need to create is how public guides will be periodically reviewed to ensure that your library does not have out-of-date information in the system. Every library will have a different guide review workflow that works best for its institution, but all policies should have at least three pieces of information. First, you want to have a set timeline. For example, all guides will be reviewed every twelve months, every June, or at the end of each semester. If you have different groups, they can each have their own review timeline that makes sense for them. Content tied to specific course and events will follow the schedule of events where general subject content and tutorials may be used at any time. Having a set timeline will make sure that everyone really looks at his or her guides in a timely matter. Second, you want to make sure someone (or multiple people) is identified to actually do the updating. If you have more than one person who is doing content updating (which will be the case at most institutions), you should assign one person who makes sure that the updating on all guides gets done. Lastly, you will want to create a plan for what to do with guides that are not reviewed. For example, if a guide is not checked for out-of-date content, it will be unpublished until it can be reviewed.

The last workflow that you will need to establish is when and how to remove guides. No matter how wonderful the content is, there comes a time in the life of all information when it is no longer needed. Those guides should be removed. Just as you have clear criteria for when to create a guide, this workflow starts with equally clear criteria for when a guide is removed. Many times these criteria will mirror the criteria you use to decide if a guide should be created. This workflow should define who will do the removal and what will happen to the content that is removed. For example, guides that have been marked for removal from the LibGuides system will be unpublished for a year and then deleted if no one has accessed them in that year. You also want to make a plan for what will happen to any content on that guide that might be shared with another guide.

MOVING FROM SETUP TO YOUR LIVE LIBGUIDES SYSTEM

If you have followed the steps in this chapter, you have finished setting up a robust and sustainable LibGuides system. You are ready to move it from the LibGuides system setup to a live, active, usable website. To make sure your system stays in good working order, you will need to train your content creators on the purpose and goals of your LibGuides, how the LibGuides system works, and the workflows that you have set up. Many LibGuides administrators also find it helpful to create LibGuides help documents and examples for each guide type or group that are specific to your institution. Content creators can refer to these when they are creating their own content.

After your content creators have published their initial content following the guidelines you have laid out for them, you want to go live and add connections to your LibGuides from the appropriate places in your library's web presence. Once these connections are set, your LibGuides system will be live and your content available to your users. The rest of the book will focus on ways to enhance your LibGuides system, but if you have gotten this far, you have the good foundation you need for the rest of your enhancements.

2

Manager, Librarian, and Web Developer

How a Multidisciplinary Team Reimagined LibApps

Stefanie Metko, MLIS, Virginia Tech
Lauren Pressley, University of Washington Tacoma
Jonathan Bradley, PhD, Virginia Tech

OVERVIEW OF LIBGUIDES/LIBAPPS ADMINISTRATION

Many libraries use the Springshare suite for a variety of functions. These include, among others, creation of subject and course guides and website design. This presents a need for strategies and policies related to implementation and management of LibApps. As libraries of all types and sizes strive to adapt their Springshare instance to fit the needs of their unique community, many questions and challenges have developed regarding best practices for administering LibApps across library types. The LibApps suite, particularly LibGuides, offers librarians with limited knowledge of HTML and CSS a platform where they can create and share content quickly and easily (Schroeder and Zarinnia 2012). This is especially helpful to libraries that do not employ a web programmer or those with limited IT resources for updating and maintaining sites. LibChat, another great feature in the suite, makes it easy to offer virtual reference services and to embed those features on the library website, in LibGuides, in institutional course management sites, or in many other areas. LibCal makes booking library spaces much easier, and LibSurveys allows for simple design and customization of forms and surveys. These are just some of the many features available from Springshare, and all are designed for ease of use in libraries of all types and sizes.

Other concerns have emerged in the library literature regarding cognitive load theory and the use of LibGuides and LibApps features. Cognitive load theory is based on the idea that cognitive capacity for learning is limited and that learners are often "overwhelmed by the number of information elements and their interactions that need to be processed simultaneously before meaningful learning can commence" (Paas, Renkl, and Sweller 2004, 1). While librarians have been creating guides for library patrons since the 1950s, the invention of LibGuides has transformed the way that students engage with these guides as they are now digital (Little 2010). Given this shift in the way librarians create guides for their users, user experience design and website development principles have become a pressing area of need for librarian professional development.

In some ways, the ease of use of LibApps is what makes it even more imperative that policies and procedures are in place to guide the use of these systems. Despite this ease of use, there are still opportunities for looking at the development of Lib-Guides from a technical lens, and for employing experts when administering the LibApps suite. This chapter will discuss how one university approached the adoption, reorganization, and administration of the LibApps suite to address challenges and solutions across the library.

HISTORY OF LIBAPPS AT VIRGINIA TECH

Virginia Tech University Libraries (the Libraries) adopted LibGuides as a tool to help market collections. The Collections and Technical Services department had previously maintained subject guides, while Reference and Instructional Services maintained course-specific research resources. Collections and Technical Services identified LibGuides as a tool that would enable collaboration between collections librarians and subject liaisons in building subject guides, and began the process of porting content to the system as the Libraries' inaugural use of the tool.

Though LibGuides was originally a Collections and Technical Services tool at the Libraries, a cross-unit working group was established to ensure all aspects of the tool were considered, including technical setup, training, and the user experience. This volunteer group established basic guidelines for use and served as advocates for the product; several of the instruction librarians in the group also created Virginia Tech's initial course guides as a pilot.

When the library restructured in 2014, LibGuides were reframed as a Learning Environment, and the new Learning Environments unit was responsible for implementation. This shift enabled the Libraries to contextualize LibGuides through a learning context. With this change, the Libraries framed LibGuides as a learning platform that transforms the way faculty and students experience collections and the knowledge these collections provide. As work continued on implementation, the working group evolved into a facilitated learning community in which any interested library employee could participate in discussions about the use of LibGuides. This broadened the community of LibGuides users to include librarians in Research and Informatics and Special Collections.

INITIAL CHALLENGES AND SOLUTIONS AT VIRGINIA TECH

Initially, our challenges were conceptual. We in the Libraries knew that LibGuides could solve existing problems, but it was unclear what the best use of LibGuides might be. Early conversations included an exploration of how formalized subject guides should be—which interested stakeholders determined to be fairly formal. Other conversations focused on how formal course guides should be—which those with expertise in teaching determined should be flexible to meet the needs of individual classes.

Another issue that arose was the question of how to get useful data from library users. A newly formed student advisory board was consulted, though students in that group were not necessarily representative of the average student as they self-selected to serve on a library committee. Student employees were similarly helpful, though not representative of the student body. As the working group evolved, its membership and criteria for useful data also evolved. This allowed the library to move forward on several decisions.

A particularly complex issue for the Libraries was the temptation to use Lib-Guides to solve every web based problem. The Libraries purchased LibGuides at a point when the university's content management system was not easy to use and the Libraries' intranet was being reestablished. These websites were challenging to work with, and LibGuides were a breath of fresh air. People were thrilled to have the capability to create content and to do so easily. Several units adopted LibGuides as the place for their internal working documents. Some individuals chose LibGuides to make comprehensive websites for their areas of service. This decision had cascading effects as it shifted library employees' mental models for LibGuides and set the stage for later challenges in regard to defining the best online tools for various projects.

IDEAS FOR TEAM DEVELOPMENT IN LIBAPPS ADMINISTRATION

Libraries that have recently undergone restructuring or are seeking to find new ways of providing library programs and services in new and emerging landscapes may need to shift the emphasis and thinking about public services away from a collection-driven model to a more learner-centered focus. One way to do this is through the creation of new teams that can leverage existing expertise within the library and that can then fill the gaps in the teams through hiring new people with specific expertise in order to achieve the library's overarching goals. In order to create a strong program that supports both current and emerging models of instruction and self-directed learning, libraries may find it necessary to bring in expertise for help in coordinating a LibApps implementation as well as for help in becoming a catalyst for a strong online learning program in general.

At Virginia Tech, refocusing was achieved through the creation of three new positions: an online learning and education librarian, a web learning environments applications developer, and a learning services and educational technology librarian. To further strengthen the team, the library also drew from existing expertise within the library by adding an instructional designer who had been serving in another capacity within the library, who could serve as a new member of the online learning team. This is a great example of how libraries can take inventory of the human capital they already have while creating new positions to fill gaps in skill sets, and allow the library to move forward in addressing goals and objectives more fluidly.

The design of new positions or the reimagination of positions already housed within the library can be a powerful step toward designing an effective team to manage and create new online learning platforms using the LibApps suite. For example, the online learning and education librarian position was created to be a hybrid position, requiring the person to bring subject matter expertise in education to the Libraries, in addition to significant online learning experience. In this role, the online learning and education librarian could lead conversations across the libraries around online learning, create an intentionally designed and strategic approach to how the Libraries use online learning in their work, and serve as a local expert-consultant helping all liaisons determine the best way to engage in online learning.

Another example of a new position that could be created within the library to assist with the implementation of LibApps is a learning environments web application developer. This role can serve both as a web developer and also bring expertise in learning. Many libraries find themselves in need of someone who has the skill sets to both develop applications and communicate across broad audiences, from teachers to technologists. Organizationally, the Libraries imagined these positions would partner closely with each other and serve to compliment the variety of tasks that would be needed to operationalize the vision for LibGuides and ultimately the entire LibApps suite. In practice, this type of cluster hiring can be beneficial to libraries, particularly for other technology-enhanced projects. For example, at Virginia Tech, this team has partnered on the predesign stages of an online learning platform that will very much align with the mission and vision stated for LibGuides and on other projects such as design of studio spaces for teaching and learning.

GAINING BUY-IN AND LEVERAGING EXISTING PARTNERSHIPS

When creating new team dynamics, it is important for the team to quickly learn the current landscape of LibApps, online learning, and the political culture of their institution while also responding to immediate demands such as needs for the administration of the LibApps suite. In order to gain buy-in from previous people involved in the initial Springshare integration, it is beneficial to evaluate the advantages of continuing the existing system, even if just for some time, to allow people to learn your approach and to gain buy-in for any changes that will be made. One way that Virginia Tech University Libraries accomplished this was through the continuation of what had previously been created—a facilitated learning community that served as a way to onboard the new online learning team, while also establishing their expertise across the Libraries. Given the wide range in skill levels among liaisons and librarians at the Libraries, the team used the facilitated learning community that they called the Springshare Interest Group, as a way to gauge what support was needed, while also fielding questions that the group had for the team.

Finding a balance between the transfer of leadership for the Springshare suite, with the ability for librarians to maintain some ownership and voice in regard to decisions being made about LibGuides, is critical to a successful implementation plan. Developing a community that shares this leadership is one way to increase engagement and enthusiasm among library participants and gain buy-in for the work that you hope to do in the future. It also can serve as a good transition point for libraries that are slowly bringing new people into an administrative role for LibApps. Whenever possible, it is advantageous to attempt to leverage existing expertise from the original implementation team through facilitated conversations, and by scheduling low-stakes meetings that are open to everyone at the library.

There are two main advantages to this approach. First, the team will be able to use these facilitated meetings to introduce new members to the existing library faculty and staff who have a shared interest in Springshare and in turn will also able to communicate the new team's openness to the idea of learning from the history of what had come before them. In this way, implementation team meetings can become more about learning and less about passing ownership and management of the site to a new team. Second, the team can use the facilitated meetings as brainstorming sessions. By opening up the discussion to all library stakeholders, the team will be able to learn about any valuable history involved with past Springshare implementations, such as politics regarding ownership and maintenance of the site, as well as challenges, frustrations, and opportunities for the future. By offering low-stakes meetings that are open to all library staff, participants will feel included in the process and the new team can establish relationships throughout the library that could also spill over into new areas. In addition, the new team can use these meetings to take an inventory of needs within the library, particularly surrounding training needs for LibGuides.

In leading the facilitated meetings, it is a good idea to ask the outgoing leadership team to lead the transition meeting. This can serve as a positive way of introducing the new team while also allowing new conversations to happen naturally. At Virginia Tech, this approach led to high attendance at first and future meetings, and helped position the online learning team as instructional partners with those who had previously been involved in the administrative aspects of LibApps. The librarians and staff in attendance were very open about the challenges that they had faced as well as their needs going forward, and as a result, quick changes could be made.

After this initial meeting, libraries can also benefit from planning a series of future meetings and workshops that are based on feedback received at this first meeting. By creating a series of workshops based on specific feedback from both the old and new administrators as well as from all areas of the library, all stakeholders are able to maintain some ownership for the way that the Springshare instance is administered, which can go a long way toward gaining support for future changes.

In addition to a facilitated learning community, working one-on-one with individual liaisons can also be beneficial. Particularly when a library is in the very early stages of developing an online learning program or integrating Springshare into a specific program, this approach is helpful for communicating with liaisons about the customization and fine-tuning of their LibGuides. This approach also helps generate ideas for how to use other elements within LibApps when carrying out liaison work. Through offering individualized and customized trainings, Springshare administrators can meet librarians and staff at their point of need rather than trying to hold full training sessions that cover all elements of the LibApps suite.

In addition to individualized training, designing library-wide training that covers pedagogy and design of LibGuides as well as the technical aspects of LibGuides can be a successful approach. Often, this is achieved by partnering with others within the library who have specific expertise. At Virginia Tech, this was achieved by the web learning environments applications developer and the online learning and education librarian partnering together to address broad training needs.

When designing workshop content, it is helpful to look back at what feedback the library has received, particularly after holding any type of meetings where feedback was solicited. Surveys can be good for getting this type of feedback, but anecdotal feedback is just as important. Keeping track of any comments or requests that are mentioned either fleetingly after a faculty meeting, or specifically in a written email, is important for designing workshops that address the needs of the library. At Virginia Tech, the workshop design was heavily influenced by the feedback received at the Springshare Working Group meetings to ensure that the content was timely and relevant to those who would be attending, but it is important to keep in mind the culture at your institution when soliciting feedback for workshop training and when designing a multifaceted approach for transitioning leadership of the LibApps suite. All of these things are important for gaining buy-in for bigger changes that the library hopes to make in the future.

STRATEGIES FOR IMPLEMENTING LIBAPPS INTO THE SITE STRUCTURE

While communication and training are important issues to consider during the initial implementation of the LibApps suite, it is also important to focus heavily on site structure and security issues that need attention, particularly as more and more people begin to use LibApps for a range of different purposes. Often issues arise regarding library policy and privileges on the system. Without having a clearly defined policy document it can sometimes become common practice to have too many administrators assigned on the system. At Virginia Tech, this had been commonplace for training purposes so that librarians were able to see all options available to them when creating new assets and learning resources within the system. Over time, however, this practice resulted in a scenario where many people had the ability to completely alter the installation (including some users who no longer worked for the university). Avoiding this situation from the outset is optimal, and the best way to do this is to establish policy documents that address not only stylistic issues within LibApps but also security issues.

LibApps Roles

Libraries that find themselves with a large number of administrators on the system will want to begin cleanup across all of the LibApps systems. One way to approach this initial cleanup is to have clear discussions with both the library administration and the users themselves, to understand what their needs are in regard to use of the system. Once you have clearly defined who needs access to each system within LibApps and have identified administrators for each area within the library, it is important to clearly communicate the changes that will be made. When transitioning administrators to regular users, you will want to have a policy document in place that you can point to if questions arise about the change. In addition, you may want to add language that explains the details of web security and why it is important to limit the number of administrators within a given system. Direct communication with librarians and liaisons during the reassignment of privileges timeline is necessary, particularly when large changes are made.

In addition to creating policy around administration of the suite, it is also important that the implementation team develop protocols for when changes need to be made. For example, at Virginia Tech, we found that any changes made to the system had the potential to impact several users at any given time, and we decided that for future projects like this, we would need a comprehensive communication plan in place before the implementation in order to communicate changes, identify roles, and clarify reasons for changes that were being made.

LibGuides

When administering LibGuides, it is important to take inventory of the existing system and what purposes LibGuides will be used for. Often, LibGuides can become a place for the library to build web content, instead of a learning resource. In addition to the obvious purposes, such as creating subject and course guides for use by faculty and students, the system can also be used to host personnel pages and other internal documents.

Given the many different uses for LibGuides, there is always the risk that administrators will set the default for their LibGuides instance to no-indexing, meaning none of the guides would appear in a Google search. Without indexing, the guides are only marginally available to the public, which, for many institutions, conflicts with their own mission to keep things as open as possible. This is especially true for land-grant universities that share a mission of serving the public. Situations like these are great scenarios for discussion at team or working group meetings as they help the library to gain a better understanding of why these pages are being hosted on LibGuides to begin with, as opposed to the library's website or other places. One argument that often comes up is that LibGuides are easy to edit and librarians can see immediate results when making their changes, which, unlike many websites, often can take days to update once edited.

In Virginia Tech's instance, the group came to the conclusion that the no-indexing rules on the site as a whole would be removed, and a new template would be created containing its own no-indexing code. That template would be used for internal pages for the immediate future. While every institution may need its own customized settings for dealing with issues like these, this can be one solution for libraries to keep LibGuides in the public domain as a learning and information tool. An alternative to dealing with internal pages that are built within LibGuides could be to develop a library intranet, creating another place that could offer the same real-time updating features as LibGuides but that is designed to handle concerns such as security and visibility that are unique to those internal documents.

Another concern that arises when administering LibGuides is how to handle training, test guides, and templates. At Virginia Tech, librarians and liaisons created a large number of test guides and templates during initial training sessions without first establishing a clear naming convention for managing the guides on the back end. This resulted in many practice guides remaining on the site, leaving the back end of the instance cluttered and confusing from an administrative standpoint. Many of the pages had also been copied instead of referenced, resulting in a back end containing numerous duplicate entries and test files with no easy way to tell which were published on the site and which were dead. This cluttered the system.

One way for libraries to avoid a similar issue with their LibGuides instance would be to devise a naming scheme that allows for clarification and flexibility. By setting a timeline for cleaning up wayward pages on the system, the back end will remain clean and manageable. Having a new naming scheme will need to be part of the ongoing training that takes place within the library in order to ensure that it is followed, and it should also be updated in any policy and protocol documents. For instance, a document containing the details of the naming scheme and a rationale for the choices should be created and shared with all stakeholders, including a timeline for when pages will be cleaned up. The goal is to establish a system in which the cleanup would have a scheduled begin date and the document could then go online in the announcement section of the LibApps suite as a reference.

Administrators will need to create templates to help facilitate this transition to the new method of naming and organizing within the LibApps system. These templates should be varied in layout and style, mimicking the most commonly used pages on the library's LibGuides instance so as to allow for the most choice and flexibility for users. At Virginia Tech, multiple librarians identified wanting choice in their LibGuides and did not want to feel confined to a standard template. This request was possible to accommodate with multiple templates while still creating a recognizable and familiar structure for the end users. Libraries that use similar template models can also improve accessibility and usability, which will ensure that creators are following proper design practices for the web.

LibChat

The creation of templates also allowed for the implementation of another feature needing revision in this system: our LibChat functionality. Previously, the system fed all chat requests, even those originating from subject and course guides, to a central chat group that all users on the back end received. While some librarians used the system and answered chats as they came in, the most common source of answers were from the reference or circulation desks, which are staffed by doctoral students. Depending on the major of the LibChat monitor, many times the student worker would not have the subject knowledge to accurately answer questions, leading to inconsistency with the user experience when using LibChat.

With the templates, however, special contact boxes were embedded that would default the chat message to go to a librarian specialized in a particular subject area, and if no response was received, then it would pass the question to the normal chat group at reference or circulation. One challenge with this change was adoption of the new system on the part of subject librarians and other liaisons. Many of the liaisons, especially those who were specialized and had responsibilities for being embedded in departments, felt that they did not have the time to dedicate hours to virtual reference. This setup alleviated the problem because liaisons would only see questions that were relevant to their discipline and could avoid the rest just by choosing the appropriate template. They could also opt out altogether by not going online, and the system would still default to the reference and circulation desks. This is an area that the online learning team would like to address further as we move through our next phase of implementation.

Customizing LibCal and LibSurveys

LibCal is another application in the LibApps suite, which functions as an internal calendar system for booking spaces in the library. One major challenge for Virginia Tech with the LibCal booking feature is that it did not communicate actively with institutional resource calendars such as those in Exchange. However, a great benefit of using LibCal in the integrated LibApps environment is that features from other applications, such as the statistics-tracking features in LibSurveys, can be customized to generate information and visual data about the use of library spaces over time. Generally, application customizations must be negotiated with the LibApps administrators at Springshare, who are often able to create work-arounds that incorporate features in development.

The LibCal and LibSurveys integration and customization at Virginia Tech extended LibCal functionality by adding custom code to the university's instance of LibCal. This modification significantly streamlined the room booking process as imagined by Virginia Tech's library administration. While this example is specific to Virginia Tech, any library (with help from the LibApps administrators at Springshare) can create LibSurveys forms that push data to code hosted on local institutional servers.

The room reservation LibSurveys form data was provided to code hosted locally at Virginia Tech, which processed the data received and generated emails that provided the email recipients with options to approve or decline reservation requests and then transfer approved reservation data back to LibCal. In practice, this customized process would generate an email to librarians in charge of library spaces with end user–submitted data organized in a table. This email also contained two option buttons, one reading Approve and the second reading Deny. If the librarian clicked Deny, then a new email would pop up with the room request information already filled in and the librarian would only have to provide a short justification for the denial before sending. If the librarian clicked Approve, then the reservation data would pass from the email into LibCal, where it would be processed by custom JavaScript code added to the administrative side of Virginia Tech's LibCal instance. The data passed to LibCal would then propagate to the LibCal reservation form automatically. This process has saved a great deal of time for Virginia Tech librarians and has allowed for active record keeping. This is just one example of how various parts of the LibApps suite can work together to create the environment libraries may need at their particular institution.

Virginia Tech's experience with this system is a great example of the flexibility of the LibApps tools. Even when the software doesn't have the exact functionality needed, the staff at Springshare is willing to work with the library to come up with alternatives to achieve the desired result while continuing to develop new features.

BEST PRACTICES AND KEY TAKEAWAYS

Taking a look back at the historical aspects of Virginia Tech's Springshare implementation and then looking ahead to where LibApps is today, it is crucial to understand the major factors that contributed to the success of various apps that are currently working well for the library. First, when implementing LibApps at an institutional level, it is important to understand the stakeholders involved and to keep open lines of communication with them in order to ensure that the suite is used to its fullest and for the right purposes. Second, it is important to consider the strengths and weaknesses of your current team and to maximize those strengths whenever possible. At Virginia Tech, the online learning team has been fortunate to have the combination of a web developer with expertise in coding, a librarian with expertise in instructional design, and a library manager knowledgeable of the political landscape at the Libraries as well as the goals of Learning Environments when integrating LibApps into its current landscape. This configuration allowed the Libraries to bring together technical expertise, and expertise in instructional design, online pedagogy, political, and organizational management and frameworks to the project. This has led to opportunities that wouldn't have existed otherwise. From creating a facilitated learning community to open lines of communication for airing out challenges and frustrations with the LibApps suite, to customizing the actual functionality of the site, to developing and delivering training that is tailored to the staff at the Libraries, every piece of the process was instrumental in the successful implementation and the current state of the Virginia Tech's LibApps instance to date.

REFERENCES

Little, Jennifer J. 2010. "Cognitive Load Theory and Library Research Guides." *Internet Reference Services Quarterly* 15 (1): 53–63. doi: 10.1080/10875300903530199.

Paas, Fred, Alexander Renkl, and John Sweller. 2004. "Cognitive Load Theory: Instructional Implications of the Interaction between Information Structures and Cognitive Architecture." *Instructional Science* 32 (1): 1–8.

Schroeder, Eileen E. and E. A. Zarinnia. 2012. "Creating a Students' Library Website." *School Library Monthly* 28 (7): 29–32.

3

Making the Case for Migration

Enhanced Functionality with LibGuides Version 2 CMS and the A–Z Database List

Christine Tobias, MLIS, Michigan State University

The Michigan State University (MSU) Libraries has a prolific collection of Lib-Guides that serve as an excellent example for other academic libraries. Consistently ranking highly in the number of published guides, the MSU Libraries currently ranks in the top ten overall amongst LibGuides version 2 (LGv2) subscribers with nearly eight hundred published guides, according to Springshare (n.d.). With this degree of visibility and depth of content, it is essential for guides to be organized, findable, usable, and relevant for the teaching, learning, and research community at large. The option to migrate to LGv2 CMS provided the opportunity for the MSU Libraries to achieve these goals. The MSU Libraries is better able to organize and display our guides and electronic resources, increasing the findability and relevance to our students and faculty. This chapter will not only describe the planning and processes undertaken by the MSU Libraries to migrate to LGv2, but also share the philosophies and pragmatism behind the decision to migrate and provide guidance to those libraries that wish to make their own cases for migration.

MIGRATION TO LIBGUIDES VERSION 2 CMS

Selling the Vision

When making an argument to upgrade to a new version of software or to switch to the use of a new product, it is essential to prepare your case in order to sell the vision to stakeholders (e.g., librarians and library administration) before pursuing any course of action. In the case of migrating to LGv2, not only was it important to understand the purpose and subsequent benefits of migrating, but it was also criti-cal to prepare a timeline and outline action steps and expectations for the librarians to ensure a smooth transition. Given that the MSU Libraries had undertaken the grueling process of migrating guide content from an open source system, Libdata, into LibGuides version 1 (LGv1) just a few years earlier, the MSU LibGuides Team wanted to make sure the benefits for migrating to LGv2 CMS would be substantial, while also providing reasonable expectations and minimal burden on librarians.

The MSU LibGuides Team at the MSU Libraries viewed several webinars provided by Springshare to learn about the new features and functionalities in LGv2 CMS and to better understand the technicalities, timelines, and requirements surrounding the migration process. Having a solid understanding and foundational knowledge about LGv2 CMS made migration an easy sale. The benefits of migrating to LGv2 and reasons for purchasing an upgrade to LibGuides CMS were outlined in an email message to the assistant director of public services. The basic premise of the message stated that, in general, LGv2 CMS enhances the visibility and usability of our current LibGuides system. With LGv2 CMS, organization of resources and display of information can be streamlined to enhance findability and increase the relevance of guides for students and faculty. Specifically, the MSU LibGuides Team wished to take advantage of the following benefits available in LGv2 CMS:

- The capability to organize our guide content more efficiently and effectively through the use of Groups. Groups can be assigned to a particular subset of guides based on the type of content (e.g., course, research, collection development policy) or to a particular subset of librarians (e.g., area studies, health sciences, digital humanities).
- Enhancement of the findability of our resources, guides, and subject librarians through the assignment of Subjects.
- Improvement of the presentation of our databases and related resources through a centralized asset manager (A–Z Database List), including the capability to highlight New and Trial Resources and Best Bets.
- Provision of access to guides or Groups based on IP range or password protection. This is an important feature for embedded librarians who teach courses or who work closely with faculty in providing course content within their guides. The protection of guides would ensure that only enrolled students are able to access a guide containing course content (e.g., syllabi, course readings, etc.).

Another selling point of LGv2 CMS for the MSU Libraries was the back-end interface improvements that enhance user friendliness of guide creation, maintenance, and management. Also, in LGv1, customization was possible, but only with a high level of CSS hacking at the system level by the library's web designer (Brandon, Sattler, and Tobias 2011). In LGv2 CMS, however, the system could be customized with moderate skill level in HTML and CSS, so designing the interface of the new system could easily be done by the LibGuides Team.

Preparing for the Migration

Fortunately, Springshare provides a detailed, sequential checklist for migrating content into LGv2 CMS (Burke 2015). In particular, the "Migrating to LibGuides v2 (and Going Live!)" guide outlines the five basic steps of migration, providing guidance for developing a timeline and managing the project. The MSU Libraries determined that it would be best to train librarians on the new system and prepare for the migration to LGv2 CMS throughout the summer with the goal of going live one week prior to the start of the fall 2014 semester. Once the migration to LGv2 CMS was approved by library administration, the MSU LibGuides Team requested a beta site from Springshare, an empty site in LGv2 CMS containing no guide content or interface customizations. Since there are more layout options in LGv2 CMS, having a beta site provided an opportunity to take a closer look and become familiar with the various enhancements such as layout options, column options, header and footer options, tabbed boxes, and image manager. Furthermore, since having a beta site has no effect on the live guide content in LGv1, this was an opportunity to dig deep and explore the new system in great detail to prepare for training and customization of the new interface.

It was essential for the MSU LibGuides Team to establish the information architecture for LGv2 CMS prior to introducing the librarians to the new system. In LGv1, the MSU Libraries had not used the Subjects in the traditional sense; subjects in LGv1 represented categories of guides, such as Course Guides or Research Guides, rather than the academic subject. This setup left much to be desired as it caused confusion for our users who were looking for research help in specific subject areas, thus stifling the findability of our guides. With LGv2 CMS, the MSU LibGuides Team was able to significantly improve the organization of the library's guides through the establishment of Subjects. With this functionality, individual guides and databases could be assigned to one or more subjects. Additionally, the use of Subjects in LGv2 CMS provided an opportunity for the MSU Libraries to highlight subject liaisons by assigning librarians, or guide owners, to their subject(s) of expertise.

Subjects served a different purpose in the organization of the library's LGv1 site, so it was necessary to start from scratch in populating the beta site with Subjects. Rather than reinventing the wheel, the MSU LibGuides Team used a preexisting list of subjects from the library's electronic resources portal to develop the Subjects list in LGv2 CMS. Subject pages were then developed not only as a basic structure for the organization of the LibGuides home page, but also as a starting point for research.

The use of Subjects and the establishment of Subject pages in LGv2 CMS provided the opportunity to categorize guides into groups. To maintain some familiarity in structure between LGv1 and LGv2 for the librarians, the MSU LibGuides Team opted to establish Groups in LGv2 based on the types of guides already present in LGv1. Thus, the following groups were established in LGv2 CMS—Course Guides, Research Guides, Collection Development Policy Statements; customized home pages for each group were designed. To further simplify the categorization of guides, it was decided that all guides would be assigned to General Purpose as the Guide Type. The LibGuides home page was set up to default to the complete list of Research Guides and Course Guides by Subject with the options to display lists of guides by Group or by Expert (i.e., subject librarians).

In LGv1, the MSU Libraries had developed a set of Getting Started guides, highlighting two to three databases as starting points for research in a particular subject area. However, the usage statistics for this collection of guides was disappointingly low despite the value of the content. It was determined that utilizing the features of LGv2 CMS would allow the MSU LibGuides Team to repurpose this set of guides, and the use of Subjects would be particularly beneficial with the development of Best Bets pages as a replacement to the Getting Started guides. By highlighting guides and databases for each subject and providing a profile of the subject liaison(s) with contact information, the Best Bets pages would enhance the findability of the most appropriate guides and resources for each Subject area and improve the usability of the guides.

In LGv1, the A–Z Database List displayed as a list of links in a guide. In LGv2 CMS, the A–Z Database List functions as a central repository in the Assets section of the system. Due to this difference in functionality and to prepare for the integration of the A–Z Database List as an electronic resources management system in LGv2 CMS, some manual labor had to take place. Although Springshare offers the option to specify databases for automatic import into the A–Z Database List in LGv2 CMS, there were two reasons the MSU LibGuides Team did not pursue this option:

- It was not entirely certain that the A–Z Database List in LGv1 was correct and current.
- The MSU Libraries had made the decision to use the A–Z Database List to replace the homegrown system for managing electronic resources and had not yet determined a process for populating the appropriate data accordingly.

Thus, to set up the Best Bets pages at this early stage of migration, the descriptions and URL for the databases listed in the Getting Started guides were manually copied and pasted into the A–Z Database List. Each database entry was assigned its appropriate subject area(s) and identified in the system as a Best Bet for the subject. The development of the Best Bets pages represented the end of an era as the Getting Started guides were slated for deletion once the migration to LGv2 CMS was complete. To help provide context, transparency, and direction to librarians in this transition, a "Death to Getting Started" presentation was given at a monthly Reference Services meeting. To provide context, get buy-in from librarians, and ease the transition between the Getting Started guides in LGv1 and the use of Best Bets in LGv2 CMS, the differences between the two applications were outlined and an explanation of the action steps required by librarians were outlined in an email message and a "Death to Getting Started" presentation was given to the Reference Services staff.

The implementation of Best Bets in LGv2 CMS as a replacement to the Getting Started guides in LGv1 enhanced the findability and usability of the MSU Libraries' guides. By associating content with Subjects and identifying the best starting points for subject-specific research, the relevance of the MSU Libraries' collection of guides was enhanced for the teaching and learning community. Furthermore, the design of the Best Bets pages brought an element of personalization to the research process by highlighting subject librarians through the placement of Profiles on the Subject pages. The MSU LibGuides Team planned hands-on training sessions for librarians, referred to as blank slate training, during the summer of 2014. The blank slate training sessions were used as a means to get buy-in from librarians by introducing them to the beta site and giving them an opportunity to experiment with the new and enhanced features of LGv2 CMS. During these sessions, librarians were also informed about the expected tasks and timelines required for a smooth, successful migration process. The LibGuides Team's main goal was to ease any worries about extensive individual work required for the migration. Six two-hour training sessions were scheduled during June 2014 and librarians were required to register for a session as a prerequisite to having an account created in LGv2 CMS. The objectives for the blank slate training sessions included

1. An introduction to LGv2 and CMS.
2. Providing a timeline for migration and communicating deadlines for the various steps in the migration process.
3. Explaining procedures for migrating to the new system and managing both the LGv1 and LGv2 CMS systems simultaneously.
4. Outlining the steps to clean up guide inventory prior to migration and encouraging evaluation of guide inventories as a means for saving time and effort after the migration.

Fortunately, Springshare provides support documentation with checklists outlining and providing directions for the various steps in the process of migrating to LGv2 (Burke 2015). Since the content framework in LGv2 CMS is different than LGv1, an additional and important step in preparing for the migration to LGv2 CMS is the cleaning up of guide inventory. Due to differences in the structure between the two systems, it may be necessary for guide owners to redesign their guides to take advantage of the new functionalities of LGv2 CMS, such as layout and content options. Some box types would not transfer over from LGv1 to LGv2, so librarians were required to adjust the content appropriately prior to migration. Springshare suggested a time frame of two minutes to two hours per guide after migration to LGv2 CMS for fixing formatting issues. Based on this suggestion and the fact that the MSU Libraries had almost nine hundred published guides in LGv1, the MSU LibGuides Team strongly encouraged guide owners to evaluate their guide content and consider reducing inventory prior to migration as a means for having less work to complete after the migration. Once the beta site was established and librarians had been introduced to LGv2, it was time to clean up the LGv1 system in preparation for a smooth migration. This also provided an excellent opportunity for librarians to evaluate the content of their individual guides using the basic premise that less content to move over resulted in less work in the future. Springshare had emphasized that since the LGv1 and LGv2 frameworks were different, guides would need to be reformatted after migration to take advantage of the full functionality and features in LGv2.

To help librarians and guide owners evaluate their guide content and inventory, the MSU LibGuides Team followed the first step of the "Migration Checklist for Admins, Part I: Cleaning Up LibGuidesv1" (Springshare 2014) to generate reports to identify opportunities to clean up the LibGuides system prior to migration. The series of reports included identifying accounts with no guides, inactive users, guides with stale content (e.g., no updates to content in past six months), duplicate guides, and guides with low hits (e.g., fewer than one hundred hits per year). Reports could also be generated for content boxes that would not be migrated into LGv2 to identify necessary adjustments prior to migration. The MSU LibGuides Team requested Stale Content and Low Usage reports from Springshare, and these reports were shared via email individually with guide owners. Guide owners were asked to consider factors such as relevancy, usage, redundancy, and duplication.

Librarians are dedicated to creating guides, often feeling strong ownership about guide content, and may find it difficult to remain objective when told that a guide has low usage. To get buy-in and motivate librarians into taking steps to evaluate their guide content and clean up accordingly, it was important to provide context in these explanatory messages to preempt defensiveness or push back. To elevate the transparency of the process, each message sent along with the stale content and low usage reports included an outline of the steps with a proposed timeline for the migration process. Naturally, there were librarians who interpreted this message to mean that the MSU LibGuides Team had made a judgment call on the relevancy and usage of their guides and felt as if it was insinuated that the guide was not relevant and should be deleted due to low usage. The MSU LibGuides Team reassured librarians that no judgment calls had been made; this was simply an exercise in sharing information to help assess guide inventory and content appropriately in preparing for migration.

Migration, Clean Up, and Going Live with LGv2

The MSU LibGuides Team requested the one-time migration from LGv1 to LGv2 CMS from Springshare in July 2014. This process simply copied the content over from one system to the other. After the migration was completed, the MSU Libraries kept the LGv1 system as the live system to allow librarians time to clean up any content and address any formatting issues in LGv2 CMS. The librarians had been told at the blank slate training that there would a short time frame in which maintenance of both the LGv1 and the LGv2 CMS systems would be required.

For the remainder of the summer, librarians worked to ready their guides in LGv2, making use of the various design templates, fixing formatting issues, and updating content to take advantage of the new features in LGv2 CMS. Working with the library's systems department to provide a redirect URL and coordinate the logistics of changing the back-end settings, the launching of LGv2 CMS successfully took place a week prior to the start of the fall 2014 semester.

IMPLEMENTATION OF THE
A–Z DATABASE LIST IN LGV2 CMS

Functional Requirements and Task Force Recommendations

The MSU Libraries had used a home-grown system, locally referred to as Erasmus, as a silo for managing and displaying information about the library's vast collection of electronic resources. The existing system was quite old, developed when electronic resources were just emerging onto the landscape. It was never intended to handle a large and diverse number of entries, and while it was painfully obvious that a newer and better system was needed, talks of an in-house redesign did not progress as the level of programming requirements was unrealistic. The Erasmus Redesign Task Force was formed and charged with assessing the front-end interface and making recommendations for improvement. The Electronic Resources Team also developed functional requirements for a new platform. While preparing for migration to LGv2 CMS, we realized that the A–Z Database List offered functionalities recommended by the Erasmus Redesign Task Force, such as assigning Subjects to databases and creating Best Bets pages to highlight databases as starting points for research. Simultaneously, LGv2 CMS was emerging onto the scene and the MSU LibGuides Team noticed that many of the new and enhanced features available in LGv2 CMS were very similar to the programmatic requirements recommended for an improved Erasmus. So, while LGv2 CMS was not initially purchased for the purpose of replacing Erasmus, we quickly realized that the A–Z Database List, a central repository for managing and organizing electronic resource information, would meet the library's needs in managing our electronic resource records and could serve as a portal to our wealth of resources in a user-friendlier interface.

During the summer of 2014, the MSU LibGuides Team worked with the Electronic Resources Team to study the A–Z Database List in LGv2 CMS and analyzed its capabilities against the functional requirements needed for Erasmus's upgrade or replacement. Most of the current functions in Erasmus were found to be available in the A–Z Database List. Additionally, the A–Z Database List offered functionalities recommended by the Erasmus Redesign Task Force, such as assigning Subjects; organizing databases by type, subject, or vendor; and creating Best Bets to highlight subject-specific databases. Another consideration for switching to the A–Z Database List was the level of familiarity held by the MSU librarians for LibGuides. With minimal loss in functionality between the two systems, the implementation of the

A–Z Database List was a practical solution to giving the front-end interface of the electronic resources portal an updated look. Usability would also be enhanced as the management of electronic resource records would be streamlined through the integration of multiple systems into LGv2 CMS.

Functionality and Design of the LGv2 A–Z Database List

The MSU LibGuides Team was charged with handling both the functionality of the system and the design of the interface for the A–Z Database List. Implemented prior to a time when the library catalog held records for single-title e-books and electronic journals and before library users understood how to navigate the Internet efficiently, records were made in Erasmus for proprietary databases, electronic books, electronic journals, and freely available websites. Since librarians had data entry access to Erasmus, workflows and maintenance policies and procedures had to be considered and greatly revised in order to keep the A–Z Database List manageable and unwieldy. The MSU LibGuides Team worked closely with the Electronic Resources Team to revise policies about the population of content and management of data in the A–Z Database List.

Records listed in the A–Z Database List would represent proprietary online databases purchased by the MSU Libraries. Only asset managers, librarians who had admin access to the A–Z Database List in LGv2 CMS (e.g., Electronic Resources Team and LibGuides Team), would have permission to add, change, or delete entries in the A–Z Database List. This procedure varied significantly from the management of Erasmus when all librarians had the freedom to add records for single titles and free websites to Erasmus as desired (resulting in an unwieldy mess of two thousand records). Although we determined that not all of these electronic resources would be transferred to the A–Z Database List, we deemed it necessary to include a selection of nonproprietary resources meeting the following criteria:

- Resources created by the U.S. federal government, access to which fulfills depository obligations.
- Resources created by the state of Michigan.
- Resources created by Michigan State University.
- Resources created by an intergovernmental organization that have compelling reason for inclusion in the A–Z Database List, such as interdisciplinarity and findability.
- Resources created by a major research institution that have compelling reason for inclusion in the A–Z Database List, such as interdisciplinarity and findability.

Landing pages for electronic resources were developed as guides in LGv2 CMS to provide access to resources by format in the categories of Databases, Newspapers, Primary Sources, Media, and Data. The entries in the A–Z Database List would appear on the appropriate landing page for the database type. Librarians would share links with library users via guides by using the Add Database function in LGv2 CMS and mapping to the appropriate entry in the A–Z Database List to display the description and URL for the database. While descriptions were added by asset managers for each entry in the A–Z Database List, librarians had the option to customize the description on the individual guides if desired. Entries in the A–Z Database List will be owned by the Electronic Resources account rather than by individual librarians. Eventually, librarians will map database information in their guides to the appropriate entry content in the A–Z Databases List, but would have an option to provide a Custom Description of the database on guides. Any other settings for a database entry could be changed only by the MSU LibGuides Team or asset managers. The option for providing a Custom Description would alleviate the duplication of entries in the A–Z Database and the mapping functionality would simplify maintenance for the Electronic Resources team.

During the migration from LGv1 to LGv2 CMS, only a few of the databases were automatically populated into the A–Z Database List because the infrastructure of the new system as a replacement to Erasmus had not yet been determined, and it was not clear how the manual transfer of data between Erasmus and the A–Z Database List would be handled. The MSU LibGuides Team and a library support staff member handled the manual process of copying and pasting description, URLs, and subject associations from Erasmus. Upon completion of moving data from Erasmus to the A–Z Database List, the list of electronic resources records included 895 entries to be centrally maintained. The LibGuides Team, along with a support staff member and a student employee, performed quality control, ensuring that all entries had the correct proxy settings and correct LibGuides account owner, and providing any missing information such as Vendor, Database Type, Description, Resource Icon, or Subject Association. The exclusion of freely available websites that are easily found via a Google search helped to keep the volume of entries in the A–Z Database List to a much more manageable level. Librarians were reminded that free websites could be requested for cataloging in the online library catalog. A process was also put into place for requesting the addition of a freely available website into the A–Z Database List. The MSU LibGuides Team was charged with the future responsibility of conducting an annual review of freely available websites in the A–Z Database List including analysis of usage statistics as a means for maintaining the list appropriately.

Once the quality control process for the almost nine hundred entries was complete, the Electronic Resources Team had to be trained on the workflow for the management and maintenance of the A–Z Database List. Prior to the implementation of the A–Z Database List, the Electronic Resources Team had not used LibGuides and lacked familiarity with its interface. Training included review of the criteria for entries in the A–Z Database List and the procedures for adding, changing, or deleting entries as information about electronic resources changed or as errors were found. The Electronic Resources Team was also introduced to the new landing pages created for electronic resources and learned the mapping functionality of the A–Z Database List in LGv2 CMS.

It was necessary to maintain both Erasmus and the LGv2 CMS A–Z Database List simultaneously for a few months to allow librarians time to clean up and change the links to electronic resources in their individual guides, mapping content appropriately to the A–Z Database List to replace any direct links to Erasmus entries. An email message was sent to introduce librarians to the changes brought forth by the transition from Erasmus to the A–Z Database List. The message outlined a set of action steps and explained the how and why of the process to provide transparency. In-person, hands-on training was scheduled during Spring Break week in early 2015. In these sessions, librarians were trained in the functionality of the A–Z Database List, including an understanding in the difference in content from Erasmus; were introduced to new policies and procedures for managing the new system; and were made aware of the action steps required on their part for the maintenance of two systems.

A timeline for switching systems was openly shared with the librarians, and steps were outlined for each part of the process of transitioning from one system to another. Librarians were encouraged to begin using the A–Z Database List instead of Erasmus to present information about databases in their guides. They were also advised to get into the habit of using the A–Z Database List immediately to prevent the pain of fixing broken links, changing URLs, or revising outdated content later. Furthermore, librarians were encouraged to review the content in all of their guides and change any database information originally created as either rich text/HTML or List of Links in LibGuides by mapping any and all database information to the appropriate entry in the A–Z Database List using the Add Database function. From that point on, librarians were advised against entering new information into Erasmus, especially single titles or freely available websites, as these types of resources would appear as guide content only, mapped to the appropriate entry in the Content Items section of Assets in LGv2 CMS. Librarians could have information or settings for an entry changed in the A–Z Database List by sending an email message to a group email address established for the Electronic Resources Team and the Lib-Guides Team. The final deadline for switching systems and implementing the A–Z Database List provided sufficient time for librarians to perform the action steps on their guides and learn the new procedures. The A–Z Database List with corresponding electronic resources landing pages was launched in May 2015.

MAKING THE CASE FOR MIGRATION

With the degree of visibility and depth of content in the MSU Libraries' use of LibGuides, it is essential for guides to be organized, findable, usable, and relevant for the teaching, learning, and research community at large. The enhanced features available in LGv2 CMS help meet these goals, particularly with the application of the Subjects, Groups, and Best Bets. Additionally, the implementation of the A–Z Database List as a replacement to an outdated, local, overextended database was a practical solution for improving the functionality and presentation of electronic resources on the library's website.

The process for implementing the solution was complex, requiring a great deal of time, energy, and commitment, but by breaking down the project into smaller steps, the transition to LGv2 CMS was manageable. One critical element was planning, developing, and customizing the information architecture for the LGv2 CMS prior to migration. Furthermore, it was essential to work closely with various stakeholders in the planning phase, particularly with respect to establishing workflow procedures and policies. Early, frequent, consistent, and ongoing communication throughout the migration process provided transparency and helped sell the vision to library staff. Ongoing training and technical support for LGv2 CMS throughout the implementation helped reduce angst about the process. Overall, this project management approach used by the MSU LibGuides Team sets a good example for other libraries to follow for making their own case for migration and improving the findability and usability of library resources through the implementation of LGv2 CMS.

REFERENCES

Brandon, Jennifer, Kelly Sattler, and Christine Tobias. 2011. "LibGuides Interface Customization." *Online* 35 (1): 14–18.

Burke, Anna. 2015. "Migrating to LibGuide v2 (and Going Live!)." Springshare. Accessed October 23, 2015. http://support.springshare.com/friendly.php?s=libguides/migration.

Springshare. n.d. "LibGuides Community Site." LibGuides Community. Accessed October 23, 2015. http://libguides.com/community.php.

Springshare. 2014. "Migration Checklist for Admins, Part I: Cleaning Up LibGuides LGv1." Accessed November 2, 2015. http://support.springshare.com/ld.php?content_id=70149.

II

ADMINISTERING AND MAINTAINING LIBGUIDES

4

Using LibGuides CMS and Customized Templates to Create and Maintain Your Library Website

Brighid M. Gonzales

Libraries that wish to maintain an independent, easily managed website separate from a centrally managed university or government website have a number of options. Many libraries that manage their own website turn to various commercial or open-source content management systems for easier maintenance, which include Drupal, WordPress, Joomla, and others. Another option libraries may use to manage web content is LibGuides. Familiar to many in libraries as a platform for creating and publishing online research guides, the LibGuides CMS platform includes additional features and functionality that also enable it to be used as a website content management system.

While open-source content management systems are often employed by libraries and can be completely usable with minimal technical knowledge, they often require more complex technical skills to customize or operate at the level necessary for running an entire library website. These open-source systems have the benefit of being freely available and highly customizable; however, what a library saves in the cost of software may be made up for in the cost of employing knowledgeable staff to install, configure, and maintain it. While many such systems do have a community of users to offer support and resources, as well as extensive documentation, they lack the ability to offer personalized assistance.

LIBGUIDES

While not open-source software itself, LibGuides version 2 (LGv2) uses the open-source Bootstrap framework, making LGv2 mobile-first and mobile-responsive right out of the box, so there's no need to maintain a separate mobile site in addition to a desktop site. With so many libraries currently using LibGuides to create, publish, and organize their library guides, many librarians are already familiar with the LibGuides platform. LGv2 CMS offers additional functionality on top of the basic platform, including the ability to create groups, limit access by IP or password, customize individual guides, and use LibGuides APIs. LGv2 CMS also allows an unlimited number of customized templates that can be used along with a custom CSS file to create any look and feel the user wishes. Though users can also upload their own JavaScript files, a thorough knowledge of HTML and CSS are the only technical skills necessary to create a completely custom, independently managed website.

One advantage of using LGv2 as a CMS over open-source software is the full and robust support system offered by Springshare. Users have access to full documentation online, as well as the Springshare Lounge, where a community of LibGuides users come together to post questions and find solutions. Springshare also offers numerous live and recorded online training sessions, as well as personalized online support via email.

Built on Bootstrap

Bootstrap is an open-source web framework that allows for fast and easy web development and comes with built-in components such as a navigation bar and CSS helper classes. Bootstrap uses a simple grid system to lay out content in rows and columns upon which LGv2 is built. The grid is mobile-first, meaning it is created with the mobile view in mind from the beginning rather than accounted for as an afterthought, and scales up to accommodate increasing browser sizes.

In its simplest form, the grid starts out as twelve equal-sized columns, each of which is designated with a class such as .col-md-1, which represents its unit of width. Each set of twelve columns is organized into a row designated by the class .row, and each set of rows is held by a container designated by the class .container. On a mobile device, the twelve columns would appear stacked vertically, while on a larger desktop, the twelve columns would stretch out horizontally as the screen size increased. When the screen size is smaller, the width of the twelve columns automatically scales down until reaching a breakpoint, the point at which the columns will start to drop down into a second row. Figure 4.1 shows a container div holding a single row made up of twelve columns, each representing one unit of width. Table 4.1 is a visualization of what the row would look like with twelve equal-sized columns laid out horizontally.

The total units of width in one row must add up to twelve, but the number of columns can vary. For example, one row can have twelve columns of one unit each as in the preceding example, or three columns of four units each. It can even have one column with the entire twelve units. However, the total width of the row cannot be greater than twelve, or it will cause the extra to wrap onto a second line. Figure 4.2 shows code that produces three columns of four width units as shown in table 4.2.

Columns can also be nested within a single row. Columns that are nested within another column must also add up to twelve. For example, a row might contain two columns, each with a width of six units. But if each of those two columns contains

```
1.  <div class="container">
2.    <div class="row">
3.       <div class="col-md-1">content</div>
4.       <div class="col-md-1">content</div>
5.       <div class="col-md-1">content</div>
6.       <div class="col-md-1">content</div>
7.       <div class="col-md-1">content</div>
8.       <div class="col-md-1">content</div>
9.       <div class="col-md-1">content</div>
10.      <div class="col-md-1">content</div>
11.      <div class="col-md-1">content</div>
12.      <div class="col-md-1">content</div>
13.      <div class="col-md-1">content</div>
14.      <div class="col-md-1">content</div>
15.    </div> <!--end of row-->
16. </div> <!--end of container-->
```
Figure 4.1. Example code showing twelve one-unit columns.

Table 4.1. Example of twelve one-unit columns.

X1	X1	X1	X1	X1	X1	X1	X1	X1	X1	X1	X1

```
1.  <div class="container">
2.    <div class="row">
3.       <div class="col-md-4">content </div>
4.       <div class="col-md-4">content </div>
5.       <div class="col-md-4">content </div>
6.    </div> <!--end of row -->
7. </div> <!--end of container -->
```
Figure 4.2. Example code showing three four-unit columns.

Table 4.2. Example of three four-unit columns.

X4	X4	X4

three inner columns, the width of those three columns would also have to add up to twelve. The code in figure 4.3 will produce the layout shown in table 4.3. The first column is six units wide and contains three inner columns of four units each. The second column is also six units wide but contains two inner columns, one eight units and the other four units.

```
1.  <div class="container">
2.    <div class="row">
3.      <div class="col-md-6">
4.        <div class="col-md-4">content </div>
5.        <div class="col-md-4">content </div>
6.        <div class="col-md-4">content </div>
7.      </div>
8.      <div class="col-md-6">
9.        <div class="col-md-8">content </div>
10.        <div class="col-md-4">content </div>
11.      </div>
12.    </div> <!--end of row -->
13. </div> <!--end of container -->
```

Figure 4.3.   Example code of nested columns.

Table 4.3.   Example of nested columns.

X4	X4	X4	X8	X4
X6			X6	

When laying out columns for a template in LGv2, it's important to make sure the width of each column is appropriate for the type of content that will be placed in that area. Nested columns will allow you to have greater control over the placement of your content, especially as it relates to other elements on the page.

TEMPLATES

With templates, LGv2 lets you exercise full control over the layout of your website. To start with, all web pages in LGv2 have a system default template with tabs at the top of the page and another default template with side tabs. For those who don't like or trust the effectiveness of having tabs along the top of the page, side navigation provides an alternative option. By default, the side tabs will appear on the left side of the page, but by restructuring the template, the layout can be flipped to provide navigation on the right-hand side of the page instead.

Templates are made up of basic HTML and consist of everything that is between the opening and closing body tags of the website page (header and footer content is handled in a separate area). The Mustache template system is used, which enables "content keywords" that dynamically add content to the page later on. LGv2 templates can be accessed in the Admin tab, under Look & Feel, and then under Page Layout. LGv2 admins have the option to allow guide creators to use any template they choose, or they can restrict use to a single, specific template. Allowing guide creators to choose their own template allows for greater flexibility and creativity in the creation of library guides and other web pages, while restricting guide creators to a single template ensures a greater level of consistency across all guides. One thing to keep in mind is that if an admin does lock down the guide layout option to a single template, all guides, including those that have already been created, will be changed to that template, and even the admins themselves will be forced to use only that template. When using LGv2 to create a library website, there may be a need to use more than one template—for example, one template for the library home page and another template for all subpages in the website—making it necessary to leave the choice of template open.

Customizing Templates

Customizing a new template is done using one of the default templates, so it's not necessary to start from scratch. LGv2 administrators can start with all of the basic default information and then remove, hide, or move various elements as they see fit, as well as add in additional elements. When creating a new template, it's a good idea to first enter in the template name and then immediately scroll to the bottom of the page and choose Save as a NEW Template. This prevents accidentally overwriting another template that you may be working off of. While it's possible to edit and save the template code right in the browser, it's good practice to copy the code from the browser and paste it into a text editor to edit. It's also a good practice when making changes to save a version of the code you start with, in case there's a need to go back. Text editors offer several features that can be useful when editing templates, such as syntax highlighting, automatic code indentation, and linking opening and closing tags. Some popular text editors include Sublime Text, Notepad++, TextWrangler, and BBEdit.

Much of what the user will see on the website is produced from the Guide Content section of the template. In the default template, this code is found between the <!--BEGIN: Guide Content --> and <!--END: Guide Content --> comments. This section in the default templates includes the Mustache keyword {{content}}. Including this keyword means that someone creating a guide or web page from this template will be able to add any content they wish to the page, in the form of LibGuides boxes. They will also be able to choose the layout of the page, including the number and width of columns. The rest of the code around the {{content}} keyword could be edited to ensure a specific look and feel to the overall web page, but including just the {{content}} keyword in the template allows the guide creator to have full control over the content he or she adds to the page and its layout.

When using LGv2 to create a library website, you may wish to create a more structured template with a specific number of rows and columns. Using the grid system provided by Bootstrap, you can lay out the page in whatever format you wish.

Each row must have the class .row, while each column must have a class that specifies its width as an increment between one and twelve (.col-md-#). Content for each column can then be put directly into the template or left open for guide creators to add their own content.

Specific content keywords can be used to add content directly to the template. For example, if there is a box within LGv2 that needs to be included in the same location on every page in the website, such as a Contact Info or Ask a Librarian box, that box can be added to the template with the keyword {{content_box_<ID>}}, where <ID> is the ID number of that box (the box ID number can be found by hovering over or clicking on the pencil icon in the upper right corner of the LibGuides box). Once it is in the template, the box will then appear on every guide or web page created with that template, without any extra work on the part of the guide creator.

To allow guide creators to add their own content to a specific area of the template, the {{content_col_<ID>}} keyword is used, where <ID> is the number of the column where the content will be added. For example, a template where a column had the ID #s-lg-col-1 would include the keyword {{content_col_1}} to allow guide creators to add their own content to that column. Column #s-lg-col-2 would include the keyword {{content_col_2}}. A second level of div tags, as shown in figure 4.4, is needed in the template in order to automatically refresh the page when new content is added. Without this second level, after adding a box to a guide you would need to refresh the page before the box would appear.

```
1.  <div id="s-lg-col-1" class="col-md-4">
2.     <div class="s-lg-col-boxes"> <!--second div
    level that allows automatic page refreshing-->
3.        {{content_col_1}}
4.     </div>
5.  </div>
```

Figure 4.4.   Example code showing two levels of div tags.

The Guide Content section of a template is wrapped inside a div that encompasses the entire section. In LGv2 default templates this "wrapper" div has the ID #s-lg-guide-main and the class .container. The .container class is another part of Bootstrap that provides a fixed width based on the browser size and is controlled by media queries. For example, on large desktop browsers over 1200 pixels, a div with the .container class would appear as 1170 pixels in width, while on a tablet the same div would appear as 750 pixels wide. While the LGv2 templates default to this fixed-width container, Bootstrap also provides a full-screen option that allows the div to expand to fit the entire browser window no matter its size. The .container-fluid class achieves this result. A combination of these classes can also be used to achieve the look of a full-width background image or graphic with other content staying within a fixed width. Figure 4.5 shows that the code that controls the image background_image.jpg would span the width of the entire screen, while the content in column 1 would stay at a fixed width of 1170 pixels on a large desktop.

```
1.  <div id="s-lg-guide-main" class="container-fluid" style="background-
    image: url('background_image.jpg');">
2.      <div class="row">
3.          <div id="s-lg-col-1" class="container">
4.              {{content_col_1}}
5.          </div>
6.      </div>
7.  </div>
```

Figure 4.5. Example code showing the use of the .container and .container-fluid classes.

Using some of the built-in classes from Bootstrap gives you more flexibility with your customizations than you would have found in LGv1. These Bootstrap classes can also carry over into the header and footer code of your site. Creating a custom header and footer, as explored in the next section, will tie the entire page together with the template customizations you've already accomplished.

CREATING A CUSTOM HEADER AND FOOTER

The header and footer code for the website can be accessed in the Admin tab, under Look & Feel, and then under Header / Footer / Tabs / Boxes. In the Page Header and Page Footer sections of the accordion, there is a box to enter custom HTML code. The header and footer also use the Bootstrap framework, so any HTML code entered in these areas can also take advantage of Bootstrap's capabilities. The Page Header section also gives the option to upload a banner image rather than using HTML. When uploading a banner, it should ideally be around 1170 pixels wide, the default width for viewing on a desktop. Images that are smaller than 1170 pixels will be stretched to that size when viewed on large screens and may become distorted. Likewise, larger images will be compressed and may also end up distorted.

Like in the templates, the header and footer code can also be wrapped in an encompassing div tag and given either a .container or .container-fluid class to control their width. Also like in the templates, these classes can be used together to create the effect where the background of the header or footer reaches across the full browser window while specific content in each section remains within a fixed-width area.

The Bootstrap NavBar

Bootstrap contains a number of components that are used throughout LGv2 and can be employed within LibGuides customizations, including Glyphicons, Buttons and Dropdowns, and Navs and the NavBar. Documentation for these and other Bootstrap elements can be found on the official Bootstrap website. A beneficial aspect of using Bootstrap to build a NavBar rather than using pure CSS and HTML is that the Bootstrap NavBar is already mobile-responsive. The horizontal NavBar will collapse at a certain screen width called the breakpoint and be replaced with the familiar mobile "hamburger" icon, a square box with three horizontal lines that a user can click or tap to open the hidden menu. The basic code for the default

Bootstrap NavBar can be found on the Bootstrap website (http://getbootstrap.com/components/#navbar-default). With some tweaks and CSS customization, this default NavBar can be tailored to match the rest of the library website and modified to meet any specialized needs.

Changing the Breakpoint

In Bootstrap, the default breakpoint, or the screen width at which the horizontal NavBar will collapse and be replaced with the hamburger icon, is 768 pixels. This can be an issue if, for example, your horizontal menu options start to wrap onto a second row before reaching the breakpoint. The following block of code found on the Coderwall website (Skelly 2014) works as a CSS fix for changing the NavBar breakpoint in Bootstrap. Using the code in figure 4.6 will cause the NavBar to collapse when the browser reaches a width of 1000 pixels.

```
1.  @media (max-width: 1000px) {
2.      .navbar-header {
3.          float: none;
4.      }
5.      .navbar-left,.navbar-right {
6.          float: none !important;
7.      }
8.      .navbar-toggle {
9.          display: block;
10.     }
11.     .navbar-collapse {
12.         border-top: 1px solid transparent;
13.         box-shadow: inset 0 1px 0 rgba(255,255,255,0.1);
14.     }
15.     .navbar-fixed-top {
16.     top: 0;
17.     border-width: 0 0 1px;
18.     }
19.     .navbar-collapse.collapse {
20.         display: none!important;
21.     }
22.     .navbar-nav {
23.         float: none!important;
24.     margin-top: 7.5px;
25.     }
26.     .navbar-nav>li {
27.         float: none;
28.     }
29.     .navbar-nav>li>a {
30.         padding-top: 10px;
31.         padding-bottom: 10px;
32.     }
33.     .collapse.in {
34.     display:block !important;
35.     }
36. }
```

Figure 4.6. Example code that will cause the NavBar to break at 1000 pixels.

Add this code to your custom CSS file and change the "max width" in the first line to the width at which the NavBar should be collapsed. Other customized code can help you make adjustments to other Bootstrap defaults. The next section explains how to change the drop-down menu in the NavBar from opening on click to opening on hover.

Changing the Drop-Down Menu

By default, drop-down menu options in the Bootstrap NavBar only open when a user clicks on the down arrow. The code shown in figure 4.7 can be added to your custom CSS file to cause the drop-down menu to open when a user hovers over it with their mouse. The code is wrapped inside a media query so that the menu can be opened by clicking instead of hovering when the page is viewed on a tablet or mobile device.

```
1.  @media (min-width: 1000px) {
2.      .dropdown:hover .dropdown-menu {
3.          display: block;
4.      }
5.  }
```

Figure 4.7. Example code that will cause the drop-down menu to open when a user hovers over it with their mouse.

In the previous example, the media query is set to a minimum width of 1000 pixels, so at the same point at which the menu collapses it would also revert to opening by a click or tap instead of by hover. This ensures that users viewing the menu on a tablet or phone and not using a mouse will still be able to open and view the menu options.

CSS FOR STYLE AND APPEARANCE

The CSS code determining the overall look and feel of the website can be accessed in the Look and Feel section of the Admin tab in LGv2, in the area for Custom JS/CSS. Before writing any CSS code, it may help to inspect the HTML code of the website to isolate the element IDs and classes that require CSS styling. One way to do this is to view the website's source code. To view a website's source code, right click anywhere on the page and select View Page Source. This will display the HTML code for the entire page. In the Firefox and Chrome browsers, the element inspector will display the source HTML code for a particular element as well as the CSS code that has been applied to it. To use the element inspector, right click on the specific element and select Inspect Element from the menu. The element inspector will also expose the ID and any classes applied to the element.

Table 4.4 shows some specific elements within LGv2 that you may wish to customize and some possible customizations with example code.

Table 4.4. Customizable IDs and classes with code examples.

Element ID or Class	Example Customization

#s-lg-guide-name
The ID that defines the name of the guide/page in LibGuides
	``
	01. #s-lg-guide-name {
	02. display: none;
	03. }
	``
	Code to hide guide name from the display page.
	
	Causes the page to not display the guide name. This can also be accomplished by removing the {{guide_title}}: {{page_title}} content keywords from the template.

#s-lib-scroll-top
The ID that defines the Scroll-to-Top arrow in LibGuides
	``
	01. #s-lib-scroll-top {
	02. bottom: 25px;
	03. right: 25px;
	04. color: blue;
	05. font-size: 2em;
	06. }
	``
	Code to relocate default scroll-to-top arrow.
	
	Moves the Scroll-to-Top arrow to a different fixed location, changes its color and its size.

.s-lib-box .s-lib-box-title
The classes that (together) determine the appearance of a box's title
	``
	01. .s-lib-box .s-lib-box-title {
	02. font-family: Sans-serif;
	03. font-size: 1.375em;
	04. text-align: center;
	05. }
	``
	Code to change the font of box titles within LibGuides.
	
	Changes the font family and size of the title and centers the title within the box header.

Element ID or Class	Example Customization

.s-lib-box-content
The class that determines the appearance of the content inside of the boxes in LibGuides
	``
	01. .s-lib-box-content {
	02. padding: 0;
	03. background-color: gray;
	04. }
	``
	
	Code to change the default padding and background color of boxes within LibGuides.
	
	Removes padding from inside all boxes and makes the background color of box content gray in all boxes.
	
	#s-lg-box-<ID> .s-lib-box-content where <ID> is the ID number of a specific box will change the inside of just that particular box.

.s-lib-box
The class that determines the appearance of the outer part of the boxes within LibGuides
	``
	01. .s-lib-box {
	02. box-shadow: none;
	03. border: 0;
	04. padding-bottom: 50px;
	05. }
	``
	
	Code to remove the default box shadow and border on boxes within LibGuides, as well as adjust padding.
	
	Removes the drop shadow, removes the border and adds 50 pixels of padding to the bottom of all boxes.
	
	#s-lg-box-<ID>-container .s-lib-box where <ID> is the ID number of a specific box will change the styling of just that particular box.

#s-lg-box-<ID> The ID that identifies a particular box within LibGuides	Where <ID> is the ID number of a specific box, apply styling to this element to make any changes to one box that you would have made on all boxes using the .s-lib-box class, including customizing the border, margins, padding, background color, box shadow, etc.

These are just a few of the customizations that are possible when creating a website using LGv2. However, any ID or class within LGv2 can be changed using CSS. Just use the element inspector in Chrome or Firefox to determine the ID or class of the element you want to change, and then apply new CSS accordingly.

Helper Classes

Since LGv2 is built on Bootstrap, it incorporates the use of "helper classes" that are included within Bootstrap and that can make implementing certain features much easier. Adding a helper class to the HTML code means that there's no need to write any CSS code to adjust the style of that element because the CSS is already written into Bootstrap. One very useful helper class, as shown in table 4.5, is the .img-responsive class. By adding this class to an image in LGv2, the image becomes responsive and will scale up or down in size along with the size of its parent container. The .center-block helper class can also be added to the image to center it.

Table 4.5. Helper classes for images.

.img-responsive	Applies a max width of 100 percent, a height of auto, and block display to the image so that it scales up or down in size depending on the size of the browser window.
.center-block	Centers the image within its container.

Another part of Bootstrap is semantic color variables that use a specific set of colors that are assigned a meaningful context. In LGv2 these are assigned to a specific set of colors, as shown in table 4.6, which can be used with helper classes to add semantic context to text or background areas. The following are the various helper classes that can be applied to text or backgrounds within LGv2.

Table 4.6. Helper classes for text.

.text-muted	Applies a "muted," or light gray color (hex #777) to text.
.text-primary	Applies a blue color (hex #337ab7) to text.
.text-success	Applies a green color (hex #3c763d) to text.
.text-info	Applies a lighter blue-gray color (hex #31708f) to text.
.text-warning	Applies a dark orange-brown color (hex #8a6d3b) to text.
.text-danger	Applies a dark red color (hex #a94442) to text.
Helper classes for backgrounds.	
.bg-primary	Applies a blue color (hex #337ab7) to an element's background.
.bg-success	Applies a light green color (hex #dff0d8) to an element's background.
.bg-info	Applies a light blue color (hex #d9edf7) to an element's background.
.bg-warning	Applies a light yellow color (hex #fcf8e3) to an element's background.
.bg-danger	Applies a light pink color (hex #f2dede) to an element's background.

The class .text-danger can be applied to static text or links and will output red text that can be used to provide a warning. Likewise, the class .bg-danger will apply a light pink background to whatever element it is applied to, such as a div. These classes can be used together to create alerts, warning messages, and success messages similar to the way they are used within the LibGuides platform (an example is the warning message you receive when deleting a guide, which displays red text inside a box with a pink background).

Helper classes are built into Bootstrap and can make applying customizations to your site much faster. Explore both the documentation on Springhare's website as well as Bootstrap's official documentation to learn more about helper classes and how they can be used.

CONCLUSION

With advances from the LGv1 system to Springshare's current LGv2 system, LibGuides CMS can be nearly as customizable as various open-source content management systems, without requiring nearly the same level of technical expertise. With basic HTML and CSS knowledge, your LibGuides system can be customized to the extent that visitors to your site may not even be able to recognize it as a LibGuide.

The ability to create your own templates in LGv2 is the main advantage to the new LibGuides system. These templates are highly customizable and the use of content keywords to add dynamic content to your guide pages makes them highly flexible as well. Because LGv2 is built on Bootstrap, you won't need to worry about creating a mobile version of your website or making your website mobile-responsive, because it comes that way out of the box. This will be a great relief to library web developers everywhere who have struggled with creating a desktop site that also looks good and functions well on mobile devices of varying size.

LibGuides' Bootstrap foundation also allows the use of helper classes that will help to add customizations with little effort. As you become more familiar with Bootstrap, customizing your LibGuides website will become easier and more possibilities for customization will become apparent.

Springshare provides a great deal of documentation to walk you through some of the possible customizations, including changing the layout of your templates and applying CSS to LibGuides-specific classes. There are also a large number of resources available online that will help you as you begin to customize your LibGuides website. Some of the most useful online resources are listed in the next section.

ONLINE RESOURCES

The following websites can provide useful information or answer questions for those using LibGuides to create a library website.

- Bootstrap (http://getbootstrap.com/)
  Full documentation for Bootstrap is available at the official Bootstrap website, including the basic code for components like the NavBar, examples of how to implement specific features, and information on additional components and CSS features included with the framework.
- LibGuides Website Examples (http://buzz.springshare.com/producthighlights/libguidescms-as-website/academicexamples)
  Springshare's Springshare Buzz website shows multiple examples of academic libraries that have used LibGuides CMS to create their library websites. Additional links along the left side of the page lead to examples from school libraries, public libraries, and districts/consortia as well.
- Springshare Support (http://support.springshare.com/libguides)
  Springshare provides easy-to-understand documentation on how to accomplish basic customizations within LibGuides. They also provide live online training classes and recordings of previous training sessions. You must be logged into your LibApps (LibGuides version two platform) account to view Springshare's documentation.
- Springshare Lounge (http://springsharelounge.com/)
  The Springshare Lounge is Springshare's online community of users. It's a place where you can ask questions, get answers, and share ideas.
- Stack Overflow (http://stackoverflow.com/)
  Stack Overflow provides another online community of users, this time for developers and coders of all kinds. Googling almost any HTML- or CSS-related question is likely to bring you to an answer on Stack Overflow. If you don't find an answer to your question through Google, you can ask it here.
- W3Schools (http://www.w3schools.com/)
  W3Schools provides a great deal of reference information on HTML and CSS as well as a variety of other web-related information. Also included are lessons, tutorials, and practice areas for getting up to speed quickly.

REFERENCE

Skelly, Carol. 2014. "Change the Bootstrap NavBar Breakpoint." Coderwall, February 28. Accessed October 23, 2015. https://coderwall.com/p/wpjw4w/change-the-bootstrap-navbar-breakpoint.

5

LibGuides Administration

Paul Thompson, the University of Akron

You've set up LibGuides and you're staring at the default settings wondering how you'll go about changing them. Or you've got twenty-seven emails in your inbox from new LibGuides users asking what their password is. Or maybe all you really want to do is find out how many people are visiting your LibGuides pages. Take heart. In this chapter, we'll explore the answers to these questions and set you up to be a successful LibGuides admin.

For most of the topics in this chapter, you'll need no prior website knowledge or skills. You already have the tools you need to review statistics, change passwords, and adjust colors. However, you'll also need a few tools we won't have time to talk about here. Having a working knowledge of HTML and CSS will be necessary to adjust the way your visitors interact with your LibGuides pages. To get the most out of the LibGuides APIs (Application Programming Interfaces), you'll need to know JavaScript. LibGuides is built upon additional frameworks like Bootstrap and jQuery, so it wouldn't hurt to learn those as well. At the end of this chapter is a list of resources to get you started learning these tools.

A note about the syntax used in this chapter. Oftentimes you'll be instructed to click links, and sometimes follow a chain of navigation. Directions like this will appear in the format shown in figure 5.1.

Follow the arrows! If you get stuck and can't find a link or button, use Ctrl+F (Command-F for Mac users). This will pull up a search bar and your browser will highlight every place your search term is used, making finding strings of text a breeze! Finally, make sure your account is at the "admin" permission level. If it isn't, you'll need to request a LibApps promotion from another admin.

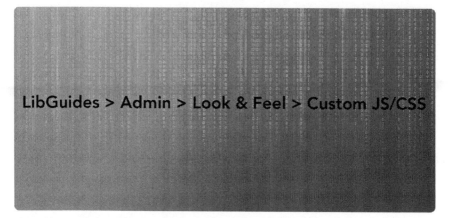

Figure 5.1. Navigate web locations in this chapter left to right. Follow the arrows!

USER ACCOUNTS

Springshare has developed a suite of sweet software (say that out loud for full effect) for libraries. Your institution may subscribe to more than one product, and to provide organization to the software, user account controls can be found in more than one place. System-wide controls can be found in LibApps, while more specific account options fall under the LibGuides umbrella.

LibApps is the container for all Springshare products and comes with its own dashboard. Think of LibApps as the parent of the Springshare family, and the various software products such as LibGuides, LibCal, and LibSurveys as the children. When we view it like this, it makes sense that the options we find in the LibApps Dashboard are different than the ones in the LibGuides Dashboard. Applying this idea to user accounts, we find that indeed, there are different actions we can take that will be determined by whether we are in the dashboard for LibApps or LibGuides.

Fire up your favorite web browser and log in to LibApps. In the top orange bar click Admin > Manage Accounts LibApps will generate a table with user account data from *all* the Springshare products your institution has purchased. Of note here is the ability to see in which products a user is active (labeled Site Count), when the user last logged on, and quick edits to the user's email, password, name, and LibApps account level. These "quick edits" are available by clicking the gear icon to the right of the user on which you'd like to perform the edits (it's always a good idea to let the user know first).

Advanced Account Management

For more in-depth control, you'll need to switch over to the LibGuides Dashboard. Do that now by clicking the blue LibApps button and selecting LibGuides.

Next select Admin > Accounts. You're now able to see the LibGuides accounts in a similar interface. The number of guides owned by a user is displayed to the right, as well as three action icons. Notice the familiar one: gears. While it looks the same as the icon in LibApps, there is a different set of options available here. You can change the user's permission level (LibGuides only) and assign the user to groups if your institution has purchased LibGuides CMS, an optional upgrade to the base software. Recall, to change the user's name, email or password, you'll need to navigate back to LibApps > Admin > Manage Accounts. Also available as an action is the delete icon, symbolized by a gray *x*. Exercise caution when deleting an account. LibGuides will ask you if you're sure and ask you to reassign any assets owned by the user you're about to remove. Deleting the user will remove her from LibGuides, but she'll still have a LibApps account.

Notice the arrow icon sitting to the left of the gears. This is the God mode of LibGuides. Upon clicking this icon, you'll be logged into the user's account, with full access to his owned assets and guides. You'll have the user's level of permissions as well, so keep in mind options available to you as an admin won't be while you're impersonating the him. Use this feature sparingly. Logging in as another user brings great power, but comes with great responsibility. Just in case you turn out to be an evil admin, LibGuides will inform the user that you have logged in as him. Checks and balances, my friend.

Finally, if you wish to add a new user account, this is the place to do it. Click the Add Account button and fill in the required information. LibGuides will check against the account list in LibApps and add the user to LibApps if she does not already exist.

Communicating with Users

Whether you need to let your LibGuides users know you'll be making a system-wide change or just inform them about a new feature, there will come a time when you need to communicate with every user account in LibGuides. This can be accomplished in two ways. If you're still on the LibGuides > Accounts page, notice there is a tab near the top titled Account Emails. Navigating to that tab will show you a list of all emails that you can copy and paste into your favorite email client or mailing software.

But sometimes you're only sending a quick update, or you need your message to persist in a highly visible place for days or weeks. Enter alert boxes. Alert boxes will display your message on the LibGuides Dashboard of all users, and will stay there until you decide otherwise. To create an alert box, be sure you're in LibGuides and navigate to Admin > Alert Boxes. On this page you can create two kinds of alerts—one that will be displayed on the dashboard, and one that will be displayed on the Create Guide page. At the time of this writing, you can have one of each kind of box. You'll be asked to name the box and then you'll be able to add rich text/HTML content to it. To keep your alerts visible, color your text in red or highlight it in another bright, expressive color. Once you save your alert, it will be displayed until you return to this page and delete it. Super handy for that really funny joke you know.

SYSTEM SETTINGS

Find your way into your LibGuides Dashboard, and from there click Admin > System Settings to change, well, system settings. Settings you change here will take effect across all guides. For example, if you add a custom analytics script, it will be placed on every guide, on every page. Other options on this page allow you to set a proxy URL and database vendors, and connect to social media accounts.

The first box visible when your browser loads the System Settings page is the System Information box. You can view your System Version and ID here, as well as change the System Name, Admin Email, and your institution's URL. Below this are tabs for Proxy & Library Systems, Guide Options, Search Options, and Social Media Accounts. Clicking through each of these tabs will display the options available to you and most are straightforward. If you aren't sure what a particular setting does, hover your mouse over the "i" icon next to it (where available).

A couple options bear closer scrutiny. Under Proxy & Library Systems, make sure you have set the proxy URL correctly if you have databases, links, or books that require your institution validate an off-campus network connection. Students at home will not be able to access these resources if your proxy URL is not set correctly.

Under the Guide Options tab you can choose default behaviors for your Lib-Guides. The Default Page Layout option allows you to specify how many columns and the percentage of their widths are presented when a user creates a new guide. If you have particular marketing or branding guidelines, this setting can help develop a consistent look and feel across your guides. More on the LibGuides Look & Feel administration functions later.

The final option of note is the ability to enable or disable Sharing Restriction. Keep in mind that enabling Sharing Restriction will not allow other institutions to copy your guides into their LibGuides system. By default, this restriction is disabled. If you have sensitive, internal data on your guides or you're Scrooge McDuck, you might choose to enable the Sharing Restriction.

While we're speaking of Scrooge, hop on over to the Access Rules tab at the top of your System Settings page. These rules can help you further restrict access to sensitive data, but be careful! It's easy to set up an access rule only to find yourself locked out. Springshare suggests that the first thing you do is set a site-wide rule for your IP address (it is displayed so you know what it is) to avoid looking like the admin that left his keys locked in the running car. Once you've followed this advice, proceed to add rules as you see fit.

Access Rules work like this: First specify the type of rule, Site Rule (Danger! See previous paragraph), Group Rule (LibGuides CMS only), or Guide Rule. Next, set your starting and ending IP addresses. Be sure to coordinate with your network admin to make sure the range you set will have the desired effect. Finally, add a note describing the rule; good administrators document their modifications. The note could read "This rule restricts the Cataloging Manual Guide to be visible only to cataloger workstation IPs." Be descriptive so that someone else can look at the note and understand what the rule is attempting to accomplish.

The final option we'll discuss here is the ability to add custom analytic code to your guides. LibGuides comes built in with robust statistic gathering scripts, but you may want to incorporate a third-party analytic script as well. If you choose to add your own analytic script, be sure to enclose it with <script> tags. Otherwise, when LibGuides inserts this code into your pages, it won't work. As a final step, choose whether to place the script within the <head> tag or before the </body> tag by clicking the appropriate button. Check with your analytics provider to see which spot they require.

SUBJECTS, TAGS, AND GROUPS

Subjects

Properly identifying your guides with subjects and tags will help your users find the information they seek. Any guide listed as a subject guide should also be associated with a subject (you can set a guide as a subject guide either at the time you create a new guide, or by clicking the gear icon in the upper right corner of the guide and choosing Guide Type & Group from the drop-down menu). Before you can do this, however, you'll need to add the subjects relevant to your institution. Navigate to Admin > Subjects, Tags & URLs. If you have added a subject or two, you'll see them listed in gray. If you haven't, you'll need to click the Add Subject button, type in a name, and hit Save.

Once you have your subject list, you can begin to assign *subject experts* and *subject guides*. To assign a subject expert, select a subject then click the Subject Experts drop-down. You'll be able to select from the list of all accounts in your LibGuides system. You can select more than one librarian if your institution is lucky enough to have multiple experts in a given subject. Same goes for guides; you'll usually have more than one guide for a particular subject, and you can multi-select them from the list when you click the Subject Guides drop-down. Subjects can also be applied to guides while in edit mode. If you navigate to a guide while logged in, you'll see the subjects assigned to the guide just below the guide title. Clicking the pencil icon to the right will allow you to change or update the subjects for this guide.

Tags and Friendly URLs

Tags help identify the type of content in your guides and allow users to easily search for the information they need. To add tags, click on the Tags tab on the Subject, Tags & URLs page, then click Add Tag. You can only assign tags on the guide pages in edit mode. Navigate to a guide and look just below the guide title for Tags. Click the pencil icon to the right to add or change tags. You can create new tags here as well as select from existing tags. Back on the Subject, Tags & URLs page, you'll see a Guide Count column that tells you where your tags are being used and an edit icon to the right that will let you update the tag itself. If you update or change a tag, keep in mind that your change will go in effect for every guide using that tag.

URL stands for uniform resource locator. It's a fancy term synonymous with web address. Friendly URLs are another tool at your disposal to help make your content and information discoverable and accessible by your users. It's not easy to remember or type a URL like this: http://libguides.uakron.edu/c.php?g=226551&p=1501167. Adding a friendly URL to your guide will alleviate those annoying trailing symbols and leave your users with something easy to remember and type, such as http://libguides.uakron.edu/3d. On your Subject, Tags & URLs page, you can view all the friendly URLs in your system. As the all-powerful admin, you may want to review this list from time to time, to make sure the friendly URLs being created are, in fact, friendly. If your institution has naming conventions for URLs, this is the place to make sure those are being followed.

Groups

If your institution subscribes to LibGuides CMS, you'll also have the ability to assign guides to Groups. Groups can be public, restricted, or internal. Restricted and internal group settings make it easy to create guides with sensitive content. Internal guides also make great testing environments. Before assigning a guide to a group, the group must first be created. You can do so by navigating to Admin > Groups > Add Group. After you enter the details to create the group, you can then click on the gear icon on your guide edit page and select Guide Type & Group from the drop-down. Your newly created group will appear in the list for easy assignment.

LOOK & FEEL

Here's where the fun begins. Springshare has done a fantastic job making LibGuides fully customizable. With a little knowledge of HTML, CSS, and JavaScript, you can transform the base look of LibGuides into anything you want. Set aside for a moment the ability to make your LibGuides pages look exactly like your existing library website (an essential component of integration), and consider an added benefit: total customization future-proofs your site when the fads of design change. You're in control of how your pages look. Ah, the sweet taste of power.

Before we get into the heavy hitting, let's look at basic customization. For a majority of users, these will be the only changes you'll need. Make sure you're in LibGuides Dashboard and head over to Admin > Look & Feel. The page will load with the gray tab Page Header open; ignore it for now. Skip down to the last gray tab, Tab & Box Options. Would you like to change your color scheme? Here we go . . .

You can set four colors for both tabs and boxes. For tabs, your options are Active Background, Active Font, Inactive Background, and Inactive Font. Think of the words *active* and *inactive* as placeholders for *selected* and *not selected*. A selected tab will show the Active Background and Active Font colors, while all other tabs will display the inactive options. You can choose a color two ways: either use the color picker that appears when you click, or enter the hex code of the color you want (a hex code looks like this: #7BAECA). If your institution has already determined what colors you may use, check with your marketing department for the specific hex codes. Clicking the camera icon next to Tabs or Boxes will show you what you're changing, but it is not a preview for your selections.

The color options for boxes are slightly different. A box in LibGuides is a container that holds your content, so these colors adjust how the box looks but not the content inside. Choose a Border, Background, Header Background, and Header Font color just like you did for the tabs. There's one more option for boxes, and that's Border Width. This determines how thick your box border will be and it is given in pixels. A value of 5 pixels will result in a medium-sized border. If you don't like borders, enter 0 and, like magic, they'll be gone. Both tabs and boxes can also have either square or round corners. You need not feel constrained to select the same option for both. If you want more or less roundness, we'll be able to adjust that with some custom CSS.

Finally, you might want to force all guides to conform to your color choices. Do this by selecting the Lock All Guides option at the bottom of the page. If your institution desires to promote its brand and wants consistency across all user interfaces, this is the option to pick. On the contrary, if you have several groups or departments using LibGuides, you could choose to make your color choices the default for new guides, but allow guide owners to customize their guides. No matter which direction you go, make sure that the tab and box colors are of a high enough contrast to be accessible to those with disabilities.

Custom Header and Footer

You'll need to know HTML to change the way your header and footer look. In case you are a tad rusty on your markup skills, we'll go over some of the basics. For further study, take a look at the books and websites listed in the Additional Resources section of this chapter. It's likely that your institution's website already has HTML code for your header and footer. In this case, integrating the look of your website into LibGuides can be as simple as copy and pasting. If header and footer HTML code is available to you, copy it into the appropriate boxes on the Look & Feel page and then skip ahead to the section on Custom JavaScript and CSS.

Open the Look & Feel page. The Page Header gray tab is open by default. One code-less option exists here: you can add a banner to the header of your page. If you walk this path, you'll need to create or download an image and then upload it on this page. Note: do not add this image to your Image Manager as it will not be available for this page. Another note: when you add an image, you cannot remove it! You can change it or choose not to use it, but as of this writing, it will always be there, perhaps in hopes that you will one day see its worth and put it back into active service. You can overwrite it with another image, but never will it go away. You're also given the opportunity to upload an image for display on your Admin/Guide pages. This image would be visible while users are logged in and editing guides. By way of example, this could be another way to communicate with your users.

You may already know that HTML stands for hypertext markup language. The nitty-gritty of the language means that you add "tags" to your text that define how a web browser interprets your content. For example, the <p> tag identifies the following text as being in a paragraph; a <strong> tag identifies text that should be bold. There are many tags you'll use as you write HTML. Table 5.1 lists the most common, with how they're used. HTML 5 adds some useful tags. Some of the more common tags set aside parts of your page for a specific purpose. Table 5.2 shows you some of the new HTML 5 tags.

Table 5.1.   A list of common HTML tags and examples for when to use them.

Tag	How To Use It
<div>	Used to create divisions of area on a page.
<p>	Separates blocks of text into paragraphs.
<a>	Creates a link to another page or resource. Needs "href" attribute.
<ul>	Identifies an unordered list.
<li>	Defines a list item; used within <ul> or <ol> (ordered list).
<img>	Tells the browser you want to put an image here.

Table 5.2. HTML5 tags* and how you can use them.

Tag	What It Does
<header>	Identifies content placed at the top of the page.
<nav>	Used to indicate the following will be used for menus.
<aside>	Helpful in creating sidebars or inserts.
<section>	A generic tag that helps separate content.
<footer>	Goes at the bottom of the page.

*For more in-depth study of HTML5, take a look at the Additional Resources section at the end of this chapter.

You'll run across many more, but you should be able to get started marking up your text with these basic tags. After your opening tag, you simply write the content you want displayed. A paragraph of text might look like figure 5.2.

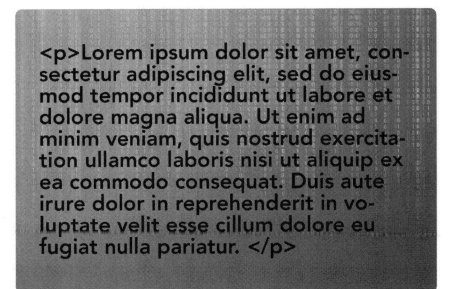

Figure 5.2. Paragraphs in HTML are created with the opening and closing <p> tag. "Lorem ipsum" text is commonly used in graphic and web design as filler-text. As you are creating the desired Look & Feel for your LibGuides, you may consider using "lorem ipsum" text to get a sense of your layout. When everything is like you wish, replace it with actual content.

Almost every HTML tag needs to be "closed." That is, once you write <p> you need to tell the browser when you're finished making a paragraph. This is done with the closing tag </p>. Each tag can be closed in this manner. Together, they make a set: <div> </div>. The only tag from our list in table 5.1 that doesn't need a separate closing tag is <img>. The accessibility chapters in this book will cover important elements to include in your image tags for accessibility. When talking about the coupling of opening and closing tags, the pair forms what is called an element. Elements can have classes and IDs, which we'll talk more about in the Custom JavaScript and CSS section of this chapter.

It's customary to use indentation when writing HTML, so that you can better see how the code is organized and can make sure you have closed all your tags. Browsers don't like it when you've forgotten to close a tag, but they will try their best to display your code anyway. This can result in some pretty weird effects. Indentation will help you avoid goofy-looking pages. See figure 5.3 for an example of indenting your HTML tags:

We can easily see that all our tags are closed, and each part of our markup is clearly defined. This looks like a good start to a custom navigation that we can add to our LibGuides system. Keep in mind that LibGuides does not check for errors in your code, nor does it validate that everything is correct. So I suggest you write your

```
<header>
  <nav>
    <ul>
      <li><a href="/home.html">HOME</a></li>
      <li><a href="/home.html">ABOUT</a></li>
      <li><a href="/home.html">CONTACT</a></li>
    </ul>
  </nav>
</header>
```

Figure 5.3.   Indentation makes your HTML easier to read. It has no impact on how the browser displays your site, however. If you or someone else needs to make changes to your code, you'll be thankful you indented.

HTML code in a code editor designed for this purpose, then copy and paste it into the Page Header box on the Look & Feel page. If you don't have an editor you like, do a Google search for best HTML editors and pick the one that strikes your fancy. There are also free, online editors that will get the job done.

Once you've put your HTML code into the box under Page Header, be sure to click Save HTML. If you don't click Save HTML, then your changes will not be implemented on your pages. As soon as you save, guides across your system will be updated with this code. Instant save and propagate is a good feature, but it doesn't make for a good testing environment. If you haven't gone "live" with LibGuides yet, no problem! Test away knowing that no one but you will see the changes you're making. You want to present your users with a polished web experience—not the rubbish middle steps that are necessary to get the final product. Here is where a development environment will be invaluable. If your institution is a subscriber to LibGuides CMS, you can create a development environment with Groups. Simply create a group with a name like "zTesting." A name like this makes it easy to sort and find the guides you are testing. Assign guides you want to test to this group and keep them unpublished or private while you play with new content. When you're ready, reassign the guide from the zTesting group into an appropriate group and you're ready to go! If you're using an HTML code editor, see if it will let you preview the code you've written. Make sure it looks like you want before inserting it into LibGuides. If your institution has a web team or employs a web design company, consider asking them for help.

The Page Footer gray tab is nearly identical to the Page Header tab, the only exception being no option to use a static image as banner. Code you place in this box will be inserted at the bottom of your guide pages. The same suggestions on testing apply here:

create and develop your code in another environment before loading into LibGuides. With your header and footer code in place, it's time to make it look pretty.

CUSTOM JAVASCRIPT/CSS

Make sure your browser is pointed to Admin > Look & Feel > Custom JS/CSS. In this section, we'll talk a bit more generally about how to add custom scripting and styles to your LibGuides pages. The world of JavaScript, jQuery, and CSS is large; many excellent books have been written on these topics so we won't go in-depth here. We will talk about the basics and offer tips to get the most out of LibGuides. For further study, look over the books and websites in the Additional Resources section of this chapter.

Developer Tools

If you aren't familiar with the developer tools in your web browser, now is a good time to begin experimenting. In most modern browsers (including Internet Explorer) you bring up the developer tools by pressing F12. Let's try it out: Load up your favorite web page and press F12. You'll see the HTML code for the page in one frame, and its CSS code in another. The cool part is that you can change the code and see the results in your browser. Don't worry, you aren't messing with the actual web page. You're just playing with a locally stored copy of the code. This makes the developer tools your best friend. Well, developer tools won't get drinks with you or help move your mammoth couch, but they will make your life easier as you are integrating LibGuides into your existing website.

Another useful feature of your browser's developer tools is the ability to inspect an element. As an example, have your LibGuides Dashboard open and right click (Ctrl-click for you Mac users) the blue button in the upper left corner. Select Inspect Element from the menu. If the developer tool isn't open, this will load and will highlight the HTML code containing the element you clicked. You'll also see all the CSS styles that apply to that element. Notice the browser shows us the HTML code with easy-to-read indentations, an example of how to write clean HTML. Take some time and explore the element you're inspecting. You can change its color, size, font, and more. Again, don't worry about ruining your dashboard: none of the changes you make are permanent.

Before we leave the developer tool, notice two things about HTML elements. First, most, if not all HTML elements, have an ID attribute. The ID uniquely defines the element so that it can be found in your JavaScript and CSS code. For example, the ID attribute on a <div> element might look like figure 5.4.

Second, most elements will have a *class* attribute in addition to the ID. If we added a class to our example <div> element in figure 5.4, it might look like figure 5.5.

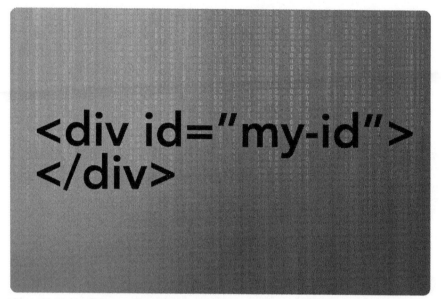

Figure 5.4. Applying an ID makes selecting the element more precise. CSS and Java-Script can use the ID to find the elements you want. Note the syntax: id="my-id." Everything inside the double quotes is the ID and can include letters, numbers, and special characters such as underscores and hyphens. Do not use spaces; plus, it is good practice to avoid characters such as periods, colons, and hashtags.

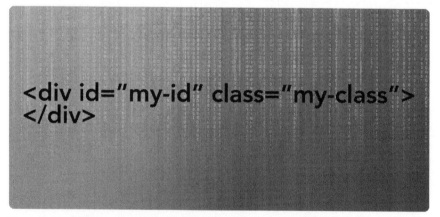

Figure 5.5. Adding a class to an element is similar to adding an ID. The same syntax rules should be followed. Note: where an ID must be unique, an element can have multiple classes, and classes can be assigned to multiple elements. If giving an element more than one class, separate the classes with a space.

Classes can be applied to multiple elements and are used to apply similar styles and functionality to different elements. Both ID and class attributes are important. If you want to adjust the way your LibGuides pages look and feel, you'll need to be able to find these attributes (inspect element) and write code to change their behavior with custom JavaScript and CSS.

CSS

With that out of the way, let's talk about the format of CSS code. When you add CSS to the Custom JS/CSS page in LibGuides, you'll need to first wrap it with a <style> tag. When LibGuides inserts this code to the web pages, the browser will know to interpret it as CSS code when it sees the <style> tag. Remember to close the tag with </style> at the end of your code. CSS code consists of a selector, properties, and values. Selectors are always followed by curly braces, properties are always followed by colons, and values are always followed by semicolons. Figure 5.6 gives an example.

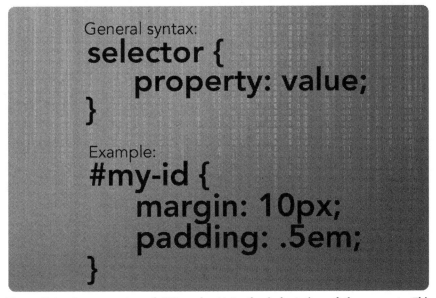

General syntax:
```
selector {
    property: value;
}
```

Example:
```
#my-id {
    margin: 10px;
    padding: .5em;
}
```

Figure 5.6. Proper syntax of CSS code. Note the indentation of the property. This makes your code easy to read.

A "selector" is another name for the elements, classes, and IDs we write into our HTML code. Essentially, they identify a particular section of code in your pages. Elements, classes, and IDs each have a different format in CSS. Table 5.3 shows you the differences.

Table 5.3.   Elements, classes, and IDs all have a different format in CSS code.

Type	HTML Format	CSS Selector Format
Element	<div>	div { ... }
Class	<div class="s-lib-side-borders">	.s-lib-side-borders { ... }
ID	<div id="s-lg-col-2">	#s-lg-col-2 { ... }

To select classes in CSS, prefix the class name with a period. For IDs, the prefix to use is a pound sign (or hashtag for you Twitter-savvy folks). Elements can simply be written as is, but be aware that the CSS rules you write for an element will be applied to all elements of that type on your page. Tread carefully! Also, it's very easy to forget a curly brace, a colon, or semicolon. If things aren't looking the way you expect, make sure you've (figuratively) dotted all your *i*'s and crossed your *t*'s.

CSS has dozens of properties and values, far too many to explore here. If you dive into your LibGuides page code with the inspect element feature in your web browser, you'll see the properties and values that are being applied to elements on your page. You'll see things like margin: 10px; or color: #fff; or font size: 14px (px stands for pixel; #fff is hexadecimal shorthand code for the color white). You can change these properties and values in the developer tools inside your web browser, but if you find something you like, you can also copy and paste it into the Custom JS/CSS page in LibGuides. When you do so, the CSS you enter will permanently override the default style that comes with LibGuides. This is powerful because it means you are not locked into the basic design and standard options you get out of the box. Your LibGuides can look just like other web pages your institution publishes, or you can make them unique—completely unlike anything the world has seen before. With a little practice with HTML and CSS, you'll bask in the power to transform your LibGuides. We recommend you use this power for good, but ultimately it's your choice.

JavaScript and jQuery

Just as CSS code must be wrapped in <style> tags when inserted into your Custom JS/CSS page, JavaScript and jQuery code must be wrapped in <script> tags. You do not need to add links to the jQuery library (a jQuery library is a collection of code used to make certain tasks easier to implement), as Springshare includes those on every page in your system. JavaScript is a rich coding language that puts a wealth of functionality and enhancements at your disposal. Writing JavaScript code can be complex, and unless you are looking to add a specific feature to your LibGuides, you probably won't need to mess with it too much. If you want to learn more about JavaScript and jQuery, there are excellent books and websites listed in the Additional Resources section of this chapter.

Wrapping Up Look & Feel

When you're finished entering code into the Custom JS/CSS box, make sure to click Save. Once you do, your code will be included on all of your guides. If you've had LibGuides for a while, you may want to test your code in another environment before placing it here. We never want to present our users with weird and buggy code. However, if you're setting up LibGuides for the first time, you can generally plug code in and play; just make sure everything is working as you want before you "go live" to your users. As a final note, the alternative to placing code in the Custom JS/CSS box is to save your JavaScript and CSS code in external files. LibGuides allows you to include these custom files. You can upload your files by clicking the Customization Files tab near the bottom of the Custom JS/CSS page. Keep in mind that you'll still need to enter code into the Custom JS/CSS box, but LibGuides will generate that code for you. From there it's an easy copy and paste. You should now have the basics down and be ready to spread your wings. So go ahead! Flap those wings and make your LibGuides look amazing.

ADVANCED LIBGUIDES TOOLS

Gathering Statistics

There will come a time when you want to know how many people are visiting your guides. You may wish to know what search terms they're using or which assets are being accessed the most. LibGuides offers robust statistic-gathering tools. You may also use third-party analytics such as Google or Adobe, but while powerful, these third-party tools aren't tailored for your LibGuides like the built-in reports. From the LibGuides Dashboard, hop over to the Statistics page from the top orange bar and you'll see what I mean.

You can choose to view a number of reports for your home page, guides, sessions, even the browser and operating system used to access your guides. The basic format is the same for each of these. You'll select a time span and hit Run Report. The default time span is one week; you'll get more data by expanding the time span, but the trade-off is that it will take longer to generate. From here, you can drill down into the data. LibGuides will give you a graph of the report and a sortable table with the raw data. As you'd expect, you can export the statistics to an Excel spreadsheet or PDF for further study or distribution. You are also given the option to save the graph LibGuides generates. Formats include .png, .jpg, and .pdf, among others. To save a graph, click the "hamburger" icon in the upper right-hand corner of the graph.

The report for guides can be generated for all guides in your system, or you can choose to focus on a specific guide or group. Whether you generate reports for all your guides or a few, you'll still be able to jump into an individual guide page's report. After running the broad report, click the guide you want to inspect. You'll be presented with data on all the pages of that guide. Notice the eyeball icon to the right of each page. Clicking the eye will show you the referring URL to that page. This is like looking back in time. The referring URL is the web page a user visited directly before your page. This feature is powerful because it lets you see how users are getting to your LibGuides and can help you determine bottlenecks and common entry points.

Search terms provide a similar insight into how your users are finding the information you publish in LibGuides. An important note should be made here: the search terms you find here are words users have entered into the LibGuides search box. They are not words they entered into Google, Bing, or another search engine to find your site. You will see a total number of searches on the Searches report page, as well as the terms used and page from which the search was made. In many libraries, search privacy is important. LibGuides does not gather personal identifying information, but be careful to use these reports in a responsible manner.

Widgets and APIs

So far in this chapter we've talked about making your LibGuides pages look and feel like your institution's existing web pages. However, a necessary component of integration is the ability to include LibGuides content on non-LibGuides pages. Perhaps you want to embed a LibGuides box full of useful links on your institution's home page. Or maybe you want to use your A–Z list as a starting point for research. What if you wanted the ability to search LibGuides from outside your guide pages? All of these features and more are possible with widgets.

What is a widget, you ask? In web design, a widget is a small bit of code that is designed to be portable, that is, it can be used on more than one page, more than one time. Think of widgets like kitchen utensils. Each utensil can be used over and over, may come in many different designs, and serves a distinct purpose. In this analogy, your kitchen is made up of many widgets, and we see that a widget looks a lot like a tool. Tools they are, and the primary purpose of LibGuides widgets is to deliver information. Much like a measuring cup, the widget ensures you get the right amount of an ingredient into your recipe. LibGuides widgets make sure you can use your information anywhere you please.

The best part about widgets is that LibGuides does all the real work—you just pick your options and watch the magic happen. From your LibGuides Dashboard, navigate to Tools > Widgets. You can select from a number of different types of content: Guides, A–Z List, Users, Subjects, and more. Most of these widgets will generate a list of links that point back to your LibGuides. For example, generating a widget of the Guides type will create a list of all your guide titles. Users would be able to click on the link to visit that guide. There are three widget types that are not lists, however. They are Content Box, Guide/Page, and Search Box. We'll talk about those in a moment.

Your first order of business is to choose options. The options available are listed on the left, and as you pick which options you want, a preview is created for you on the right. This makes it easy to see exactly what you'll get when you embed the widget on your site. Each widget allows you to adjust the output format, which can be a bulleted list or drop-down box. Widgets for Guides, A–Z Lists, Users, and Groups give you the option to filter what is displayed to the user. For example, you may have more than five hundred guides, but you might only want to show those owned by a specific librarian or that have certain tags.

After you have decided on which options you want in your widget, click anywhere in the box titled Embed Code. The entirety of the code will be selected for you, and you may then either right click and choose copy or press Ctrl+C (Mac: Command-C). This code can be sent to your institution's web team for inclusion on your site, or you can paste it directly into a web page. The Embed Code contains everything you need, including styling, size information, and access to your LibGuides.

What if you want to lift an entire box of content out of a LibGuide for use on another web page? Enter the Content Box widget. As an administrator, you may choose from any box on any guide, and LibGuides will generate the widget code for you. If you choose Framed under the Look & Feel options, the color and style settings you created by working through the Look & Feel section of this chapter will be applied to the widget. If you choose Simple, your widget will have basic coloring and style. Notice, the widget code places several scripts into your web page that you may not need. If your institution already uses jQuery, jQuery UI, and Bootstrap, you may want to delete the <script> and <link> tags that look like the ones in Textbox 5.1.

You aren't limited to just content boxes, however. You can place entire pages or guides on external web pages. The widget creator for Guide/Page operates similarly

TEXTBOX 5.1.

These script and link tags call special libraries of code that LibGuides automatically includes on every guide you've created. Adding them an extra time will cause users to experience performance drops, and in some cases (if you include an older version of these libraries) ruin the visual appearance and functionality of your LibGuides.

```
<script type="text/javascript" src=" "//lgapi.libapps.com/web/jquery/js/1.10.0
_jquery.min.js">
```

```
<link rel="stylesheet"href=" //maxcdn.bootstrapcdn.com/bootstrap/3.3.4/CSS/
bootstrap.min.css" />
```

to the Content Box widget. Again, you'll have access to all guides for this widget, but be careful the guide you select is published and accessible. The widget creator will generate code for unpublished, private, or internal guides, but guides with these visibility settings will not be viewable when you paste your code into a web page.

The Search Box widget will create code that will enable your users to search through your LibGuides from any web page. Conveniently, search terms entered in a Search Box widget are saved for statistics gathering (see the Gathering Statistics section of this chapter for details on how to retrieve this information). You can elect to have the search box look through guides or your A–Z Database List. Unless you've become proficient in writing your own Ajax calls in JavaScript (Ajax stands for Asynchronous JavaScript and XML, which we'll mention in the next section), it'll be best to let the widget do it for you; keep the Embed Type set to JavaScript Code. This Search Box widget can go anywhere on your web pages. If your institution's web presence is predominantly LibGuides, the Search Box widget can function as a global search. Otherwise, it's a nice entry point into LibGuides that makes it easy for patrons to begin their research.

APIs

API stands for Application Program Interface, and as such requires a greater knowledge of programming than we can cover in this chapter. APIs do, however, offer greater control over your data than widgets. The LibGuides APIs available as of this writing enable you to get guide, account, subject, and asset information. Where widgets of these types return a simple list, the API will give you much more data. With proper coding, this information can be used in any way you like. If you're interested in learning more about how to write code for LibGuides APIs, research and learn about the following topics and how to implement them into your HTML. The Additional Resources section of this chapter is a good place to start.

- jQuery
  jQuery takes some shortcuts with JavaScript code and makes it easier to write. Beyond its uses for API development, jQuery can transform the look and functionality of your web presence.
- JavaScript
  This is the foundation for all client-side code. You'll need to know proper syntax and how and when the browser executes code.
- JSON—JavaScript Object Notation
  This is the format in which the API returns data. You'll need to know how to parse it and its syntax in order to use the information the API gathers.
- Ajax—Asynchronous JavaScript and XML
  All LibGuides APIs use Ajax to collect data. What this means is that the API can be off gathering information while your web page loads and does not hinder

user interactions. jQuery can assist with making Ajax calls, but you'll need to understand how it works to get the most out of your APIs

SUMMARY

Let's recap. At the beginning of this chapter we discovered how LibGuides disseminates user accounts—some options are available in your LibApps Dashboard, while more can be found in your LibGuides Dashboard under Admin > Accounts. From there we explored ways to communicate with your users. Springshare conveniently provides a list of user email you can copy into an email client, or you can add an alert box that will display on the Dashboard of every user when they log in. We saw that creating subjects, tags, and groups will help our public users find the information they need. Assigning subject experts and friendly URLs can greatly increase the usability of your LibGuides and enhance the experience for your users. Taking the time to set up your system correctly from the start can save you, and your users, a lot of headaches later. In the Look & Feel section, the true power of customization became ours for the taking. By leveraging Springhare's standard settings and knowledge of HTML, CSS, and JavaScript, your LibGuides are not confined to the basic out-of-the-box look. Your LibGuides will look how you want them—and don't let anyone tell you otherwise (unless it's your boss or the director of marketing; you should listen to them for sure). Finally, we saw how easy Springshare makes it to gather statistics for our guides and scratched the surface of using widgets and APIs. We certainly covered a lot of ground in this chapter. So where do you go from here?

I've compiled a list of resources for further reading. With them you'll learn more about writing code for the web and, in turn, how to provide a seamless transition from your institution's existing web pages and your LibGuides. When you come across a LibGuides-specific question, the Springhare support team is ready to help. Click the black Support tab that appears to the right of every page on your dashboard, and a Springshare representative will get back to you quickly. That's it! Now off you go; we can't wait to see how awesome your guides turn out!

ADDITIONAL RESOURCES

Websites

http://www.codecadamy.com. Free, interactive tutorials on HTML and CSS, JavaScript, and more.
http://developer.mozilla.org. Extensive reference and examples for all web coding technologies.
http://CSS-tricks.com. Blog and videos dedicated to solving real-world problems with CSS.
http://api.jquery.com. Complete reference for the jQuery library.
http://www.stackoverflow.com. Forum-type site with searchable knowledge base.
http://codepen.io. A free web development playground that shows you results as you write code.

Books

Duckett, Jon. 2014. *JavaScript & jQuery.* Indianapolis: Wiley.
Duckett, Jon. 2014. *HTML & CSS: Design and Build Websites.* Indianapolis: Wiley.
Verou, Lea. 2015. *CSS Secrets.* Sebastopol, Canada: O'Reilly.
Nixon, Robin. 2014. *Learning PHP, MySQL & JavaScript.* 4th ed. Sebastopol, Canada: O'Reilly.
Smith, Ben. 2014. *Beginning JSON.* Berkeley, CA: Apress.
Spurlock, Jake. 2013. *Bootstrap.* Sebastopol, Canada: O'Reilly.

6

LibGuides Administration

Road Map to Engaging Content

Jennifer W. Bazeley, Miami University
Jennifer J. Natale, Miami University
Elizabeth Sullivan, Miami University

Libraries purchase LibGuides software in the effort to provide all users with easy access to engaging library content. Active administration of the software is a vital component in realizing this goal. In the summer of 2014, Miami University Libraries migrated from LibGuides version 1 (LGv1) to LibGuides version 2 (LGv2). A small group had traditionally overseen the administrative aspects of the LibGuides software that included managing accounts and troubleshooting. The migration to LGv2 created a unique opportunity for the group to reevaluate their administration and take a more active role in implementing a broader vision of the use of LibGuides in order to meet the needs of faculty, staff, and students.

BACKGROUND

Miami University is a public university located in Oxford, Ohio, and is a primarily undergraduate institution, with a full-time enrollment of approximately 16,500 students. The Miami University Libraries (the Libraries) are comprised of six individual libraries—the main library, the music library, the art and architecture library, the science library, and two regional campus libraries. These libraries employ a total of ninety-nine staff (forty-nine librarians and fifty staff) and support numerous bachelor's degrees in more than 120 areas of study, sixty master's degrees, and twelve doctoral degrees. The Libraries have supported a number of subject areas with subject guides for several decades, with the most recent online iterations on the LibGuides platform. Springshare offers a suite of complementary software products; however, the Libraries currently only utilize LibGuides. At the time of the Libraries migration from LGv1 to LGv2, the Libraries were maintaining almost 200 guides in support of the programs previously mentioned. Since migrating to LGv2, the Libraries

LibGuides have increased to well over 250. Of the total staff employed by the Libraries, fifty-four have accounts in LibGuides.

ACTIVE ADMINISTRATION

Like many other academic university libraries, Miami University Libraries have maintained research and subject guides online for faculty and students for many years. While Staley (2007, 124) indicates that students do not use subject guides with regularity, there is still a need for both subject and individualized course guides. In an era where online learning is becoming the norm, subject and course guides are finding new life and purpose.

The necessity to be active (and proactive) in centrally administering a library's subject and research guides (on any platform) is evident in the scholarship on subject guides. The literature contains numerous articles on all aspects of subject guides, from those created in print formats to later iterations created electronically and/or online. A study by Dahl (2001) demonstrates that the first electronic guides created (sometimes called electronic pathfinders) may have ignored recommendations regarding consistency, resulting in user confusion and lower usage of guides. Dahl's study (2001, 236) also found that the ease of creating electronic pathfinders led authors to provide an overwhelming number of links to resources instead of providing a focused research portal. This tendency to create overly complex subject guides can be mitigated in part by an administrative group or committee that is active in creating and maintaining standards and best practices.

With the advent of software like LibGuides, it has become easier for library staff to create subject guides and to standardize messaging and communications with patrons (Brooks-Tatum 2012, 16–18). An evaluation of a LibGuides pilot at the University College Dublin Library determined that "having a common core and 'look and feel' for each guide increased the ease of navigation for students across different guides, whilst also helping to reinforce branding" (Dalton and Pan 2014, 519). The LibGuides platform is ideal for supporting standards in layout, requires little knowledge of HTML to implement and maintain, and has the added benefit of enabling guide owners to reuse existing content, allowing for both collaboration *and* consistency. LibGuides' intuitive interface and flexibility allows libraries to easily implement a common core and "look and feel" across guides, which favorably benefit users.

The Libraries developed an administrative group to oversee the implementation process of LibGuides in 2009. Post-implementation, this small group continued to oversee a few administrative aspects of the LibGuides software, including managing user accounts and troubleshooting. The Libraries' migration to LGv2 in 2014 created a unique opportunity for the group to reevaluate their administrative role and take an active lead in creating a unified vision of library LibGuides. Prior to the migration, the group conducted a literature review; an environmental scan of the use, look, and function of guides created at other universities; and usability testing with existing LGv1 guides. This research led to the creation of standards, best practices, and trainings in an effort to provide resources to meet the needs of the user community in an accessible, consistent, and professional way. This active committee has had a significant impact on the way the Libraries interact with users through LibGuides.

An active administrative presence to oversee LibGuides can be the work of a single individual, a pair, or a committee, depending on university library resources. If resources allow, establishing a committee creates efficiencies and allows a beneficial division of labor. When establishing a committee, it is essential to select a diverse membership to seed the committee with the variety of knowledge needed to administer an entire library's guides. Knowledge of web design and accessibility, library technology, library instruction practices (both in person and online), and library resources are integral pieces in creating a self-sufficient group.

In their chapter on administering LibGuides in the LITA Guide *Using LibGuides to Enhance Library Services*, Kumar and Farney (2013) suggest five potential scenarios to use for setting up an administrative structure:

1. Single lead
2. Task specific
3. Large team
4. Divided leadership
5. Buddy system

A *single-lead* scenario may be ideal for institutions with fewer staff, where one librarian serves as the LibGuides administrator to oversee basic format and layout while giving librarian guide owners and editors more control over content. The *task-specific* scenario divides technical administrative duties among a group of people, allowing each person to focus on a task. The *large-team* solution may work best at larger institutions, as it is comprised of two administrative teams, where one team oversees administrative duties and the other team oversees content. Like the large-team solution, the *divided-leadership* scenario creates multiple administrative teams where the division of duties is by subject area (e.g., social sciences, humanities, sciences). The fifth suggested scenario, *buddy system*, has the potential to work at an institution of any size, as it pairs an administrator with a guide owner (Kumar and Farney 2013, 44–47).

The Libraries administrative group used a combination of three of these scenarios—single lead, task specific, and buddy system. The group is comprised of five members—the user experience librarian, an academic resident librarian, two liaison librarians, and one technical services librarian. The user experience librarian brings web design and accessibility skills to the table, along with the knowledge of technologies already in use in the library. The academic resident and liaison librarians bring knowledge of instruction practices (both in person and online) used across the university's community of users. The technical services librarian brings knowledge of the library's print and online resources (both the resources themselves and the infrastructure that makes them discoverable) to the group.

All five group members were given administrator privileges in LibGuides, were owners of numerous LibGuides themselves, and were intimately familiar with LibGuides functionality and features. This allowed the group to lead by example, by following standards, providing reusable content, and encouraging collaboration in their own guides. Group members were able to address migration challenges in their own familiar guides first, which allowed them to provide expert guidance when colleagues experienced similar challenges. After standards and best practices were created, administrative group members implemented them in their own guides first, which demonstrated the benefits of the standards and paved the way for asking colleagues to follow the same guidelines.

Responsibilities of the individuals in the group can be assigned to some degree based on corresponding responsibilities in the job description of each individual. For example, at the Libraries, the technical services librarian was assigned the role of primary liaison to Springshare customer service (a version of the single-lead scenario). This aligned with similar job responsibilities in managing vendor relationships for library materials and also prevented duplicative and redundant communication and troubleshooting between group members and Springshare customer service. It was also extremely helpful during the migration process from LGv1 to LGv2, a process in which Springshare assigns a primary contact to manage the migration process for a library. A second example was to assign the liaison librarian in the group (who is also responsible for overseeing the library's role in the university's growing e-learning program) to focus on the creation, maintenance, and accessibility of video content on LibGuides, an expertise that the librarian utilizes in his daily job (a version of the task-specific scenario). At different times throughout migration and implementation, all group members paired themselves with guide owners in order to ease migration and training anxieties (a version of the buddy system).

As a group, the Libraries administrative group performed three essential functions before, during, and after the migration to LGv2. The group's initial priorities were migration-related tasks, such as transferring accounts, troubleshooting page migration issues, learning new features and functions, and training colleagues on the changes brought about by migration. Once migration was complete, the group's priority shifted to performing usability testing and comparing that usability testing with results from previous studies completed with LGv1. This allowed the group to determine if students' needs had changed significantly between 2009 and 2014, and to make site-wide decisions based on those needs. In the post-migration, post-usability period, the group consciously elected to take a much more active role in evaluating and overseeing LibGuides than they had after the 2009 implementation.

Migrated guides exhibited a wide variety of formats, features, styles, and aesthetics, many were branded inconsistently with university and library branding, and many contained outdated references and broken links. Taking an active role meant creating and enforcing standards and best practices in the LibGuides site-wide customization options, which created consistency across subject guides and between subject guides and the Libraries' other online presences. For guide owners with an overwhelming number of guides to be updated, administrative group members absorbed the work of the standard content changes, such as reformatting page layouts; making text consistent in font style, size, and color; and updating broken links. This eased the challenges of migration and paved the way in helping colleagues to accept the perceived imposition of standards and best practices.

STANDARDS

Best practices and standards are a necessity for any site-wide product implementation. A product like LibGuides affords many people editing rights to both content and layout, presenting administrative challenges such as determining how restrictive policies should be, electing how to enforce those standards, and developing a strategy for revisiting and updating standards as needed. The impending transition to LGv2 served as a natural opportunity for the Libraries administrative group to assess and update their own set of standards and best practices.

Importance of Standards

Academic libraries offer a breadth of resources and information that is sometimes overwhelming to users seeking information on a specific topic or within a particular discipline. Subject guides play an important role in helping librarians highlight useful resources and reinforce information literacy skills to a specific target audience. However, there are common pitfalls that detract from developing and maintaining guides that are user-friendly and practical for the intended audience. As we create and maintain guides, it is important to keep our audience and their needs at the forefront. This includes following basic web design principles and periodically employing usability testing to update standards.

In 2009, when it was first implemented at Miami University, LibGuides replaced a fairly static alternative. The dynamic format of LibGuides was a breath of fresh air. It allowed librarians with only basic web-authoring skills to create content. All librarians were encouraged to explore the varied functionalities of the platform. At the point of adoption, Springshare was just two years old and LibGuides was growing quickly, but little about best practices had been presented in any scholarly setting.

The Libraries' initial best practices were too basic and vague. A template for subject guides was developed to ease creation by librarians and present a common look and feel. One early misconception was that subject guides would largely serve as stand-alone pages. As shown in figure 6.1, guide home pages were welcoming but offered no functional use and added yet another click between the user and the content they sought.

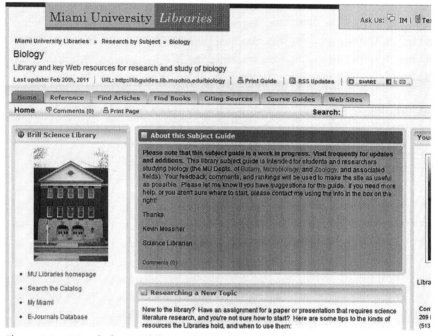

Figure 6.1.   LGv1 before usability testing.

Casually observing both what users were seeking on the guides and how they were trying to find it led us to conduct a formal usability study in 2011. Initial findings indicated that students expected a common experience across all guides and found even slight differences jarring. This observation along with analysis of results led us to make the following changes:

- Standardize all nomenclature across all guides to simplified terms instead of library jargon (e.g., "find articles" instead of "databases and indices").
- Require specific tabs on all subject guides, including Find Articles, Books, and Citing.
- Eliminate any embedded search boxes.
- Require a centered Quick Start guide at the top of each subject guide home page, as shown in figure 6.2, which reiterated tabs. We found users failed to notice that each guide had tabbed content so were often confused when met with a welcome box and little to no resources.

One of the primary goals was to create a common user experience across all guides. Guide owners were informed about usability testing and asked to implement changes prior to the start of the 2012 spring term. While some guides were updated, others were not, and little was done to enforce conformity. By 2014, the total number of

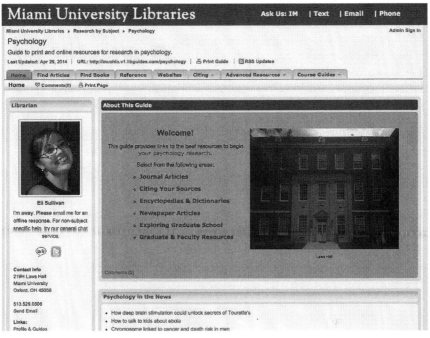

Figure 6.2. LGv1 after usability testing.

guides had increased by more than 60 percent with little commonality among them. With Springshare gearing up to roll out LGv2, the administrative group decided to take another in-depth look at all Miami guides. Usability testing and a literature review were conducted, and best practices from other institutions were analyzed to inform updating local standards. Some common themes emerged including consistency, simplicity, accessibility, and maintenance.

Consistency

One important aspect of developing subject guides is presenting a consistent experience for the user to ease navigation and use. Developing standards that brand your LibGuides to match institutional and library aesthetics indicate to the user that the guides are part of that bigger effort (Gonzalez and Westbrock 2010, 642). Strutin (2008, para. 24) found that students' goals are "speed and simplicity" and that "familiarity and consistency seemed to be key" when selecting what research tools to employ. Consistency in layout and style is not only best practice in web design (Jasek 2004, 4), but also aids users in navigating to what is needed quickly and efficiently. If students have to learn how information on subject guides is organized each time a different guide is accessed, they will opt for other resources that are easier to use.

While users could find a common experience across *some* guides, overall, consistency was lacking in any meaningful way. Testing determined that while users are initially drawn to images, they quickly shift their gaze to the middle of the page. Standardizing content of the guide home page allowed the administrative group, in essence, to predict and prioritize what users see and experience. Therefore, the home page of each subject guide adopted the same layout and basic content. All guides moved from a 25/50/25 three-column format to a 25/75 two-column format. Additionally, font style, font color, and box colors were standardized to create a consistent look throughout. Profile boxes were shifted to the left side of the page and the larger column offered two key features: a Quick Links box that replicated tabbed content and a Best Bets box that contained the most commonly used resources for the particular subject area. The administrative group found that most users were commonly seeking subject-specific databases, so the group opted to bring that content forward and showcase it on the home page. Users who required more options or alternatives could find a more exhaustive list on appropriate secondary tabs as shown in figure 6.3.

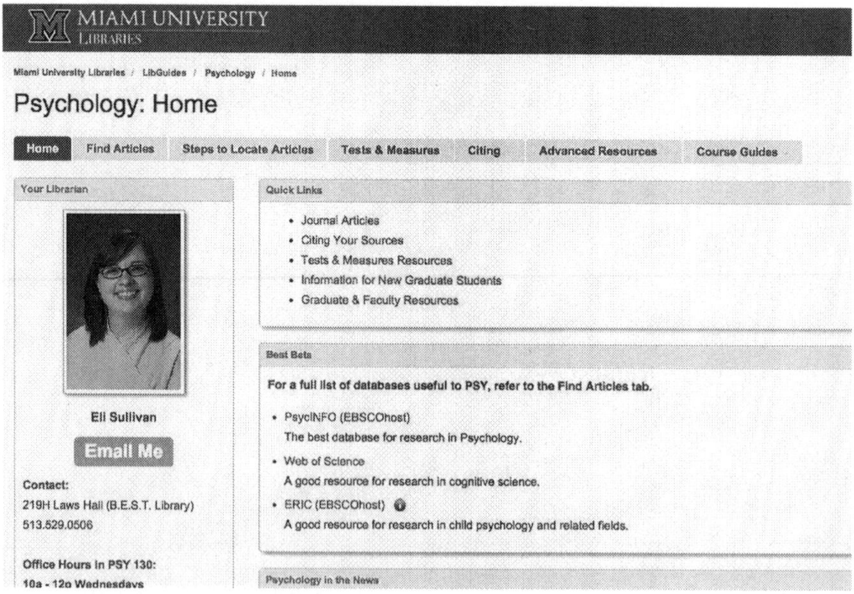

Figure 6.3. LGv2 home page.

The Libraries administrative group also opted to require professional photos for all guide owners. The initial practice of allowing owners to use any headshot resulted in images of varied quality and backgrounds. Requiring 225 × 275 professional photos was a small change but played a big role in developing consistency. It also made librarians and staff more identifiable to users.

Simplicity

Along with consistency, simplicity is pivotal both in designing and populating guides. LibGuides ushered in easy web design for libraries, offering each owner the ability to customize every aspect of their guide. While this offers flexibility to guide owners, too much customization can counter the consistency of the collective guides, creating a cluttered or chaotic aesthetic and failing to meet basic web design standards. Subject guides should serve as an extension of a library's website and therefore reflect the same aesthetic with "few colors and minimal graphics" (Jasek 2004, 7). A case study at York University Library by Dupuis, Ryan, and Steeves in 2004 found that organization and simplicity were key factors in guide creation (272). A simple organizational scheme using common language allows users to easily find the information they seek.

The quantity of content, too, should be strategically simple and selective. Vileno (2007, 448) notes that even though librarians create tools with the intent of aiding a specific audience, frequently that population's input or feedback about their needs is never sought. Too often, librarians design guides to address *any* need a user might have, but the more tabs and pages of information there are within a single guide, the more opportunities users have of being confused (Dahl 2001, 236). According to Kapoun (1995, 96), tools like LibGuides should not be exhaustive, but rather serve as an introduction to resources.

It became clear during testing that Miami users struggled to prioritize content on a text-heavy page and found many guides to be "cluttered." A conscious effort was made to rework the guides with the user in mind. Best practices included the following:

- Standardize the home page content and create a Best Bets box.
- Prioritize resources, listing them strategically instead of alphabetically.
- Be selective, focusing on the needs of most users, not all users.
- Direct more advanced questions to course guides or a librarian.

Accessibility

Accessible content has been part of web development best practices for a long time but is not universally employed. Spindler (2002, 152) found that many libraries struggle to meet accessibility standards on their websites. In 2011–2012, the United States Department of Education (2015, 1) reported that more than 11 percent of students enrolled in higher education had at least one disability and those numbers are on an upward trend, making compliance with accessibility standards critical. Our goal is to ensure compliance with Section 508 of the Rehabilitation Act of 1973, which covers information and technical assistance of the Americans with Disabilities Act (United States Department of Justice, Civil Rights Division 2013). The LibGuides software complies with Section 508 through the creation of alternate public pages intended for screen readers, as well as hidden "skip to" links, seen only by those using adaptive technology. In order to create a standard experience for all users, it is recommended that all images have alt-tags, all videos be captioned and have text equivalents, and all "click here" linked text be replaced with descriptive text for the URL.

Maintenance

Beyond developing standards for guide creation and layout, standards were also developed for maintenance of guides. Regular maintenance requires ongoing time and energy but is integral to the value and usability of guides. The administrative group is encouraged to set standards, including a biannual schedule for owners to review and update guides, evaluate usage statistics, and remove or reorganize content and links that are not getting used in order to ensure a healthy and relevant resource. Our administrative group sends reminders and offers workshops on strategic maintenance in addition to periodically checking guides to ensure standards are met. The group further supports guide owners and trains new employees who are inheriting and developing guides by maintaining a guide that details standards, how-to processes, and expectations.

In addition to creating a professional and reliable aesthetic, it is important to maintain the currency of information and functionality of resources in each guide. Springshare offers some useful built-in tools such as a link checker, link-level statistics, and a centralized assets feature that aid greatly in maintenance. The link checker tool simplifies the process of ensuring external links on guides are functional, though it is worth noting that it fails to detect web pages that have moved. Link-level statistics provide owners a snapshot of what resources are being utilized and with what frequency in order to assess their value to users. The assets feature allows administrators to maintain a master list of resources, which, if utilized by guide owners, allows the update of links across all LibGuides.

TRAINING AND DEVELOPMENT

A high rate of compliance with standards by guide owners likely reduces the need for frequent maintenance by the administrative group. The introduction of training and development opportunities is one way to ensure that LibGuides owners comply with standards and create engaging content. For guides to be most effective, they must be refreshed with new ideas and content on a regular basis. Dalton and Pan (2014, 519) noted that "regular outreach and evaluation activities should be undertaken to ensure that the content of LibGuides keeps pace with changing student needs and preferences, and that offerings remain relevant." Finding time in the schedules of busy librarians to create and maintain vibrant content can be a challenge. A LibGuides administrative group can lead the way by providing training, new ideas, and support.

In the process of migrating to LGv2, the Libraries administrative group met with the LibGuides owners to provide insight into the upcoming migration and to share the results of the recent usability testing that compared an LGv1 guide with a beta LGv2 guide. From the outset of the planning process, the administrative group recognized the importance of communicating information and a migration timeline. In the first meeting with owners, usability testing results were shared, including directly quoted remarks from participants. This evidence gave credibility to the suggested changes for the layout of guides after the migration. Implementing new standards would require owners to plan significant time and effort to reformat the layout and content of their guides. By outlining the rationale for new standards, the timeline for the process, and how the group would provide support, the administrative group gained the trust and cooperation of guide owners.

Training

Training sessions were planned shortly after the migration. Multiple time slots were offered in an effort to accommodate the availability of all owners. Administrators reviewed the most significant changes from LGv1 to LGv2 and presented a step-by-step walk-through of the changes needed to comply with the new standards. Through this process, it became clear that LibGuides would be an appropriate format for sharing this information. An internal guide entitled "LibGuides Standards & How-tos" (http://libguides.lib.miamioh.edu/MULGStandards) was created in order to provide a single point of information that serves current and future owners. All presentation materials as well as tips and answers to commonly asked questions were added to the guide.

LibGuides owners have varying levels of skill and comfort in using the software based on their technical abilities and previous experience with the tool. During the migration process, an administrative group can offer open sessions where owners can drop in to ask specific questions and get help. This time can be used by owners and the administrative group to proactively update guides or work collaboratively. These sessions can continue to be offered semiannually to educate owners of changes and encourage adherence to standards.

The migration process allowed work on the LGv2 guides while the LGv1 guides were still available to the public. The timeline required owners to complete changes during the summer of 2014 in order to go live with LGv2 prior to the start of the fall 2014 semester. As a proactive measure, members of the administrative group were assigned to support those individuals who owned numerous guides, had less comfort in using LibGuides, or had other competing responsibilities. Offering personal support and guidance was positively received and helped to reinforce the team effort of the process. In some cases, guide owners allowed others to make basic changes to guide format so they could focus on reviewing content.

The administrative group has continued to offer training since the LGv2 migration in order to address key issues. The first training topic involved how to access usage statistics to evaluate guides. This functionality in LibGuides helps owners to evaluate the number of visitors to a guide, the specific use of tabbed pages and links, and the time frame of usage. Training was provided on how to access the statistics, including examples of how they could be used. For example, an owner could see if a guide was accessed after a library instruction session or see if a link to a particular resource was being used. Analysis of this data reinforced the need for guides to be concise, with the most important resources prominently placed on a page for improved visibility.

Accessibility was another training topic that involved online information, in-person training, and administrative oversight. Pickens and Long (2013, 107) noted that while many new librarians may have learned about web accessibility, less technologically experienced colleagues may have little to no training. In order to ensure compliance with accessibility standards, the administrative group trained owners on technical aspects such as adding alt-text to images, creating accessible documents and videos, and using the WAVE web accessibility tool (http://wave.webaim.org/). Additionally, links to accessibility resources and tools were included on the "LibGuides Standards & How-tos" guide.

Development

The growth of online learning expedites the need for integrating library resources into learning management systems (LMSs) (Tumbleson and Burke 2013, 3). LibGuides are an ideal tool to provide this integration because they are easily embedded into the LMS. The administrative group aided owners in meeting the demand for online instructional resources by creating video content for librarians to reuse in subject guides. This shared content addresses core information literacy skills that are foundational for all subject areas. To ensure a consistent and professional aesthetic, all videos incorporate a standard library introduction and are uploaded to a high-definition Vimeo account owned by the library.

The focus on updating guides has led to the creation of new content to meet the needs of users. The administrative group has created or collaborated on topic guides that provide content across disciplines. For example, the administrative group partnered with other owners of citation guides and worked to create a single, concise, and uniform offering of citation resources and citation managers. LibGuides can also serve to provide a concise pathway to information relevant to specific demographics. The administrative group created a "Faculty Resources" LibGuide (http://libguides.lib.miamioh.edu/oxfordfaculty) in order to provide faculty-specific information in one central location. The guide is promoted during faculty orientations, is easily shared with faculty who request information, and may promote the serendipitous discovery of additional library resources. LibGuides content can also be focused on providing information to library staff. For example, a "Library Professional Development" guide (http://libguides.lib.miamioh.edu/ProfDev) was created to promote internal and external learning opportunities as well as highlighting the library science collection.

Marketing

A library website re-design coincided with the launch of LGv2, offering the opportunity to create a more prominent link to LibGuides on the new website. This increased visibility provides users with direct access to guides. The administrative group strongly encouraged subject librarians to market their LibGuides to faculty members. Subject and course guides were promoted during new faculty orientation as well as in training sessions for faculty preparing to teach online courses. This opportunity promoted the use of guides in all courses, whether online or in person. Librarians were asked to promote their guides through contact with faculty at the start of the semester through email, newsletters, or in-person meetings. The administrative group recognized that faculty members may not know how to integrate subject guides in the LMS, so a how-to video was created that could be attached to promotional email correspondence. Guides are also promoted in library instruction classes and individual research consultations with students. Gonzalez and Westbrock (2010, 652) found that guides introduced when a practical context is demonstrated during instruction sessions served as an instrumental marketing technique to student populations.

CONCLUSION

An administrative team can help to coordinate and oversee significant changes due to a software migration or determine the necessity for global updates. The Libraries administrative group used the opportunity to increase the usability of guides by implementing new standards. The administrative group consistently performs the responsibilities of contact with Springshare, orienting new guide owners, providing support and troubleshooting, maintaining database links, and training. New efforts are undertaken on a semester or annual basis to address broader issues such as the recent focus on accessibility.

Miami University Libraries' experience has clearly shown that a model of active administration can improve the overall quality of the LibGuides that are provided to users. With the changes implemented during the migration to LGv2, usage of guides increased, accessibility improved, creation of guides increased, and collaboration improved between guide owners. The keys to our success were forming an administrative team with the right balance of expertise, creating standards, and providing instruction on changes in a collaborative and inclusive way, training to continue improvements and keep guides updated, and continued oversight and maintenance.

REFERENCES

Brooks-Tatum, Shanesha R. F. 2012. "Delaware State University Guides Patrons into More Effective Research with Standardized LibGuides." *Against the Grain* 24 (1): 16–18.

Dahl, Candice. 2001. "Electronic Pathfinders in Academic Libraries: An Analysis of Their Content and Form." *College & Research Libraries* 62 (3): 227–237. doi: 10.5860/crl.62.3.227.

Dalton, Michelle, and Rosalind Pan. 2014. "Snakes or Ladders? Evaluating a LibGuides Pilot at UCD Library." *Journal of Academic Librarianship* 40 (5): 515–520. doi: 10.1016/j.acalib.2014.05.006.

Dupuis, John, Patti Ryan, and Merle Steeves. 2004. "Creating Dynamic Subject Guides." *New Review of Information Networking* 10 (2): 271–277. doi: 10.1080/13614570500082931.

Gonzalez, Alisa C., and Theresa Westbrock. 2010. "Reaching Out with LibGuides: Establishing a Working Set of Best Practices." *Journal of Library Administration* 50 (5–6): 638–656. doi: 10.1080/01930826.2010.488941.

Jasek, Chris. 2004. *How to Design Library Web Sites to Maximize Usability.* San Diego, CA: Elsevier. http://digital.csic.es/bitstream/10261/2926/1/howtodesign%5B1%5D.pdf.

Kapoun, Jim M. 1995. "Re-thinking the Library Pathfinder." *College & Undergraduate Libraries* 2 (1): 93–105. doi: 10.1300/J106v02n01_10.

Kumar, Beth Larkee, and Tabatha Farney. 2013. "Administering LibGuides: Planning, Implementation, and Beyond." In *Using LibGuides to Enhance Library Services: A LITA Guide,* edited by Aaron W. Dobbs, Ryan L. Sittler, and Douglas Cook, 43–64. Chicago: ALA TechSource.

Pickens, Kathleen, and Jessica Long. 2013. "Click Here (and Other Ways to Sabotage Accessibility)." Paper presented at the annual meeting for the Association of Research & College Libraries, Chicago, Illinois, April 10–13. http://www.ala.org/acrl/sites/ala.org.acrl/files/content/conferences/confsandpreconfs/2013/papers/PickensLong_Click.pdf.

Spindler, Tim. 2002. "The Accessibility of Web Pages for Mid-Sized College and University Libraries." *Reference & User Services Quarterly* 149–154.

Staley, Shannon M. 2007. "Academic Subject Guides: A Cast Study of Use at San Jose State University." *College & Research Libraries* 68(2): 119–140. doi: 10.5860/crl.68.2.119.

Strutin, Michal. 2008. "Making Research Guides More Useful and More Well Used." *Issues in Science and Technology Librarianship* 55 (5). http://www.istl.org/08-fall/article5.html.

Tumbleson, Beth E., and John Burke. 2013. *Embedding Librarianship in Learning Management Systems: A How-to-Do-It Manual.* Chicago: Neal-Schuman.

United States Department of Education, National Center for Education Statistics. 2015. "Fast Facts: Students with Disabilities." *Digest of Education Statistics.* Accessed October 23, 2015. https://nces.ed.gov/fastfacts/display.asp?id=60.

United States Department of Justice, Civil Rights Division. 2013. "Section 508 Surveys and Reports." *ADA.gov.* Accessed October 23, 2105. http://www.ada.gov/508/.

Vileno, Luigina. 2007. "From Paper to Electronic, the Evolution of Pathfinders: A Review of the Literature." *Reference Services Review* 35 (3): 434–451. doi: 10.1108/00907320710774300.

7

Content Wrangling for LibGuides Administrators

Aida Marissa Smith, MLIS, American Public University System

With a LibGuides account and a Springshare webinar under their belt, content authors can seamlessly create a bevy of research guides with links, widgets, RSS feeds, document files, and images. Content authors can further grow their guides by adding an unlimited number of tabs, and reusing content that already exists in their LibGuides website. To simplify content creation even further, vendors make product-specific LibGuides available that can be incorporated in part or entirely into library-authored research guides. The LibGuides platform ease of use and flexibility makes it a favorite tool among librarians for creating and delivering content on the web.

Creating content in LibGuides is such a simple process that librarians can quickly find themselves dealing with runaway content problems (Ghaphery and White 2012). Poor content presentation and dated content can confuse users, tarnishing the reputation of the library. Unused assets quickly multiply and clutter the Content Items index. Unused research guides can drain personnel resources and keep content authors from other responsibilities.

A carefully crafted web content management strategy is a key solution (Kumar and Farney 2013; Yu 2005). Applying a content management strategy to a library's LibGuides website can delineate boundaries before content gets out of hand, reducing the need for wrangling out-of-control content. With an overview of the processes involved, a sensible content management strategy can be crafted that addresses the relationships the platform has with stakeholders and draws on the platform's management features.

GENERATING SUPPORT AND MOVING FORWARD

Developing a solid content management strategy for a LibGuides version 2 (LGv2) website that will be accepted by all library stakeholders is important. Thinking about the concerns of all those involved, before the process begins, helps to ensure a solid foundation for its development and adoption. Library administration will need to ensure the strategy is in line with institutional and library goals (Yu 2005). Buy-in will be needed from content authors and owners, who will be asked to comply with the strategy's guidelines (Gonzalez and Westbrock 2010). Academic libraries may have departments outside of the library that depend on LibGuides content. Public libraries may have Friends groups with an interest. School libraries may have parent groups or clubs with an interest. Special libraries will have other interested groups. And, it is likely that each library will have additional stakeholders unique to their communities. With the many potential parties with an interest in the outcome, be sure to proceed methodically and transparently through the process of creating a library's content management strategy. Seek input and offer status updates from the various stakeholder groups when possible.

Start with Library Administration

A good place for LibGuides administrators to formally begin the process of initiating the development of a content management strategy is with library administration (Gonzalez and Westbrock 2010). Depending on the LibGuides administrator's position within the library, it may be as simple as reaching out to a direct supervisor. Support from library administration is essential in carrying out a successful content management strategy. When approaching library administration about the possibility of using a content management strategy, LibGuides site administrators should be prepared to address these issues:

- Benefits of a content management strategy for the library's LibGuides website. Significant reasons are to tame the quantity of LibGuides content created and to be better able to manage the quality of content created (Springshare 2014). Also, address the long-term and short-term benefits, specific to current state of the library's LibGuides website.
- Recommended scope of the content management strategy. Ideally, the content management strategy would address all LibGuides, but it may be expedient to initially limit the scope to one subset of guides.
- Likely perspective of the library's various stakeholders. Will all library stakeholders see this as a positive step? Why or why not?
- Collaboration with content authors and library work groups (Yu 2005). How will collaboration be facilitated? What can library administration do to enhance cooperation and reduce resistance?
- Coordination and standardization issues pertaining to the library website (Kumar and Farney 2013). Are any standards in place for the library website that would be useful to apply to the LibGuides website? Are there any workflow coordination issues that should be addressed?

- Rough time estimate. How long would it take to develop and implement a content management strategy?
- Time commitments for maintaining the content management strategy (Spring-share 2014). How much time would likely be spent on ensuring the completed content management strategy is uniformly applied? Which individuals or groups will be tasked with the responsibility? The more detail included in a content management strategy, the more time needed for its application.

Create a Content Management Strategy Development Plan

Once support is received for moving forward, create a development plan by dividing the process into key manageable components. A practical approach to breaking down the major tasks involves the following:

1. Project definition
2. Production guidelines defined
3. Maintenance guidelines defined
4. Implementation

Create a timeline for the plan's major tasks (Hernandez and McKeen 2015). The size of the LibGuides website, and the number of content owners and stakeholders, will impact the time needed for each step. This will also affect how thorough the timeline should be. Include details in the timeline to account for sign-off points from library administration and key library groups. Also consider adding feedback and update points for other interested stakeholders. The timeline will be useful to everyone involved in the process, and will let library administration know how the project fits into the library's strategic planning.

1. PROJECT DEFINITION

Define the project boundaries for developing the content management strategy. The plan can then be used as a reference point to explain the project to stakeholders and to outline the task and give focused direction to others working on the project. It can also be used to ward off scope creep, the casual expansion of the project. When defining the project, include what the content management strategy intends to accomplish and the mechanism for doing it (Gonzalez and Westbrock 2010). Elements to consider addressing when defining the project:

- Scope: Indicate which LibGuides will be addressed in the content management strategy. Will it be all guides? Only those in one group (if using LGv2 CMS)? Will the content management strategy include a workflow approval process?

- Responsibilities: Identify which individuals, groups, or committees will be responsible for the various aspects of the project from development to implementation.
- Format: Address the format of the final content management strategy. Will a LibGuide be created for this purpose? Will a Word, PDF, or Google document file be used?
- Implementation: Address how content owners and editors will learn about the completed content management strategy. Will distributing a copy of the document suffice? Will training workshops be needed?

While defining the project, think ahead to the types of metadata needed to organize and manage the collection. When addressing metadata, keep in mind how the collection will be used by authors and patrons. What types of internal sorting mechanisms may be useful? What terminology might users be familiar with? Maximize metadata functionality in LGv2 by defining how these fields are implemented and applied:

- Guide type: A grouping designation for sorting on the default LGv2 home page and internal sorting and filtering on the admin index. The six default type labels can be changed in the Language Options area of the Admin settings. Note that the Internal and Template Guide types are not made available for external indexing by search engines, and access is restricted to those logged into an LGv2 account.
- Guide group (LGv2 CMS): Allows distinct design customization based on group designation.
- Guide title syntax: Consider syntax standards for clarity and uniformity.
- Guide description: Consider terminology standards for clarity and uniformity.
- Subjects: Establish meaningful and clear subject designations. Consider adding scope notes for their use and associations.
- Friendly URLs: Consider establishing syntax standards for friendly URLs for ease of use and uniformity.
- Tags: For authority control issues, consider selecting a recommended list of tags to be uniformly applied. Consider using designated tags to bring together a subset of LibGuides that cannot be easily grouped together through other methods. Think about offering suggestions to content authors on how to select additional meaningful tags within the production guidelines.
- Custom metadata: If other metadata options methods for organizing and identifying guides are not suitable, consider the custom metadata fields available through the settings (cog) icon. This option embeds additional metadata into the head tag area of a web page. Custom metadata can be used to improve external site indexing and to identify published content for integration with external websites.

2. PRODUCTION GUIDELINES

The LibGuides platform gives content authors and editors many options and choices for developing content. A practical set of production guidelines for a LibGuides content management strategy draws on the strengths of the platform, to give parameters and definition to the information presented. Production guidelines can address guide content, design, and editorial standards.

Content Standards

Content standards address issues associated with creating new LibGuides and types of content added to them. Addressing content standards gives content authors focused direction on which guides are appropriate to create and what content to include or exclude (Kumar and Farney 2013; Springshare 2014). Strong content standards go far in curbing quantity and strengthening quality of assets and LibGuides. Consider addressing these content issues in your content management strategy:

- New guide authorship: Address who can author new guides or own existing guides. Librarians, library staff, student employees, volunteers, faculty? Will guide authorship and ownership vary by guide type?
- New guide workflow approval process: A workflow for approving new guides ensures only needed LibGuides are created and that content adheres to the content management strategy guidelines. A thorough approval process includes two key steps. The first step is approval for the development of a new LibGuide, often from a department chair or a committee. The second is to verify adherence to the content management strategy guidelines, often from a designated reviewer or editorial team. The new guide approval process can address all new guides, only guides with a published status, or only particular types of guides.
- Guide scope: Indicate the proper content scope for the types of LibGuides in the library website. For example, are the LibGuides intended to be comprehensive or introductory? Limited to licensed resources or to include open access resources? Should guides duplicate information already in use on the library website or point to the library website?
- Metadata standardization: Standardize the use of metadata. This helps organize and manage the growth of guide content. It also assists in presenting an organized collection of LibGuides to users. Guide metadata includes the guide title, subject, tags, description, friendly URL, type, group (LGv2 CMS), and the optional custom metadata fields.
- Images: Provide commonly needed images. Doing so will help content authors locate useful images, add a measure of quality control to the images used, and reduce multiple uploads of the same image. Upload and organize images to the Shared Library in the Image Manager for common use. Be careful; uploaded images cannot be moved between personal and shared folders. Use descriptive

file names and consider following a locally developed file naming convention to provide context. For example, the file name "library-logo-blue-lg.jpg" conveys more meaning than the file name "logo1.jpg." Image file names cannot be changed once uploaded.

- Link consistency for Content Items: Consider making recommendations on how links are created and used for Content Items. All book links need to have been created using the Book from the Catalog content type to generate a list of books used in guides from the Content Items index. When creating links to books, applying the proxy prefix option uniformly when creating links makes it easier to make global proxy prefix changes. Using a database asset, instead of creating a new Content Item for a database, makes it easier to make global changes to databases links and descriptions. Also, think about making recommendations on which links to use for content in the library catalog. Should links direct users to the catalog record or directly to the item? Think about how this decision impacts long-term link maintenance.
- Text link use: Create guidelines for how text links created in the Full Text/ HTML editor are used. These links are easy for content authors to create, but more difficult to maintain than Content Items. Unlike Content Items, links embedded in the text are not checked by the built-in link checker and link-level use statistics are not available.
- Copyright: Address copyright issues in selecting guide content. Reinforce the library's copyright guidelines or provide copyright compliance pointers to follow. Consider providing links to open access, royalty-free image. Consider standardizing on a Creative Commons attribution or allowing content authors to select their own. Creative Commons attributions can be added at the guide level or standardized on all guides through the Look & Feel settings. When added at the guide level, they are typically found near the bottom of a guide's home page. LibGuides leaves the issue of copyright with content authors and individual libraries.
- 508 Compliance: Address possible 508 compliance issues. When adding an image in LGv2, the Image Property box allows content authors to easily supply an alternate text. This will provide a clear text alternative for image for screen reader users. The websites WAVE (http://wave.webaim.org/) and AChecker (http://achecker.ca/checker/index.php) can be used for additional help in evaluating a guide's accessibility. LibGuides support documentation offers some tips in this area; the issue is left to libraries to address.

Using a common content guide is one way that content standards can be uniformly addressed and centrally maintained. A common content guide identifies and brings together original assets intended for reuse by content authors (Kumar and Farney 2013). Since the reuse content options on a guide rely on knowing an asset's title, having a guide that brings together designated reuse content as a reference point is helpful to content authors. Additionally, bringing together reusable content on one guide makes it easier to locate reused content when updates are needed.

Common content guides bring together many types of original assets for reuse. Lists of different types of Content Items, such as Link, Book from the Catalog, Document/File, and Media/Widget, can be listed on the guide. Boxes and pages can also be added to the guide. For database assets it is generally best to rely on the Add/Reorder > Database function, rather than to list them in the text on a common content guide.

Remind content authors about the difference between reusing mapped assets, which is the default option, and copied assets. Mapped assets will reflect changes made to the original asset, except for customized descriptions. Mapping assets makes it possible to update reused content assets by updating the original asset. Copied assets will not reflect any changes made to the original asset. Addressing this difference on the common content guide helps content authors in making decisions about how to reuse content appropriately.

Use the Internal Guide type designation for common content guides. This makes locating the guide easier by using the type filter on the Guide index. It also prevents the guide from being indexed externally, and requires users to be logged into their LGv2 account before viewing it.

Design Standards

Design standards address the structure for displaying content on a guide. Addressing design in a content management strategy helps content authors display their content in a consistent manner (Kumar and Farney 2013). Display consistency will make a collection of LibGuides easier to maintain. While many important elements of design can be best standardized centrally from the Admin Look & Feel settings, there are some design points that are best addressed in the individual guide. Keeping principles of user experience in mind, consider addressing these author-level design issues in content management strategies:

- Guide navigation: LGv2 provides two primary means of navigation, Tabbed Nav or Side-Nav. Regardless of which navigation method is used, advise content authors to consider the number of pages and subpages on their LibGuides. Also, think about standardizing LibGuides page titles. For example, will LibGuides have titles that correspond to format, topic or both? Should LibGuides using format types for page names have predefined names or a predefined sequence?
- Guide home page design: Consider standardizing the layout of each guide home page, the use and position of the profile box, column options, and the use and position of standardized content boxes.
- Guide page design: Consider if any content boxes or Content Items need to appear on particular pages, which cannot be standardized centrally through the Admin > Look & Feel settings.

One way to assist content authors in applying content management strategy design standards to their guides is to use a template guide (Gonzalez and Westbrock 2010). A template guide, not to be confused with the template options available in the Admin > Look & Feel settings, is a guide created specifically to be copied by authors to be used as shell for adding content. A template guide can include standardized content boxes and the appropriate guide home page layout. It could even include several sample page layouts, helpful for presenting different types of content. Think about including links to the Springshare LGv2 user documentation, and to the completed content management strategy for additional author direction in template guides.

LGv2 offers a specific guide type designation for guides used as templates. Guides with the Template Guide type designation are not indexed externally and can only be viewed by users logged into LGv2. Using the Template Guide designation can also help authors locate the template guide using the Guide index's filter options.

Editorial Standards

Editorial standards cover how the content will be displayed. It is possible that the library has already addressed these issues in relation to the library's website. If so, consider adopting them for the library's LibGuides website as well. Editorial standards address common issues such as the following:

- Standardized terms: Think about addressing how to refer to common library services, using the same terminology. For example, what term should be used to refer to interlibrary loan services? ILL, Interlibrary Loan, document delivery? What about, eReserves, e-reserves or E-Reserves?
- Capitalization: Think about how capitalization will be used in guide titles, box titles, assets, and headings.
- Color palate: Colors can be customized at the admin level, but a content author may still be able to add HTML or CSS code directly to a guide to change the color of elements on a guide. Consider providing appropriate hex color codes for individual guide customization, and indicate how the hex codes can or should not be applied.
- Icon collections: Consider selecting a collection of icons for content authors to use. Icons to be associated with assets can be added and managed from the icon index. Icons to be used as graphic elements can be uploaded to the Image Manager's shared image directory. Alternatively, think about designating an icon collection for content authors to use. Font Awesome is an ideal choice. It is compatible with LGv2, and Springshare provides help documentation on using this collection.

3. MAINTENANCE GUIDELINES

A strong content management strategy addresses guide maintenance issues. Maintenance guidelines are useful in keeping content fresh, up-to-date, and functional.

It also establishes a routine for removing extraneous or dated content (Springshare 2014). A practical set of maintenance guidelines for a LibGuides content management strategy draws on the platform's management features to identify content in need of maintenance and includes a cyclical maintenance calendar.

LGv2 Content Management Features

LGv2 offers maintenance features for content management. Understanding how the features work will help in decision making pertaining to content retention, uniformity, and organization. A list of guides can be exported to make evaluation easier. Consider using the following content management features available in the LGv2 platform:

- Guides index: From the orange command bar, Content > Guides. Use the Guides index to identify, locate, sort, and filter guides. It can be used to identify your guides by owner, type, status, and group, in LGv2 CMS. Lists can be used to identify guide trends and characteristics. It can also be used to identify departures from established syntax and metadata guidelines.
- Content Items index: From the orange command bar, Content > Assets > Content Items. Use the index to add, identify, locate, sort, and filter Content Items. The list can be used to identify Content Items with no mapping counts, find duplicated Content Items, and discover departures from established guidelines.
- A–Z Database List index: From the orange command bar, Content > Assets > A–Z Database List. Use the A–Z Database List index to centrally add, identify, locate, sort, and filter database assets. It can also be used to see which guides are reusing the database assets and to review database descriptions.
- Icons index: From the orange command bar, Content > Assets > Icons. Use the Icons index to manage icons available for assets associations.
- Tags index: From the orange command bar, Admin > Subjects, Tags & URLs > Tags. Use the index to add and manage the tags in use.
- Friendly URL index: From the orange command bar, Admin > Subjects, Tags & URLs > Friendly URLs. Use the index to manage the use of friendly URLs.
- Link Checker tool: From the orange command bar, Tools > Link Checker. The Link Checker tool is used to identify broken links by owner, and specific asset types, link, book, and database.
- Search & Replace Tool: From the orange command bar, Tools > Search & Replace. The Search & Replace option can be used to make global text updates. It can also be used to identify instances of text occurring in the site, without proceeding through with the replace option.
- Guide statistics: From the orange command bar, Statistics > Guides. The Statistics feature can be used to track guide views and referral URLs.
- Asset statistics: From the orange command bar, Statistics > Assets. The Statistics feature can be used to track asset views.

- Permissions management options: From the orange command bar, Admin > Accounts > Gear Icon in the action column. This feature allows editing rights to all guides, to be given to designated account holders. Additional management rights can be given to designated account holders, including individual groups, assets, surveys and subjects/tags/URLs, in LGv2 CMS.
- Internal guide discussion board (LGv2 CMS): Beneath the page tabs in a guide's edit view. This board offers a method to discuss a guide internally with those who have access to the guide. It can be used for dialogue between content authors and guide reviewers.
- Publishing Workflow (LGv2 CMS): From the orange command bar, Content > Publishing Workflow. This feature enables a publishing process where designated account holders approve new guides and changes to published guides. Carefully weigh using this optional feature against a workflow approval process independent of LibGuides. Designated reviewers may spend a lot of time approving minor updates using the Publishing Workflow option.

Cyclical Maintenance Schedule

A cyclical maintenance schedule helps to ensure maintenance tasks are not overlooked (Springshare 2014). A strong cyclical maintenance schedule addresses the types of content that needs to be maintained, how often the content types should be reviewed, and which individuals or groups are tasked. Establish a cyclical maintenance schedule, drawing on the maintenance features available in LGv2. Consider addressing these common content issues in the cyclical maintenance schedule:

- Subject designations and application: Are the defined subject designations still useful and appropriate? Are subject designations being appropriately applied?
- Group designations and applications (LGv2 CMS): Are the defined group designations still useful and appropriate? Are guides being added to the appropriate groups?
- Guide retention: Are there guides that are no longer needed? Can these guides be unpublished or deleted? Are there too many guides in the collection to be sustainable at the needed quality levels? What evaluation methods will be used in making these determinations?
- Guide metadata: Are the guidelines for guide metadata being applied correctly? Are the guide metadata guidelines still useful? Do they need to be revised?
- Guide content: Is the reusable guide content up-to-date? Do guides contain dated information? Is content staying within the proper scope? Does content needed to be refreshed for interest?
- Guide design standards: Are guide design standards being followed?
- Broken links: Is the Link Checker showing broken links? Have commonly used library website URLs changed? Have links to guides that have been unpublished been removed?

- Content Items: Are the guidelines for creating Content Item links being followed? Is the Content Items index showing unused and unneeded Content Items? Can those Content Items be deleted? Can redundant Content Items be consolidated?
- Database assets: Are the database asset links being reused on the guides appropriately? Are the database asset descriptions and subject associations up-to-date?
- Link icons: Are link icons being applied constantly?
- Tags: Are tags being appropriately applied to guides?
- Copyright and 508 compliance: Does guide content meet copyright and 508 compliance guidelines?

Consider which cyclical time intervals and frequencies work best with your library. Academic libraries may want to consider a schedule that corresponds with their school's academic calendar, designating various tasks to correspond with course starts and holiday breaks. Public libraries may want to use a schedule that corresponds to the calendar year. Corporate libraries may want to use a schedule that corresponds with the organization's quarterly review processes. In addition, consider that there may be tasks that need to be completed on a monthly, quarterly, or annual basis.

Think about if individuals or groups are best suited for the various maintenance tasks. For example, if it is decided to address the Link Checker tool's results on a monthly basis, is this a task best suited for guide editors, content authors, or the site administrator? If it is decided to review guide metadata on a quarterly basis, would this task be best suited for content authors, group administrators (LGv2 CMS), or site administrators? Are content authors, subject area committees, or a department leads best tasked for reviewing guide retention? Whose role is it to oversee the application of the cyclical maintenance schedule?

4. IMPLEMENTATION

Carefully consider the best way to introduce the finished LibGuides content management strategy to guide editors, authors, and others working with guide content. Offer solid documentation and provide assistance as needed to prevent guide owners and editors from becoming overwhelmed (Hernandez and McKeen 2015). Present the topic in the context of what the content management strategy offers, and give examples of what can be done. Consider the following when moving to implement a LibGuides content management strategy:

- Documentation: Think about the format of the documentation and the content of the documentation (Hernandez and McKeen 2015; Kumar and Farney 2013). The format should be easy to use and the content easy to understand. Include directions. Define responsibilities. Offer examples and creative ideas. Provide links to the Springshare LibGuides help documentation.

- Training: Consider offering hands-on workshops and question-and-answer sessions (Gonzalez and Westbrock 2010). Periodic emails, with tips and maintenance reminders, may also be useful. Be ready to share why particular guidelines are helpful. Carefully explain new guide workflow processes, if addressed in the content management strategy, and why they are beneficial.
- Assistance: Make it easy for content authors to ask questions and encourage it (Springshare 2014). Consider including contact information to appropriate individuals that can help within the content management strategy documentation.
- Feedback: Think about how to best include feedback to improve the content management strategy (Gonzalez and Westbrock 2010). Consider adding it to the documentation. Ask for it when meeting with others.
- Engagement: Consider providing mechanisms for content authors to share ideas with each other (Hernandez and McKeen 2015). Encourage creativity, within the context of the content management strategy. Offer a venue to discuss experiences and successes.

CONCLUSION

Having strong support from library administration and stakeholder buy-in provides a strong foundation for the development of a successful LibGuides content management strategy. Library administration needs to be on board for its implementation. Library stakeholders, especially content authors, need to understand the benefit of using a content management strategy. Seek active participation from library administration and library stakeholders in the development process.

An effective content management strategy addresses content development and content maintenance. Content development is addressed through well-developed guidelines, and streamlined through the use of template guides and common content guides. Template guides can simplify the process of adhering to layout and design guidelines by providing a format to follow, complete with guideline tips and examples. Common content guides make it easy to locate and update content intended for reuse on other guides. Content maintenance is best addressed though the routine of a cyclical maintenance calendar. Indicating clearly what needs to be done and who is responsible ensures easily overlooked maintenance tasks are addressed. It is useful for maintenance calendars to also include an evaluation mechanism to identify guides that are no longer needed and can be unpublished.

Content management strategies involve effort to put into place and apply. Ensuring guidelines and maintenance schedules are being followed requires oversight. Approval process workflows require thoughtful decision making. When building a content management strategy, aim for a balance between constructive direction and professional autonomy. This distributes the LibGuides overhead responsibility among library personnel, furthering a sense of ownership. The proper balance will depend on factors such as library type, the number of content authors, personnel availability for oversight activities, and the size of the guide collection.

Implementing a content management strategy can be done at any time in the lifecycle of a LibGuides website. Ideal times to implement a content management strategy include when LibGuides is initially being deployed or when migrating to LGv2. Even if these transition points have passed, the effort spent in establishing a strong and well-implemented content management strategy is worth the effort. Library users will have access to up-to-date, well-maintained guides. Content authors will know their role in creating and maintaining a solid guide collection. Library administration will be appreciating the quality control and content alignment with organizational priorities.

A well-managed LibGuides website reflects positively on the library and Lib-Guides site administrators are well positioned to lead the way. LibGuides administrators, get out there and start wrangling up that content!

REFERENCES

Ghaphery, Jimmy, and Erin White. 2012. "Library Use of Web-Based Research Guides." *Information Technology & Libraries* 31 (1): 21–31. doi: dx.doi.org/10.6017/ital.v31i1.1830.

Gonzalez, Alisa C., and Theresa Westbrock. 2010. "Reaching Out with LibGuides: Establishing a Working Set of Best Practices." *Journal of Library Administration* 50 (5–6): 638–656. doi: dx.doi.org/10.1080/01930826.2010.488941.

Hernandez, J. J., and McKeen, L. 2015. "Moving Mountains: Surviving the Migration to LibGuides 2.0." *Online Searcher* 39 (2): 16–21. doi: dx.doi.org/10.5860/choice.51–0007.

Kumar, Beth Larkee, and Tabatha Farney. 2013. "Administering LibGuides Planning, Implementation, and Beyond." In *Using LibGuides to Enhance Library Services: A LITA Guide*, edited by Aaron W Dobbs, Ryan L. Sittler, and Doug Cook, 43–64. Chicago, IL: American Library Association.

Springshare. 2014. "Getting Ready for the Transition to LibGuides 2." *Springshare* (blog), Accessed February 29, 2016. http://blog.springshare.com/2014/01/09/transition-to-lib-guides2.

Yu, Holly. 2005. "Library Web Content Management: Needs and Challenges." In *Content and Workflow Management for Library Websites: Case Studies*, edited by Holly Yu, 1–21. Hershey, PA: IGI Global, 2005.

III

DESIGNING AND DEVELOPING EFFECTIVE LIBGUIDES

8

Making User-Friendly Guides

Navigation and Content Considerations

Joshua Welker, MISLT, University of Missouri–Columbia

LibGuides began appearing as a common topic in library books and journals around 2009. The vast majority of the literature pertains to administrative or instructional issues, such as platform setup, training, and use cases. Relatively little has been written on assessing the effectiveness of guides. And of that small portion, an even smaller subset specifically addresses web usability.

A few key studies set the foundation for the assessment of LibGuides in the context of web usability. Some of the studies focus on guide organization. Staley (2007, 132) established that the way guides are usually organized is not helpful for students and that a paradigm shift for how we organize guides is in order. Beaton et al. (2009, 3) conducted a study on the language and labels used in guides, finding that participants had difficulty organizing guide content. Ouellette (2011, 442–449) found that many guides are too cluttered and provide information that is irrelevant to students. Sinkinson et al. (2012, 80) studied guide organization and found that guides should be designed to fit the context of student research rather than traditional library categories.

Other studies focused on navigation. Corbin and Karasmanis (2009, 26–38) conducted an in-depth observational study watching students complete various tasks in LibGuides and found many shortcomings in guide navigation. Hungerford et al. (2010, 3–9) found even more problems with typical guide navigation and layout. Pittsley and Memmott (2012, 52–62) identified several methods for improving navigation within guides and implemented them with great success.

While some issues of navigation and labeling have been addressed to a degree, the literature on navigation does not thoroughly address the deeper issue of information architecture. Another gap exists in the literature regarding the creation of useful and usable guide content, which is arguably more important than navigation. We need a comprehensive and holistic view of usability in the context of research guides that focuses on both big-picture issues and minute details.

INFORMATION ARCHITECTURE

In the existing LibGuides literature, discussions of navigation usability fall into two categories. The first category is navigation proper—where to put the navigation elements on a page, what they should look like, and so on. The second and more fundamental category is about determining what navigation categories to use and how to group page content in general. While related to navigation proper, these are really issues of information architecture.

Information architecture (IA) is the underlying conceptual model used to organize a website's content and functionality (Cardello 2014). While IA is manifest most explicitly in the navigation structure of a website, it is more conceptual than a navigation scheme. Nathaniel Davis (2011) describes IA as an iceberg. Navigation is just the tip of the iceberg. Beneath navigation are concepts such as classification, hierarchies, blueprints, and metadata. At the very base of the iceberg are conceptualizations of resources, users, and processes.

Libraries traditionally have a very strong internal IA. We have complex metadata schema, strongly controlled vocabularies, and distinct types of information content. Our IA has served us well for many years and works wonderfully in the context of internal operations. However, in the context of instruction and college students, our IA is a liability. Anyone who has spent time at a reference desk has seen students struggle with concepts like journals, articles, databases, indexes, material formats, collection categories, and subject classification. Students have difficulty with these concepts not because they are unintelligent but because they think about the library in terms of fundamentally different information architectures.

Mental Models

Experts in human-computer interaction often talk about information architecture in terms of mental models. A mental model is the way a person thinks about a system—their personal IA. Every person who uses a system has his or her own mental model for how the system is organized. In the case of end users, the model is often quite simple and based solely on past experiences. A user's success and satisfaction with a website are highly correlated with how closely the user's mental model matches the website's IA (Galitz 2007, 83).

The differences between the mental models of expert users and novice users cannot be overstated. Experts possess a deep understanding of the system and understand nuanced, complex categories and jargon. Experts are less likely to get tripped up by small details and inconsistencies because they understand the big picture. Novice users think of the system in terms of a small handful of surface-level tasks and features—specifically whatever they are trying to do right now. Since they do not understand the big picture of how the system works, minor issues like inconsistent language can cause major confusion (Galitz 2007, 89).

In the case of academic libraries, the vast majority of students are novices. Librarians are either expert users or the very designers of the system itself. Therefore, it is important to acknowledge that the way librarians think about the library is vastly different from how students think about it. There is a large gap in expertise between students and librarians.

There are two approaches to addressing the expertise gap. The first and more typical approach is to educate students about the library system to help them become more expert users. Librarians give themselves the herculean task of training their entire user base—thousands of students—to be better library users.

Most librarians agree that they have a responsibility to provide some type of education to students. But there is a fundamental difference between training students to be expert *academic library users* and training them to be expert *information users*. While that is a separate debate in itself, it will suffice to say that in the context of research guides, it is unrealistic to try to make thousands of undergraduate students into library experts in the few seconds they will spend reading a guide.

Researchers suggest a second approach to the expertise gap: modifying subject guides to conform to students' mental models. The first step is to figure out what those mental models are. These models vary wildly between different kinds of students. Librarians should conduct focus groups or usability testing prior to making a guide to figure out what students need (Ouellette 2011, 449). In order to do this, a specific target audience is needed. Subject guides should not be created for broad, general topics like Literature. Topics should be as specific as possible (445). If a professor needs a guide for her Early Modern English course, a librarian should make an Early Modern English guide, not just a tiny new subsection within a master Literature guide.

Librarians commonly make guides and subdivide them by resource format, with different sections for books, journals, databases, videos, web resources, and so on. That is how the librarian mental model works because those are the categories librarians use within their jobs. But multiple studies (Sinkinson et al. 2012, 73; Sonsteby and DeJonghe 2013, 89) found that students prefer guides to be organized based on their research process rather than resource formats. When observing students writing papers, they seem not to think in terms of content format: "I'd like to find some books, and then I'd like to find a journal, and then maybe a video . . ." Rather, they seem to think, "I need to choose a topic, and then I need to find my sources, and then I need to write my paper, and then I need to cite my sources . . ." Librarians should organize guides based on these steps. But to find out what those steps are, librarians must first talk to the students who are the intended audience and find out exactly how they think about their assignments and what they need.

A distinction needs to be made between *interesting* and *necessary*. Students primarily use research guides only when all else fails and they are stuck (Ouellette 2011,

444). At that point, they are very narrowly focused on the task at hand. There is no time for serendipitous discovery of interesting information. It's not that they dislike certain kinds of information. They just don't find it useful at the moment. Web users in general are focused on specific goals and don't take time to explore out of pure interest (Nielsen 2011).

Before even creating a guide, librarians should figure out exactly why students need it. If there isn't a concrete and specific need, like a particular professor asking for a guide for a particular purpose, librarians shouldn't even bother creating the guide. If there is a real need, the guide should include only what is necessary and omit everything else.

One common finding in literature on subject guides is that students like specific labels rather than broad, vague ones. Sonsteby and DeJonghe (2013, 89) found that the words *articles* and *databases* are easily recognized. Rather than using the vague term *reference sources*, they suggest a more specific word like *encyclopedias*. Naming these categories is an essential part of constructing a guide and should not be an afterthought. Rather than going by their guts, librarians should test category names with real users (Loranger 2013).

Cognitive Load

Cognitive load theory posits that learners can only process a finite number of things simultaneously and must free up mental space before learning can happen. Little (2010, 61) conducted a study on LibGuides and cognitive load and found some practical results. Her first recommendation, which should sound familiar by now, is to "tie guides to the course-level whenever possible rather than to the broad subject area" (61). Forcing students to shift mental gears from their specific research process to broad and abstract categories causes disruption and increases cognitive load. She also recommends using clear and consistent terminology (61–62). Inconsistency is a frequent usability hurdle for students using research guides (Hungerford, et al. 2010, 6).

SUMMARY OF INFORMATION ARCHITECTURE RECOMMENDATIONS

- Think like a student when designing guides.
- Scope guides as narrowly as possible to specific courses or subdisciplines.
- Organize guides by the processes and resources that students need in the context of their assignments. Resource type should not be the primary organization scheme.
- Be specific in the naming of pages. Avoid vague terms like *resources*.
- Keep the number of pages to a minimum, and keep page content brief.
- Use consistent terms and layouts between pages and guides.

Cognitive load theory's primary implication for information architecture is that guides should be as simple as possible. Guides should avoid an overabundance of pages and categories and focus on only the most important information (Sonsteby and DeJonghe 2013, 89). Everything else just creates cognitive load as users have to try to figure out which option will work best.

NAVIGATION USABILITY

After examining the principles of information architecture underlying navigation, the more concrete subject of navigation proper can be addressed. Common navigation conventions need to be discussed in the context of usability, and there are a handful of concrete, practical recommendations for improving guide navigation.

Tabbed navigation

Tabbed navigation is one of the most recognizable features of LibGuides. In the original LibGuides version 1 (LGv1), tabs were the only navigation option. In LibGuides version 2 (LGv2), sidebar navigation is also an option. However, tabbed navigation still dominates the landscape. At the time of writing, of the sixty-three guides shown in the Most Recent section of the Best of LibGuides website, every single one used tabbed navigation (Springshare 2015).

The way tabbed navigation works in LibGuides is that each time a new page is added to a guide, a tab for that page appears in the guide's navigation menu. Subpages appear in a small drop-down menu within tabs. Tabbed navigation remains prevalent in LibGuides even though the tabs are one of the most cited usability problems in literature on LibGuides usability. While Beaton et al. (2009, 4) did find tabbed navigation to be "recognizable and meaningful," they are a minority opinion.

Corbin and Karasmanis (2009, 9) were among the first to find fault with tabbed navigation in LibGuides. They found that the tabs were often misunderstood or outright ignored. And among users who actually used the tabs, a vanishingly small number used drop-down subtabs (14). Hungerford et al. (2010, 6) found that users often didn't notice the tabs. Pittsley and Memmott (2012, 52–53) noted that tabs in their guides were not being utilized by students. The impetus for Pittsley and Memmott's study was that usage of a subject guide for a recurring course suddenly dropped one semester. It happened to be the semester they adopted LibGuides. After consulting with students from the course, they learned that students did not notice the navigation tabs and therefore did not use most pages in the guide.

Guidelines for Usable Tabs

The out-of-the-box implementation of tabs in LibGuides leaves a few things to be desired. Krug (2014, 81) and Nielsen (2007b) both emphasize that web-based tabs have to mimic physical folder tabs to be effective. They set forth these guidelines:

- The active tab should stand out from inactive tabs with a different and bolder color. Inactive tabs should appear to be in the background.
- The active tab should appear continuous with the page content below it. The tab and the page should be the same color and not separated by a border.
- Tab labels should be clear and concise.
- There should only be one row of tabs.

Figure 8.1 contains an example of the default tabbed navigation interface in Lib-Guides. Notice that there is no continuity between the active tab and the rest of the page. The physical tab metaphor falls apart. Figure 8.2 is an example of the tabbed navigation element provided by the Bootstrap CSS framework. Through the use of borders, the active tab appears to be continuous with the page content, and the inactive tabs are cut off from the content below. Bootstrap provides a much stronger example of usable tabbed navigation.

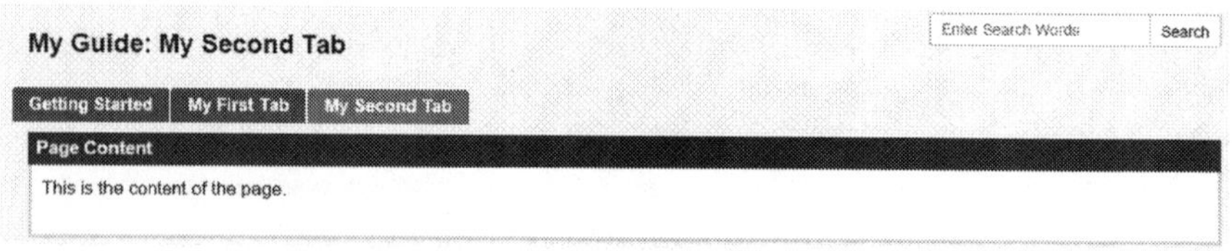

Figure 8.1.   LibGuides default tabbed navigation.

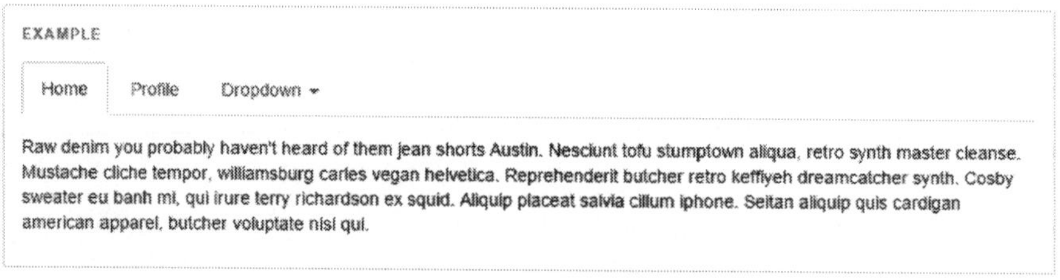

Figure 8.2.   Bootstrap tabs component.

Invisibility

A recurring finding in LibGuides studies is that users do not notice the tabbed navigation at all. The tabs do not get clicked, and content on pages other than the first page does not get viewed. One possible cause is that the default tabs are too small. Some libraries have experimented with increasing the height of tabs and have seen some success (Pittsley and Memmott 2012, 56–61). Another potential cause of the apparent invisibility of tabbed navigation is simply the location of the tabs. Top navigation can easily blend in with a website's header and needs a high level of contrast with the header to be visible (Chen et al. 2010, 3). Color and spacing should be used to make top navigation more visible (16–17).

Tab Overload

Perhaps the worst usability problem with tabbed navigation is that they create an enormous amount of visual clutter. Due to the horizontal nature of tabs, it only takes a handful of tabs before they start to overflow into multiple rows. Tabs should be limited to six or fewer (Sonsteby and DeJonghe 2013, 87). Most importantly, tabs should be limited to one row (Tidwell 2006). Too many tabs cause information overload, confusing students and causing them to ignore the tabs completely (Ouellette 2011, 444).

In addition to being harder to use, multiple rows of tabs are a red flag indicating poor information architecture (Nielsen 2007b). A guide that has been created with a specific focus in mind should not find itself including such a breadth of information as to need multiple rows of tabs. If a guide has multiple rows of tabs, its purpose and scope probably need to be rethought at a fundamental level.

Sidebar Navigation

Sidebar navigation is a new feature in LGv2. They have not yet caught on in popularity. Tabs are an integral feature of LibGuides in the minds of many librarians. After years of using tabs-only LibGuides, tabbed navigation seems to have enough momentum that few librarians want to change to a new convention. Sidebar navigation in LibGuides works in a very similar way to tabbed navigation. Upon creating a new page, an entry for that page is automatically added to the sidebar. The sidebar is on the left by default, but administrators can modify their templates to have right-hand sidebars if desired.

Sidebar navigation is a promising addition to LibGuides. In theory, it resolves many of the problems facing tabbed navigation. As discussed earlier, tabbed navigation seems to be invisible to many users. Nielsen (2006) famously describes an F-shaped pattern (figure 8.3) for how users read on the web, which includes two initial

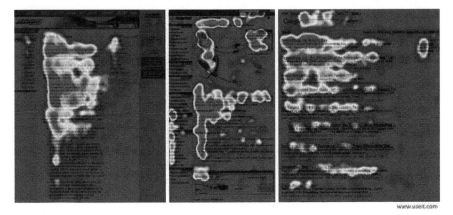

Figure 8.3. F-shaped reading pattern. *Jakob Nielsen, "F-Shaped Pattern for Reading Web Content." Nielsen Norman Group (blog), April 17, 2006, http://www.nngroup.com/articles/f-shaped-pattern-reading-web-content*

horizontal scans across upper parts of the page and a vertical scan down the left side. If Nielsen's pattern is correct, during the vertical movement at the end of the F pattern, users should see a navigation menu placed on the left.

Sidebar navigation also solves the overflow problem that tabbed navigation poses. Four or five tabs fit comfortably into a tabbed menu, but a vertical menu can easily fit a dozen items (not that it necessarily should). Another handy feature of sidebar navigation is that it has an option to show subpages in the sidebar without having to hover over a drop-down menu. Research shows that drop-down navigation menus don't work well in tabbed navigation, and it stands to reason that it probably doesn't work well in sidebar navigation. This option can be enabled in the Guide Navigation Layout menu.

Unfortunately, there is a major gap in the literature on sidebar navigation. While research abounds on left navigation versus top navigation on the web in general (and is rarely conclusive), there is virtually no research on tabbed navigation versus sidebar navigation in the context of LibGuides. Sidebar navigation seems to have promise. Librarians should be encouraged to experiment with sidebar navigation to see if it improves guide usage.

Tables of Contents

Many web designers have spent hours debating the merits of side navigation versus top navigation. Some point to eye tracking studies such as Nielsen's to decide one way or the other. But Nielsen himself admits that eye tracking data is not conclusive and must be taken with a grain of salt. Different individuals and different contexts create wide variance in viewing patterns (Nielsen and Pernice 2010, 50). When people visit a website, they are very focused on the task at hand and make quick judgments about what is relevant. Site-wide features such as branding and navigation are often discarded as irrelevant fluff, and the user jumps right into the meat of the page (Nielsen 2000).

Research on subject guides reflects Nielsen's findings. Researchers recommend adding a table of contents as the first item in the body of each subject guide (Sonsteby and DeJonghe 2013, 89). A good table of contents makes it clear to users what is in a guide. It is right in the middle of the page and can't possibly be missed. In general, students are more likely to click navigation links if they are within the content area of the page rather than being relegated to a special navigation region (Corbin and Karasmanis 2009, 11).

There are a few ways to create a table of contents in LibGuides. The most basic way is to type a list of links manually. In 2013, Springshare added a Table of Contents box to LGv1 that automatically builds a linked list of all pages in a guide and updates the list as the guide changes. LGv2 got rid of the Table of Contents box. In its place, Springshare added sidebar navigation menus, which function similarly. While by default the sidebar navigation menu appears in the sidebar column, it is possible to create a custom template that adds the menu to the main body column.

Search

LibGuides includes a search box that searches all the content across an institution's entire LibGuides website by default. Librarians understand that LibGuides is a self-contained platform and the search feature makes perfect sense for them. Students, however, find it confusing. The confusion stems from mismatched mental models. Users expect all search engines to work like the Googles and Amazons of the web (Budiu 2014). When users search Google, the scope is the whole Internet. When users search Amazon, the scope is every product on Amazon. When users search on the library's website, they reasonably expect that the scope is all the resources offered by the library.

But that is not the case. Even the most sophisticated discovery tools only search certain subsets of a library's information resources. And the search box in LibGuides is vastly narrower in scope, only searching the library's guides. To compound the confusion, research guides usually contain information about library resources. When students see a search box in the research guide, they reasonably assume that the box will search the library content related to the guide. Users will often haphazardly enter search terms into any box they can find (Nielsen 2011).

The built-in LibGuides search box is especially problematic. Students don't have a clear concept of research guides, so a search limited to research guides is meaningless to them. They end up using it incorrectly, resulting in confusion (Hungerford et al. 2010, 9). Due to the confusion caused by search boxes, librarians should exercise caution and consider removing the LibGuides search box from their guides. The search box can be removed quite easily in LGv2 by creating a custom template and removing this code as shown in figure 8.4.

```
<div id="s-lg-guide-header-search">{{guide_search}}</div>
```

Figure 8.4.   Search box code.

While not part of navigation per se, many LibGuides make use of search widgets from database vendors like ProQuest and EBSCO. Librarians often embed these within the content area of the page. But these suffer from the problem discussed already: mismatched scope. Students expect the search results to be relevant to the guide that contain the widget, but such is rarely the case (Corbin and Karasmanis 2009, 15; Hungerford et al. 2010, 4). Librarians should make sure that any search widgets are scoped only to results that are relevant to the guide at hand. If that can't be done, the widget should be left out.

CONTENT USABILITY

Compared to navigation, the usability of LibGuides content is relatively undiscussed. Much consideration is given to navigation in LibGuides, both in the

SUMMARY OF NAVIGATION
USABILITY RECOMMENDATIONS

Many recommendations in this section are only relevant to guides that used the tabbed navigation interface. If deciding to use tabs, be sure to follow these recommendations:

- Restyle tabs so that the active tab is continuous with the page content and inactive tabs are not. The active tab should be the same color as the content below it, and there should be no border between the active tab and the content. Consider making the tabs larger as well.
- Limit tabs to one row. If tabs start to overflow, consider revisiting the guide's information architecture as discussed earlier. Another option is to consolidate multiple pages into one. If all else fails, switch to the sidebar navigation template provided by LGv2.
- Use spacing and color to differentiate tabs from the website's header.
- Do not use nested subtabs. Instead of using a page with subpages, just add all that content to the top-level page.
- Consider using the sidebar navigation template provided by LGv2.

The following recommendations are relevant to all guides:

- Add a table of contents to the main page of the guide in the middle of the content area. This can be done automatically using the Table of Contents box in LGv1 or by customizing the sidebar navigation template in LGv2. Or, make one manually, but be sure to keep it updated.
- Remove the LibGuides search box by creating a custom template.
- Only add search widgets to guides if the search results are relevant and scoped exclusively to the subject matter of the guide.

literature and by librarians in the workplace. Anecdotally, librarians from many institutions have mentioned that discussions about navigation in LibGuides can quickly become heated and contentious. But navigation is much less important than having good content.

Usability experts recommend a content-first approach. Users spend much more time focusing on page content than on navigation. LibGuides strongly emphasizes navigation during the guide development workflow in its page creation tools, so librarians naturally give it a good bit of thought. A guide could have the greatest navigation structure on the web, but if its content is unapproachable, the guide is useless. Thus, a discussion of the usability of guide content is very much warranted.

Make Your Point

When a user visits a guide, she decides very quickly if it is relevant—about three seconds (Nielsen 2000). Basic information about the guide needs to be visible immediately. Users need to be able to understand the purpose and relevance of the guide right away (Krug 2014, 89). If the guide fails to make its case in that time frame, the user will leave. In addition to the guide itself, the value and purpose of all the resources listed within the guide should be immediately evident, with clear and concise descriptions (Sinkinson et al. 2012, 80; Little 2010, 62).

Facilitate Rapid Scanning

One of the best ways to help users understand what is in a guide is to make it easy to visually scan the guide. Hopefully, once the user has landed in a guide, the purpose of the guide has been conveyed in the first two or three seconds, and it struck the user as relevant. Next, the user will skim the guide and look for specific bits that pop out and look like what she needs. Librarians should make this skimming and scanning as easy as possible.

Headings

The first way to facilitate rapid scanning in a guide is to use clear headings—a tool poorly utilized in most guides (Little 2010, 56). Headings make it easy for users to tell what content on the page is relevant to their needs. Good headings have the following characteristics (Nielsen and Loranger 2006):

- They establish a clear visual hierarchy.
- They utilize native HTML heading tags h1 through h6.
- They are displayed consistently throughout the website using site-wide CSS, not through arbitrary larger, bolder, colored, capitalized, or underlined text.
- They are left-aligned, not centered.

LibGuides makes limited use of headings within guides through its box model. The title of each box is an h2 HTML tag. However, by default, the box headings are nearly the same size as the body text inside the boxes. They are instead highlighted by colors and borders, which can increase visual clutter.

Adding subheadings in LibGuides is not very intuitive. One must add a Rich Text/HTML content area, type the heading, highlight it, and change the Paragraph Format to the appropriate heading. Among the heading types are Heading 1 (h1) and Heading 2 (h2). Since LibGuides uses h1 tags for the page title and h2 tags for the box title, using h1 or h2 within a box breaks the hierarchy of the page. Although this may not cause a visual problem, it can be problematic for some use cases such as third-party table of contents widgets and screen readers. The appropriate choice for a first-level subheading within a LibGuides box is actually Heading 3 (h3)—not a very intuitive choice.

Paragraph Length

Few things on the web are less approachable than a wall of text. Huge paragraphs are extremely difficult to read on a screen (Krug 2014, 40). Usability experts recommend instead using many short paragraphs with less than five sentences each (Nielsen and Loranger 2006).

Limiting paragraphs to just a few lines makes it easier for readers to break the information down into easily digested chunks. Librarians shouldn't worry about simplistic writing rules like a single paragraph per main idea. If it makes even a modicum of sense for a paragraph to break at a particular point, it probably should.

Lists

Even better than short paragraphs are lists. Unordered (bulleted) lists are more commonly useful, but ordered (numbered) lists are good, too. Lists are great at breaking ideas down into bite-sized chunks. Lists are one of the rare cases on the web where whenever it *can* be done, it probably *should* be done (Krug 2014, 40). Numbered lists should be used less frequently than bulleted lists. Librarians should only use numbered lists when needing to convey a sequence in a specific order. Otherwise, users will look for a pattern that isn't there, leading to confusion.

False Floors

A false floor is when a web page has additional scrollable content below the visible screen but gives the appearance that the content ends at the bottom of the screen. One weakness of the LibGuides box structure is that boxes have a definitive ending point that can make it look like it is the end of an entire page. This is especially problematic in cases like figure 8.5, where a box happens to end at the bottom of the user's screen.

The best way to defeat the false floor illusion is to make page content appear continuous. If a box ends near the bottom of a page, make sure the top of the next box is visible. Of course, with varying screen sizes, there is no telling quite where a box will end for any given user. Therefore, it is advisable to either put an entire page's content into a single box or to use CSS to hide box borders. Librarians should avoid having anything that looks like an ending point until the real end of the content.

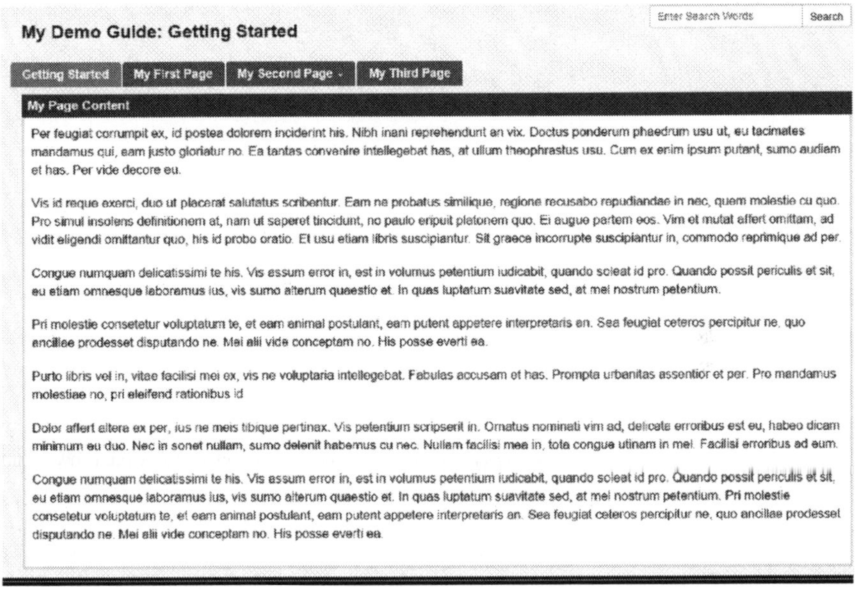

Figure 8.5. A false floor created by a box.

Columns

While they haven't been mentioned specifically in LibGuides literature, column-based layouts are a potential usability hazard. There is nothing wrong with the concept of column-based layouts per se. They are a staple of the Internet. The problem is when the columns have an identity crisis.

LibGuides makes it very easy to move content between columns—so easy, in fact, that librarians get the impression that because it *can* be done, it *should* be done. It is important for all the content of a page to stay in one column, and the location of that column should be consistent across all pages. Sidebar columns should be used for supplemental information, like guide navigation links and contact information. The stuff related to the subject of the page should stay in the main column.

There are two reasons for keeping content in one column. The first is readability. Users scan pages from top to bottom. It is very difficult to change from a one-dimensional scanning pattern (top to bottom) to a two-dimensional pattern (top to bottom, side to side). It disrupts the flow of the page. All the columns compete for the user's attention at once. It creates an enormous sense of clutter.

The second reason is that columns are not consistent across devices. Take figure 8.6, which uses a standard three-column layout common in LibGuides. The page was designed on a widescreen desktop computer and intended to look like figure 8.6. The columns should be read from left to right following the order of the box numbers.

| Box 1 | | Box 2 | | Box 3 |
| Box 4 | | Box 5 | | Box 6 |

Figure 8.6. A three-column layout on a desktop monitor.

But not all users will view this page on a full-sized screen. Figure 8.7 shows the same page as figure 8.6 when viewed on a tablet or smartphone. Now the boxes are all out of order! On small screens, multicolumn layouts collapse into a single column. The left column comes first, followed by the next column to the right, and so on. This is a major problem if the most important content on my page is in the big center column. On a small screen, that content is pushed way down beneath the left column content.

Figure 8.7. The same three-column layout on a smartphone.

This problem can be mitigated to some extent in LibGuides using custom templating and multiple rows, but it is overly complicated. It also doesn't solve the issue of left content appearing first even when center content is most important. It would be better to learn to live without a column-based layout altogether. Part of the appeal of the column-based layout is that it theoretically lets users avoid scrolling, which is seen as a great evil. This is a myth that must be dispelled.

Page Length and Scrolling

A widely cited Nielsen statistic is that only 23 percent of users scroll on web pages (Nielsen and Loranger 2006). This fact is used as evidence that scrolling is bad. Librarians respond to this information in two ways (often both): cramming as much information as possible into the top section of a guide using multiple columns, or creating guides with dozens of bite-sized pages and subpages with sprawling rows of navigation tabs.

Nielsen's 23 percent figure is taken completely out of context. It is by no means a blanket condemnation of scrolling. The 23 percent figure refers only to scrolling on home pages. On other pages that actually contained content, the scrolling rate was 42 percent. One might think 42 percent seems a bit low, and in a sense it is. But what the number really indicates is that only 42 percent made a strong enough case to make the user *want* to scroll. As mentioned earlier, users spend two to three seconds on a page before deciding whether it is worth reading. The takeaway isn't that the other 58 percent of web pages should have crammed all their content into the top part of the page. Rather, it means that 58 percent of web pages should have made themselves look more relevant. Nielsen himself makes this point in the very same book in which he published the 23 percent figure.

In the early years of computers and the Internet, scrolling was very uncommon. AOL during its peak years didn't even allow pages to scroll. But over the course of nearly two decades, web users have become increasingly tolerant of scrolling (Nielsen 1997). Since then, after the rise of Web 2.0 and its abundant white space and after the emergence of smartphones, scrolling is a regular fact of life for web users (Levinson and Schlatter 2013).

The one place to avoid scrolling is on home pages, which Nielsen's data actually indicates. The parallel in research guides is a guide's first page. Users shouldn't be forced to scroll on this page in order to learn what is in it. Convention like a table of contents should be used to grab the user's attention right away and show them exactly what relevant content is in the guide.

Web designers should avoid simple usability rules of thumb like the no-scroll rule. If a guide is designed well enough that it gives off a strong information scent and a user thinks it is relevant to her needs, she will scroll. Of course, at that point, she will be skimming and scanning, not actually reading. All the previously discussed principles about facilitating scanning apply. If pages are designed so that they are easy to scan, it can actually be advantageous to have few very long pages, compared to many short ones. It is easier to scroll up and down a page scanning headings than it is to click and scroll over and over and over navigating between many pages and hoping to find the right one (Nielsen and Loranger 2006).

Prioritize Relevant Content

Librarians like to be comprehensive. After spending so much time and money acquiring bibliographic content, librarians naturally want to advertise as much of it as possible. LibGuides in particular has a variety of box and content types that encourage adding a wealth of content: embedded videos, widgets, book images, RSS feeds, image galleries, files, polls, and more. The message librarians often take away is that since these features are there, they should be used.

In the context of research guides and the web in general, a less-is-more approach is more successful. A good rule of thumb is to try to eliminate at least half the words on a page (Krug 2014, 49). The less verbiage is in a guide, the easier it is for students to figure out what is relevant to their needs (Corbin and Karasmanis 2009, 30).

Be wary of adding anything besides text and links in guides. Everything else has a great tendency to create clutter with little real benefit to students. While, for instance, it is conceivable that an RSS feed might fill a real need in a guide, it is highly unlikely. Video is one of the more common exceptions, but the video must be relevant to the specific purpose of the guide.

A common source of verbiage is instructions. Librarians often include instructions on how to use the guide or how to use a particular database. But evidence shows that these instructions don't actually help students find research materials (Corbin and Karasmanis 2009, 30–31). The best solution is to make a process so simple and self-evident that instructions are unnecessary (Krug 2014, 51). Few people take the time to stop and read instructions, anyway.

Avoid Fonts and Colors

Fonts and especially colors are one of the worst examples of something that can be done in LibGuides but probably shouldn't. LibGuides makes it very easy to change all sorts of colors: tabs, backgrounds, box headers, and paragraph text. And a tiny snippet of CSS in a Rich Text/HTML box can change the color or font of virtually anything on the page for those willing to dabble in a bit of code.

Two common reasons why librarians change the colors and fonts in their guides are to be creative and to highlight content. Neither is a good reason. Creativity is nice, but as we discussed earlier, inconsistency between pages creates cognitive load. It breaks continuity and can make the user think, "Wait, this is different. Why did it change? What does that mean? Am I in the right place anymore?" Visual change is a disruptive experience. Creativity is great, but it should be employed at the site-wide level, not on individual guides and pages.

Highlighting content seems like a great use of colors and fonts at the surface. The problem is that it doesn't work. "Banner blindness" is real. There are some things that appear so often in ads that they automatically signal "That's an ad! Skip it!" in the user's mind, even if it is good and useful content. Any kind of fancy formatting signals advertisement in the minds of users (Nielsen 2007a). Bold colors and fancy fonts are two of the top offenders. Falling back on these tools to highlight content is a crutch that should be avoided. The appropriate way to highlight something is to locate it in a coherent and well-organized layout (Nielsen and Pernice 2010, 93).

As far as how to use colors and fonts appropriately, the rules are quite simple. Rule number one is to be consistent. The same colors and fonts should be used across all pages (Hoekman 2011). Rule number two is to pick readable choices. The best colors are black text on a low-intensity but not completely white background (Galitz 2007, 708). Fonts have few true guidelines. Use bold text sparingly

SUMMARY OF CONTENT USABILITY RECOMMENDATIONS

- Make the purpose and scope of the guide extremely clear, especially on the guide home page. Consider using a table of contents. Include clear and concise descriptions.
- Use HTML headings (h1–h6) to create hierarchy within pages. Use site-wide styles to make headings consistent across pages.
- Use many small paragraphs instead of few larger ones.
- Use bulleted lists often.
- Avoid false floors that make it look like the page ends when it really doesn't. Consider removing the borders from LibGuides boxes using site-wide styles.
- Keep all the content relevant to a page in one column. Keep the use of columns minimal. Be consistent between pages and guides.
- Don't worry about scrolling. Instead, worry about showing users why the page is relevant without regard for length.
- Make guides based on a real, specific need. Only include content that is relevant to meeting that need. Omit everything else.
- Put the most relevant content first.
- Eliminate verbiage. Remove as many words as possible. Especially avoid instructions.
- Use consistent fonts and colors across all guides.
- Avoid using fonts and colors to highlight content.

and only to highlight a few words at a time, not entire paragraphs. Avoid special display and handwriting-style fonts, especially the notorious Comic Sans. As for the debate between serif and sans-serif fonts, the current consensus is that they are both fine. In the 1990s, sans-serif fonts dominated due to looking better on low-resolution screens. Now that virtually every device has decent resolution, it is a moot point (Nielsen 2012).

CONCLUSION

LibGuides is a powerful platform loaded with functionality. It is extremely flexible and easy to use. But this strength is also its greatest weakness. LibGuides has so many features and makes them so easy to use that it almost encourages librarians to make rash design decisions that actually harm guides.

With its endless array of features, it is easy to get caught up in the features—tabs, columns, boxes, widgets, embedded content, RSS feeds, polls, colors—and lose sight of the fundamentals. Research guides should exist for a specific need, and librarians should concentrate their energy on providing content to meet that need. Creating helpful content to serve a specific need should be first priority. Everything else is icing on the cake.

When designing a research guide, librarians should consider starting off by ignoring all the features in LibGuides. Using a basic word processor like MS Word (or, better yet, MarkdownPad: http://markdownpad.com) allows one to focus on the words on the page and not bells and whistles. Once the guide is full of excellent content, it should be plugged it into a standard, consistent, minimalist template used by the whole institution, with whatever minor tweaks necessary. The tweaks should be an afterthought. Layout and navigation are only tools for highlighting *how* and *why* the content is relevant and useful. Any feature not serving that purpose should be eliminated. Once a librarian starts making great guides, she will find that she uses few features from the vast tool set built into LibGuides because she only *needs* a few of them. If it's not necessary, at best, students will ignore it. At worst, students will become confused and frustrated.

Refer back to the summary at the end of each section of this chapter for straightforward recommendations to make research guides more useable and useful. These recommendations are guidelines, not hard rules. But if they are going to be broken, this should be done intentionally and with good reason.

REFERENCES

Beaton, Barbara, Jennifer Bonnet, Suzanne Chapman, Bill Deuber, Shevon Desai, Kat Hagedorn, Julie Piacentine, Karen Reiman-Sendi, and Ken Varnum. 2009. *LibGuides Usability Task Force Guerrilla Testing*. Accessed October 29, 2015. http://www.lib.umich.edu/files/services/usability/libguides_rept_final.pdf.

Budiu, Raluca. 2014. "Search Is Not Enough: Synergy between Navigation and Search." *Nielsen Norman Group* (blog), September 7. Accessed October 29, 2015. http://www.nngroup.com/articles/search-not-enough/.

Cardello, Jennifer. 2014. "The Difference between Information Architecture (IA) and Navigation." *Nielsen Norman Group* (blog), June 22. Accessed October 29, 2015. http://www.nngroup.com/articles/ia-vs-navigation/.

Chen, Jennifer, Jenna Beck, Elizabeth Murphy, and Jennifer Romano. 2010. *Usability Evaluation of the Governments Division Public Web Site*. Washington, D.C.: U.S. Census Bureau. http://www.census.gov/srd/papers/pdf/ssm2010-02.pdf.

Corbin, Jenny, and Sharon Karasmanis. 2009. *Health Sciences Information Literacy Modules Usability Testing Report*. La Trobe University Library. Accessed October 29, 2015. http://hdl.handle.net/1959.9/398212

Davis, Nathaniel. 2011. "Framing the Practice of Information Architecture." *UX Matters* (blog), September 7. Accessed October 29, 2015. http://www.uxmatters.com/mt/archives/2011/09/framing-the-practice-of-information-architecture.php.

Galitz, Wilbert O. 2007. *The Essential Guide to User Interface Design: An Introduction to GUI Design Principles and Techniques*. Indianapolis: Wiley.

Hoekman, Robert. 2011. *Designing the Obvious*. Berkeley, CA: New Riders.

Krug, Steve. 2014. *Don't Make Me Think, Revisited: A Common Sense Approach to Web Usability*. Berkeley, CA: New Riders.

Levinson, Deborah, and Tania Schlatter. 2013. *Visual Usability*. Waltham, MA: Elsevier.

Little, Jennifer J. 2010. "Cognitive Load Theory and Library Research Guides." *Internet Reference Services Quarterly* 15 (1): 53–63. doi: 10.1080/10875300903530199.

Loranger, Hoa. 2013. "Avoid Category Names That Suck." *Nielsen Norman Group* (blog), December 15. Accessed October 29, 2015. http://www.nngroup.com/articles/category-names-suck/.

Nielsen, Jakob. 1997. "Changes in Web Usability since 1994." *Nielsen Norman Group* (blog), December 1. Accessed October 29, 2015. http://www.nngroup.com/articles/changes-in-web-usability-since-1994/.

Nielsen, Jakob. 2000. "Is Navigation Useful?" *Nielsen Norman Group* (blog), January 9. Accessed October 29, 2015. http://www.nngroup.com/articles/is-navigation-useful/.

Nielsen, Jakob. 2006. "F-Shaped Pattern for Reading Web Content." *Nielsen Norman Group* (blog), April 17. Accessed October 29, 2015. http://www.nngroup.com/articles/f-shaped-pattern-reading-web-content/.

Nielsen, Jakob. 2007a. "Fancy Formatting, Fancy Words = Looks Like a Promotion = Ignored." *Nielsen Norman Group* (blog), September 4. Accessed October 29, 2015. http://www.nngroup.com/articles/fancy-formatting-looks-like-an-ad/.

Nielsen, Jakob. 2007b. "Tabs, Used Right." *Nielsen Norman Group* (blog), September 17. Accessed October 29, 2015. http://www.nngroup.com/articles/tabs-used-right/.

Nielsen, Jakob. 2011. "Incompetent Research Skills Curb Users' Problem Solving." *Nielsen Norman Group* (blog), April 11. Accessed October 29, 2015. http://www.nngroup.com/articles/incompetent-search-skills/.

Nielsen, Jakob. 2012. "Serif vs. Sans-Serif Fonts for HD Screens." *Nielsen Norman Group* (blog), July 2. Accessed October 29, 2015. http://www.nngroup.com/articles/serif-vs-sans-serif-fonts-hd-screens/.

Nielsen, Jakob, and Hoa Loranger. 2006. *Prioritizing Web Usability*. Berkeley, CA: New Riders.

Nielsen, Jakob, and Kara Pernice. 2010. *Eyetracking Web Usability*. Berkeley, CA: New Riders.

Ouellette, Dana. 2011. "Subject Guides in Academic Libraries: A User-Centred Study of Uses and Perceptions." *Canadian Journal of Information and Library Science* 35 (4): 436–451. doi: 10.1353/ils.2011.0024.

Pittsley, Kate, and Sara Memmott. 2012. "Improving Independent Student Navigation of Complex Educational Web Sites: An Analysis of Two Navigation Design Changes in LibGuides." *Information Technology and Libraries* 31 (3): 52–65. doi: 10.6017/ital.v31i3.1880.

Sinkinson, Carol, Stephanie Alexander, Alison Hicks, and Meredith Kahn. 2012. "Guiding Design: Exposing Librarian and Student Mental Models of Research Guides." *Portal: Libraries and the Academy* 12 (1): 63–84. doi: 10.1353/pla.2012.0008.

Sonsteby, Alec, and Jennifer DeJonghe. 2013. "Usability Testing, User-Centered Design, and LibGuides Subject Guides: A Case Study." *Journal of Web Librarianship* 7 (1): 83–94. doi: 10.1080/19322909.2013.747366.

Springshare. 2015. *"Best of Home." Best of LibGuides Community: v1 & v2 Guides*, May 11. Accessed October 29, 2015. http://bestof.libguides.com/home.

Staley, Shannon M. 2007. "Academic Subject Guides: A Case Study of Use at San Jose State University." *College and Research Libraries* 68 (2): 119–139. doi: 10.5860/crl.68.2.119.

Tawatao, Christine, Rachel Hungerford, Lauren Ray, and Jennifer Ward. 2010. "LibGuides Usability Testing: Customizing a Product to Work for Your Users." University of Washington Research Works Archive. Accessed October 29, 2015. http://hdl.handle.net/1773/17101.

Tidwell, Jennifer. 2006. *Patterns for Effective Interaction Design.* Sebastapol, CA: O'Reilly.

9

To the Left, to the Left

Implementing and Using Side Navigation and Tabbed Boxes in LibGuides

Jaleh Fazelian, MA, MLS, John Carroll University
Melissa Vetter, MSLIS, Washington University in St. Louis

Libraries and librarians want to get the most out of their resources. When we use standard top navigation tabs, do we give our users the user-friendliest versions of our collections in LibGuides? At Washington University in St. Louis, two librarians chose to investigate this issue before implementing the upgrade to LibGuides version 2 (LGv2). We undertook an assessment of our users to ask them if they preferred the standard top navigation or the newly available side-navigation offerings, their thoughts on tabbed boxes, and what they might call this system when speaking to friends. We worried that using the term *research guides* or *subject guides* was not useful to our students. In this chapter we discuss the assessment process, our results, how we implemented side navigation and tabbed boxes into our LibGuides system, and the trials and tribulations associated with our upgrade to LGv2 in the summer and fall of 2014.

According to statistics provided by Springshare, roughly 92 percent of all LibGuides systems use top navigation (Schofield 2015). Prior to 2014, we asked users, including students and librarians, about their desire for a more dynamic landing page than the default provided by Springshare. While there was some interest in changing the home page, the users overwhelmingly said the default home page was fine and met their immediate needs. As we moved toward the transition to LGv2, we sought to address this question again as we thought this would be the best time to implement system-wide changes.

LITERATURE REVIEW

In writing this chapter we also looked at recent literature discussing several usability studies of LibGuides. While there is a great deal of literature on the usefulness (Castro-Gessner, Wilcox, and Chandler 2013) and best practices (Gonzalez and Westbrock

2010; Beaton et al. 2009) of LibGuides, there isn't much in the literature on the design of LibGuides themselves. However, two articles stand out as important when researching how others have assessed the look and feel of their systems. Ouellette (2011) found that when students use LibGuides they prefer both a clean and simple look to the page as well as side navigation because of its preponderance on the web. Sonsteby and De-Jonghe (2013) found that visual clutter on LibGuides overwhelmed students. When they were overwhelmed, students were less likely to use the guides.

USER TESTING: PLANNING AND EXECUTION

Before undertaking the student assessment of our LibGuides system, we met with our library's assessment coordinator to get our assessment questions approved. We also discussed how many testers would be needed to conduct a useful assessment. As a group, and in accordance with guidelines suggested by Nielsen (2000), we agreed that ten testers—five graduate and five undergraduate students—would be sufficient to give us the information we needed to assess the look and feel of the system (Nielsen 2006).

We selected two different user groups to acknowledge that undergraduate and graduate students use research guides in different ways. Our assessment coordinator also gave us a list of graduate students who had self-identified as willing to test library systems or answer library surveys. This yielded two of our six graduate student testers. The remaining testers were referred by subject librarians or were student workers in our departmental libraries. We did not offer compensation, other than our gratitude, to the testers. After introducing ourselves, we walked the students through the guides and asked the assessment questions while taking notes of their responses.

We created two templates that the students would assess. These were exact mirrors of each other, one with top navigation, as depicted in figure 9.1, and one with side navigation as shown in figure 9.2. We used a current course guide for testing.

Figure 9.1. **"Arab Spring Seminar Course Guide" with top navigation.**
Image courtesy of Washington University in St. Louis Libraries

Figure 9.2. "Arab Spring Seminar Course Guide" with side navigation. *Image courtesy of Washington University in St. Louis Libraries*

We asked the following set of questions:

- Have you ever used research guides? If so, why or for what course?
- What are the pros and cons of each type of navigation? Do you prefer one over the other?
- Do you like the tabbed boxes? Do you find them easy or difficult to use?
- What would you name a system like this when discussing it with your peers?

USER TESTING RESULTS

Undergraduate Students

We tested five undergraduate students: three who identified as female and two who identified as male. Two of the five students had used research or course guides in the past, generally tied to a specific class. Four of the five undergraduate students selected side navigation over top navigation. Their reasons for selecting side navigation were it was more visually appealing, it reminded them of other websites they regularly used such as Blackboard, and the side navigation mapped to the way their eyes moved on the page. Four of the five undergraduate students preferred the tabbed boxes. Their reasons for choosing tabbed boxes: they minimized the amount of scrolling needed and the page without tabbed boxes was too much to look at. The student who did not prefer the tabbed boxes was concerned that he might skip information if it wasn't visible on the page. Most of the undergraduate students did not have a suggestion for what to rename the guides. Those who did said that research and course guides made the most sense to them.

Graduate Students

We tested six graduate students: three of the students identified as female and three of the students identified as male. Four of the six graduate students had used research and/or course guides previously in specific classes or for general research needs. Four of the six graduate students preferred side navigation to top navigation. Their reasons for selecting side navigation: they expect to see side navigation on websites and side navigation made the site look similar to other useful websites. Only one student said the side navigation was cluttered and unexpected. The graduate students were split down the middle on their preference for tabbed boxes. The reasons given echoed those of the undergraduate students in that they preferred less scrolling and to have all the information on one page. They also liked that it made the page less busy. Those who did not prefer tabbed boxes wanted to see all the content on the page. When asked what they would call the system, one graduate student suggested we call it the Library Portal. Another student suggested we call the system "A Librarians' Guide To . . ."

After gathering and analyzing the data, we chose to implement side navigation system-wide, and lock it down as the only navigation option, as it was the preference of eight of the eleven students we tested. Additionally, the use of tabbed boxes was promoted, although their use was left to the discretion of individual LibGuides creators.

GETTING THE GUIDES READY FOR TRANSITION

We sought to curtail librarian concerns about the transition. As the system administrators, we sent out a checklist provided by Springshare that gave users two pages of items to review. These included updating links, checking rich text boxes, checking the images used on guides, and generally making sure content being migrated was still wanted. We also encouraged librarians to delete guides they had not used in several years. LibGuides administrators encouraged librarians to delete guides no longer relevant and then deleted many unused guides that had not been updated in three or more years. We also asked that all librarians focus on preparing their most used guides, such as major subject guides or course guides, for the coming fall semester. We hoped this would lessen their anxiety over the changes and give them time to get acquainted with the new system before tackling all of their guides.

We also held sessions for all staff that used LibGuides. We explained the assessment already undertaken and reasons for implementing changes to the system. We also held four hands-on migration sessions where authors could make changes to their guides while the administrators walked about the room answering questions and helping as needed. After these sessions all LibGuides creators had three weeks to make any other changes before the system was locked down into side navigation.

MAKING THE TRANSITION TO LIBGUIDES VERSION 2

Unforeseen Issues

Some aspects of the transition from the LGv1 system and three-column layout, to left-side navigation with two columns, did not go as smoothly as administrators had anticipated. All of the content created in LGv1 was transitioned into the LGv2 system without incident, but many LibGuide creators thought otherwise. One major issue that presented itself when making this transition involved hidden boxes as depicted in figure 9.3. When transitioning from three to two columns many, if not all, of the guides had boxes that were automatically hidden. Some guides, with a lot of hidden content, were obviously lacking boxes once available, and authors began to question whether the transition was a good idea if so much of their content was going to be lost.

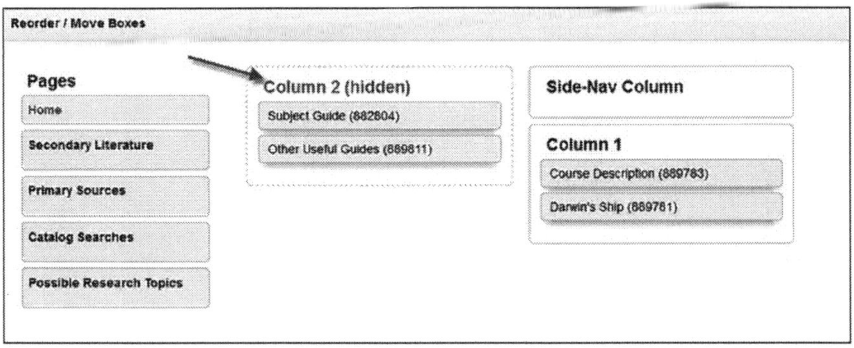

Figure 9.3. Example of hidden boxes from the Reorder/Move Boxes option. *Image courtesy of Washington University in St. Louis Libraries*

Although moving the hidden boxes into visible columns in LGv2 is simple and straightforward, many LibGuides creators initially needed assistance in understanding directions provided for making boxes visible again. Some chose to re-create their guides or particular pages in the wake of the transition while others left guides untouched. LibGuides administrators decided to log into guides lacking much of their previous content in order to see if any boxes were hidden and then "unhide" boxes for the LibGuides creators. Moving boxes is a very quick and easy process, but one that seemed to challenge LibGuides creators for various reasons.

Another unforeseen issue involved the new column-spanning box option in LGv2. Several of our LibGuides creators wanted to use these to highlight art or other images to give their guides a vibrant look. However, these column-spanning boxes do not integrate with side navigation. This was upsetting to several creators, and they wondered why Springshare would incorporate a new option that did not work in both side and top navigation settings. As far as we can tell at the time of writing, Springshare has not created a work-around for this issue.

Additional Training Sessions for Guide Creators

LibGuides administrators at Washington University in St. Louis gave our creators six months to work with the new system before offering additional training, in the spring of 2015, on features that remained unclear or confusing. We themed the workshops using language affiliated with the spring training of baseball and offered a pre-survey, shown in figure 9.4, in order to gauge interest among a "lineup" of choices.

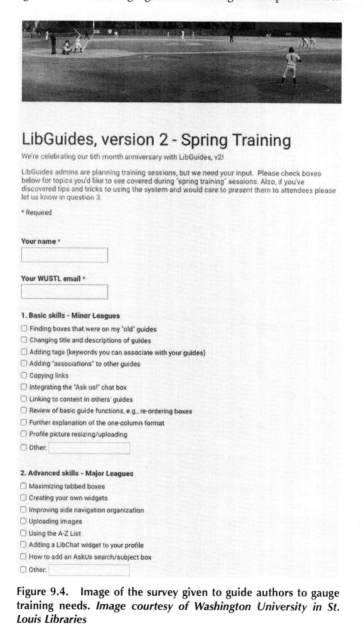

Figure 9.4.   Image of the survey given to guide authors to gauge training needs. *Image courtesy of Washington University in St. Louis Libraries*

In addition to the options available for basic and advanced skills training, creators were also asked what tips and tricks they might have learned while using LGv2 and if they would be willing to share them at the upcoming training sessions. Administrators also asked for feedback on their thoughts, six months after the transition, about the use of side navigation versus top navigation. It was interesting to see that while students liked the side navigation, many LibGuides creators did not. However, the administrators of the LibGuides system believe library staff should be giving the users what they want, especially when they tell us that in such a clear voice. Our job as librarians is to provide our users with a service that helps rather than hinders their research process. An LGv2 manual (http://libguides.wustl.edu/libguidesmanual) was created by our LibGuides administrators and was utilized as an instructional tool for subsequent training sessions.

BOX-LEVEL NAVIGATION FOR SELECTED PAGE

Some creators are taking advantage of the box-level navigation LGv2 affords. Lib-Guides creators can now choose to show box titles in the left-side navigation panel at the individual guide level. Making this designation is simple and can be performed through the use of one powerful check box in the Guide Navigation Layout settings. Our system administrators have "locked down" guide authors' ability to change the guide's overall navigation, and though they do not have the ability to switch guides to a "top navigation," they *can* still choose to show box-level navigation for each page on the guide as depicted in figure 9.5.

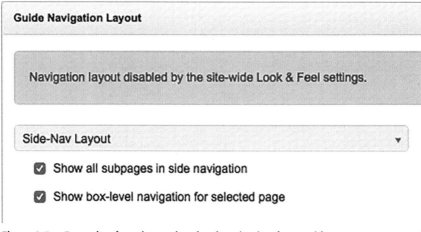

Figure 9.5. Example of turning on box-level navigation for a guide. *Image courtesy of Washington University in St. Louis Libraries*

In figure 9.6, the user navigated to the "Getting Started with Research" page. The box titles, including General Background Information, Generating Ideas, and so on, on that page are displayed in the left-side navigation when box-level navigation is enabled for a particular guide.

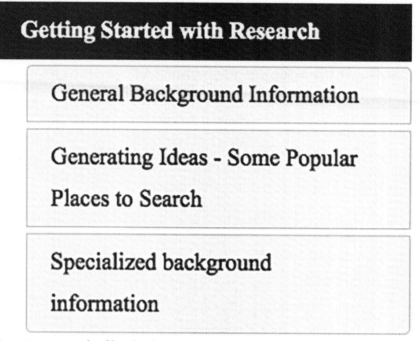

Figure 9.6. Example of box-level navigation. *Image courtesy of Washington University in St. Louis Libraries*

Tabbed and Untabbed Boxes

When usability testing was undertaken using a comparison between LGv1 and LGv2, users were asked to rate their preference of tabbed boxes versus untabbed boxes as shown in figure 9.7.

Graduate students surveyed gave us mixed results for tabbed and untabbed boxes. The graduate students highlighted the ability to scan the guide page and see all of the available content at a glance. With the tabbed boxes, these students speculated as to whether they would click on the tabs to see the information "hidden" behind them or whether they would be able to anticipate what they might find if they looked behind the tabs. But they also liked the ability to have all the information in one neat box.

The undergraduate students, especially, liked all of the content displayed before them. This enabled them to scan the page for the information needed, and they did not have to search behind the tabs. Some suspected that if all of the information were laid out on the page, they might actually look at all of it, instead of scanning only to locate what they are in certain need of.

There are some important aspects to consider when choosing tabbed or untabbed boxes. One consideration, especially when going to an overall side-navigation layout, is that box-level side navigation will not be available for all of the individual tabs in a

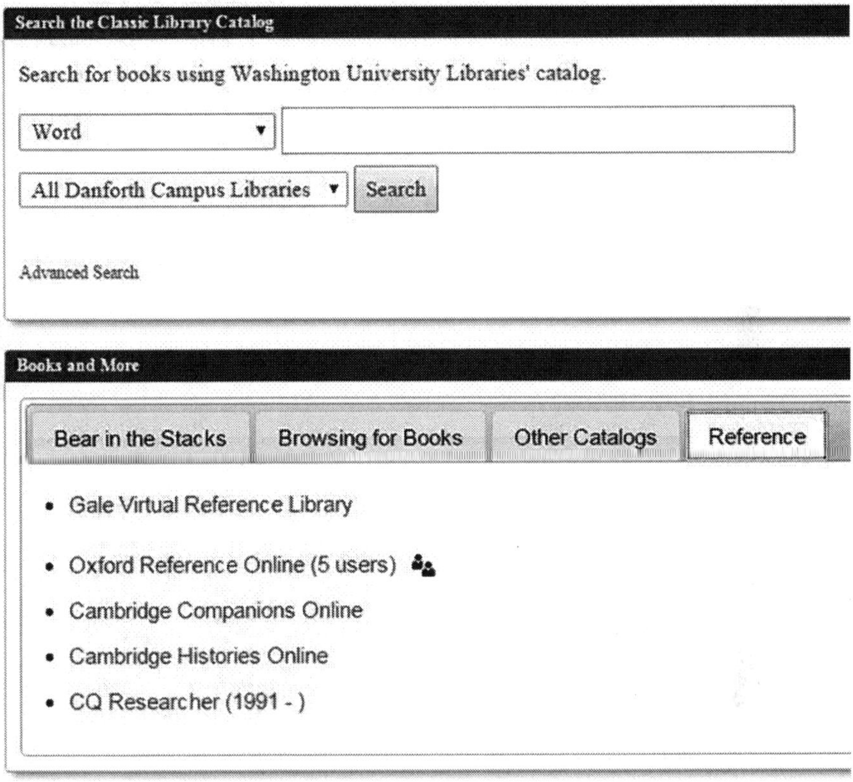

Figure 9.7. Examples of tabbed and un-tabbed boxes. *Image courtesy of Washington University in St. Louis Libraries*

tabbed box as shown in figure 9.8. The main title of the box *will* be available in the left-side navigation menu, so authors may wish to give the box a title that adequately describes all of the content a user will find contained within the tabs.

Another aspect to consider about tabbed boxes is that it is not possible to link to a specific tab either within the original guide or between two separate guides. If authors wish to create a link directly to box content, they should not put the content

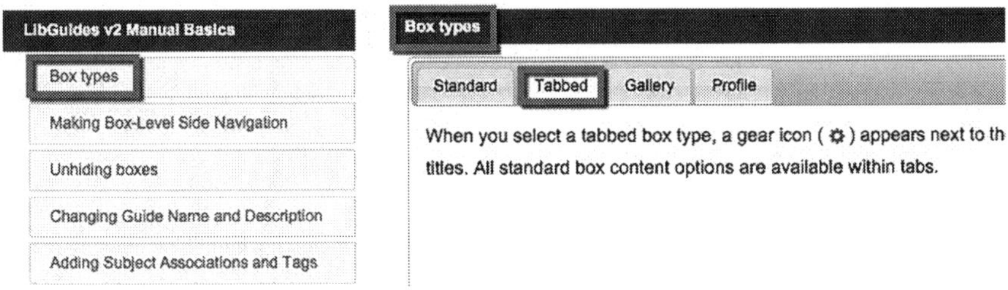

Figure 9.8. Example of box-level navigation of a tabbed box. *Image courtesy of Washington University in St. Louis Libraries*

in a tabbed box. Authors should also note that boxes change vertical length depending on the amount of box content. One solution would be to constrain tabbed box vertical dimensions and advise guide creators not to overfill tabs in order to avoid excessive scrolling. One final note about tabbed boxes is that authors can copy tabbed boxes but cannot later make them untabbed, just as untabbed boxes cannot later be made into tabbed boxes. LibGuides creators will likely wish to plan out the structure of a page before choosing box types or run the risk of having to re-create content.

CONCLUSION

LibGuides administrators who wish to make large system-wide changes should give themselves ample time to test users before instituting change. Administrators also need buy-in from LibGuides creators and need to give clear directions, plenty of training, and hands-on time with the new system to make for a smoother transition. At Washington University in St. Louis, we implemented a plan that spanned the better part of 2014 and unveiled our new LibGuides system on August 4, 2014.

Basing decisions around the demands of our users, we have successfully implemented side navigation as our template for all guides. Student assessment clearly indicated that side navigation is a style they are familiar with, especially with regard to the content management system Washington University in St. Louis currently uses. While some librarians had, and likely still have, reservations about this choice, we ultimately needed the decision to be based on the needs of our primary users—undergraduate and graduate students.

Choosing the left-side navigation option available in LGv2 came with a few unexpected consequences, as highlighted earlier, but guide administrators continue to seek effective solutions and opportunities for innovation. Encouraging LibGuides creators to incorporate tabbed boxes has aided in shortening the length of some of our more "robust" side-navigation guide pages. Further assessment will need to be undertaken in order to determine if students are moving beyond the live tabs. However, we are confident that with more web content employing the use of tabbed functionality, their use will not be completely out of the norm for our users.

LibGuides creators have been given several training opportunities in order to help them feel more at ease with the system-wide changes. Providing content creators with these opportunities helps bring the guide editing off of the backburner of overburdened schedules and highlights the importance of regular care and maintenance of content. Training sessions are also helpful in building camaraderie and buy-in to system changes. Additionally, these sessions offer LibGuides creators an opportunity to share their experiences with others in order to help us all grow and expand in our capacity as content creators.

While we have not done another assessment since the implementation, we can see from statistics provided by Springshare that hits to our guides have increased by over 100,000 hits in a calendar year. We compared data from September 1, 2013, to August 31, 2014, with data from September 1, 2014, to August 31, 2015. While this increase cannot all be placed on the shoulders of incorporating side navigation, it is enough to tell administrators that time invested by our content creators to update and publicize our LibGuides system is well worth the effort.

REFERENCES

Beaton, Barbara, Jennifer Bonnet, Suzanne Chapman, Bill Deuber, Shevon Desai, Kat Hagedorn, Julie Piacentine, Karen Reiman-Sendi, and Ken Varnum. 2009. *LibGuides Usability Task Force Guerrilla Testing*. Accessed October 29, 2015. http://www.lib.umich.edu/files/services/usability/libguides_rept_final.pdf.

Castro-Gessner, Gabriela, Wendy Wilcox, and Adam Chandler. 2013. "Hidden Patterns of LibGuides Usage: Another Facet of Usability." Paper presented at the biennial meeting of the Association of College and Research Libraries Conference, Indianapolis, Indiana, April 10–13.

Gonzalez, Alisa C., and Theresa Westbrock. 2010. "Reaching Out with LibGuides: Establishing a Working Set of Best Practices." *Journal of Library Administration* 50: 638–656.

Nielsen, Jakob. 2000. "Why You Only Need to Test with 5 Users." *Nielsen Norman Group* (blog), March 19. Accessed October 5, 2015. http://www.nngroup.com/articles/why-you-only-need-to-test-with-5-users/

Nielsen, Jakob. 2006. "Quantitative Studies: How Many Users to Test?" *Nielsen Norman Group* (blog), June 26. Accessed October 5, 2015. http://www.nngroup.com/articles/quantitative-studies-how-many-users/.

Ouellette, Dana. 2011. "Subject Guides in Academic Libraries: A User-Centered Study of Uses and Perceptions." *Canadian Journal of Information and Library Science* 35 (4): 436–451.

Schofield, Michael. 2015. "Almost All LibGuides Use the Same Template." *LibUX*, June 2. Accessed October 5, 2015. http://libux.co/libguides-use-same-template/.

Sonsteby, Alec, and Jennifer DeJonghe. 2013. "Usability Testing, User-Centered Design, and LibGuides Subject Guides: A Case Study." *Journal of Web Librarianship* 7: 83–94.

10

Making LibGuides Accessible to All

Danielle Skaggs, West Chester University of Pennsylvania

After all of the work you've put into your LibGuides, you should make sure that as many people as possible can use them. While you may be familiar with conventions for writing for the web that help readers scan and understand your content, such as using lists and being concise, do you know how to ensure that readers with accessibility issues can fully navigate and understand your LibGuides? To help you improve the accessibility of your LibGuides, we'll start with an introduction to types of accessibility issues and then cover specifics for LibGuides administrators and authors.

WHAT DOES HAVING AN ACCESSIBLE LIBGUIDE MEAN?

There are three groups of users who may have difficulty accessing your LibGuides. The group who may have the largest number of issues with your guides are readers who have visual disabilities or mobility challenges who, as a result, use a screen reader and/or need to navigate your guides without a mouse. The second group to consider is readers who are color-blind or have low vision. The third group to consider is people with hearing impairments. When you design for these three groups, it helps make your guides more accessible for those with learning disabilities. However, designing for people with learning disabilities is not specifically treated in this chapter. For more information on designing for learning disabilities, see WebAIM's "Cognitive Disabilities—Design Considerations" (http://webaim.org/articles/cognitive/design).

Designing for Screen Readers and Keyboard Navigation

Most readers who are blind or have significant vision impairment will navigate your site using both a screen reader and the keyboard (instead of a mouse). As the

WebAIM page "Keyboard Accessibility" (http://webaim.org/techniques/keyboard/) calls out, readers with mobility impairments that prevent them from using a mouse will navigate your site using a keyboard or other navigation aid; these can vary widely but designing for keyboard accessibility ensures that these readers can navigate your guides as well. You are probably familiar with designing guides that provide visual cues that readers use to navigate throughout the LibGuide. When designing for screen readers and keyboard accessibility, you need to focus on providing a properly structured guide that allows readers to easily navigate your guides.

People using screen readers cannot quickly scan the page to see all of the headings (or box titles in LibGuides). However, they can have their screen reader read all of the headings of a certain level. If the page has headings created by changing the font size and applying bold styling instead of using a heading tag, the screen reader is unable to provide this service and the person must instead go through the whole page, instead of skipping to the section they are interested in. For example, the pages in figure 10.1 are nearly identical in appearance, but the page on the left was structured with heading tags, while the page on the right used font changes to create headings.

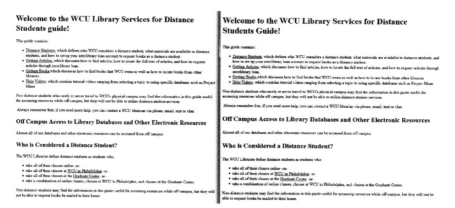

Figure 10.1.   Two near identical pages. The left is structured with headings and the right with font changes only.

To help you understand what someone using a screen reader sees when looking at your LibGuide or any other page, you can use a screen reader emulator. The emulator will help you determine if your page is properly structured for accessibility and will give you an idea of what people using screen readers face when using your guide. In figure 10.2, the identical pages from figure 10.1 now appear very different when viewed with the screen reader emulator Fangs (https://addons.mozilla.org/en-US/firefox/addon/fangs-screen-reader-emulator/).

Another aspect of properly structuring your guide for screen reader accessibility is making sure that the visual order of information on the page matches the order in the structure itself. Differences between how information displays and how it is

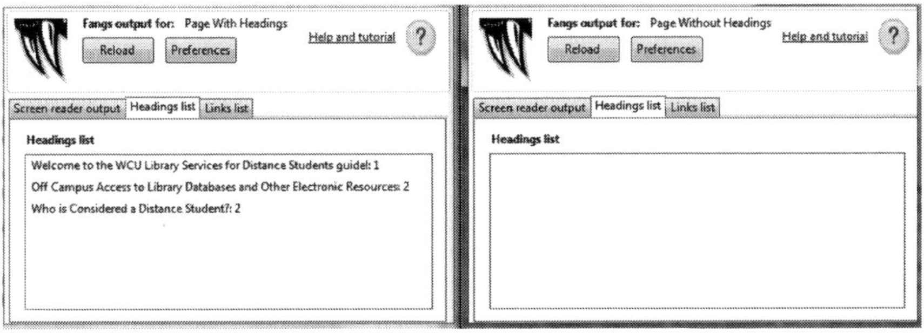

Figure 10.2. Fangs readouts for the pages in figure 10.1, showing the difference in how they appear to screen readers. *Image courtesy of Peter Krantz*

structured generally occur because of CSS styling changes. It is important that the information on the page makes sense when presented without this styling. There are several tools you can use to display a page without CSS styling, including the Web Developer add-on for Firefox (https://addons.mozilla.org/en-us/firefox/addon/web-developer/) and the no styles option in the WAVE web accessibility tool (http://wave.webaim.org/). You can quickly check LibGuides pages by viewing them on a mobile device. The order of content you see on a phone or similarly sized screen represents the order of information that a screen reader would see.

Images are another issue for screen reader users. Each image in your guide needs to have a written description associated with it, so that the screen reader has something to read about it other than noting the presence of an image. Screen reader users depend on this to understand what the image conveys visually. It's also useful for other people if the image doesn't display, whether it's because the image link is broken or they've turned off images to browse more quickly on a slow Internet connection.

While you most likely navigate the web using a mouse, readers who depend on screen readers or keyboard navigation can't use a mouse to get around your Lib-Guides. Therefore, all elements on the page need to be accessible by keyboard. In other words, you should be able to go to every link, navigate to different tabs, and start and control any videos on the page without using your mouse. A quick way to test this is to open your guide, click in the URL bar, and then use the Tab key to see if you can get to every part of the page. The Enter key or Space bar is usually equivalent to a mouse click. You may notice that there are a lot of menu links at the top that you need to go through before you get to the content of the page. To help readers using keyboard navigation, your guide should have a Skip Navigation link that enables them to jump to the main content of your page.

Screen readers can also navigate directly from link to link on a page. However, if link names are not descriptive or are repetitive, they are often confusing and not accessible. To help your readers, make sure the text of each link provides some indication of the content.

Designing for Color Blindness and Low Vision

There are several types of color blindness, or inability to differentiate certain colors. A good guideline for accessibility is to never convey information with color only. Instead, use a combination of color and text or color and shape, like the example on the right in figure 10.3.

Figure 10.3.   The circles on the left depend on color to convey information. The circles on the right use a combination of color and text.

To help readers with low vision, there should also be strong contrast between on-screen text and the background. If the visual contrast between the text and the background isn't strong enough, color-blind readers may not read the text or may only be able to see the text with difficulty. The smaller the text, the stronger the contrast between text and background needs to be.

Designing for Hearing Impairments

To make web content accessible to those with hearing impairments, the requirement is to never convey information in audio format only. In general, this means that there shouldn't be any alerts indicated only by a sound. Any videos that are included that have narration should be captioned.

Tools to Check Accessibility

Keeping these guidelines in mind while creating your LibGuides helps ensure that they are accessible. However, there are accessibility checkers that can provide a final check for your work. They can also be valuable tools if you are working to make existing guides accessible. Of the existing tools, the WAVE web accessibility tool by WebAIM (http://wave.webaim.org/) is a user-friendly, all-around accessibility checker that provides information on how to correct the problems it identifies. Among the issues it recognizes are structural problems, missing alt text, and low contrast. Figure 10.4 provides a sample of the results WAVE generates.

Other accessibility checkers you might use include

- CynthiaSays (http://www.cynthiasays.com/): Checks against specific accessibility standards such as Section 508 or WCAG 2.0 A.

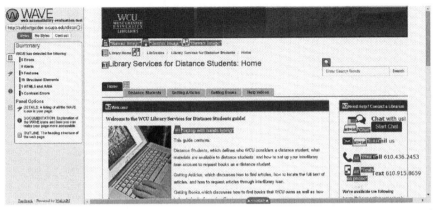

Figure 10.4. Example of WAVE results for a LibGuides page. *WAVE image courtesy of WebAIM: http://wave.webaim.org. / WCU Libraries header courtesy of West Chester University Library*

- W3C Markup Validator (https://validator.w3.org/): While this isn't an accessibility checker on its own, it does ensure that your documents are properly formatted. Having all your tags properly closed, or nested correctly within each other, helps your readers navigate your guide via screen reader or via keyboard.

ACCESSIBILITY FOR LIBGUIDES ADMINISTRATORS

As a LibGuides administrator, you control a variety of settings that impact the accessibility of all your institution's guides. When you set up the look and feel of your system, there are several accessibility items to keep in mind. Fortunately, LibGuides comes with some accessibility features built in:

- Properly structured: The page title is an h1 heading, and the box titles are all h2 headings.
- Keyboard accessible: Keyboard navigation is possible and a skip navigation link is included by default.

The following sections detail some known issues and items you should keep in mind when designing the look and feel of your LibGuides. When you are finished designing, you should create a guide page that uses all box types and all content types and run it through an accessibility checker to make sure there aren't any issues. If you have multiple templates, it's worth doing this for all the templates, as well.

Contrast Issues

When you set up the color scheme for your tabs and boxes, Admin > Look & Feel > Header / Footer / Tabs / Boxes > Tab and Box, be aware of contrast issues. You can use the Color Contrast Checker (http://webaim.org/resources/contrastchecker/) to test your proposed color scheme. There are three known contrast issues in the default LibGuide color scheme. You can correct these contrast issues by specifying high-contrast color schemes using CSS styling that overrides the LibGuide defaults. For more information about CSS styling, see the W3C Schools page on color (http://www.w3schools.com/cssref/pr_text_color.asp) and font-size properties (http://www.w3schools.com/cssref/pr_font_font-size.asp). Since the new color schemes should be applied to your entire LibGuides installation, you need to add the CSS styling in the Admin settings: Admin > Look & Feel > Custom JS/CSS.

- Footer text defaults: The light blue, small font used as the default footer text also does not provide strong enough contrast. You can correct this by enlarging the text or changing the font color. There's a specific section to add your html or CSS styling for the footer text: Admin > Look & Feel > Header / Footer / Tabs / Boxes > Page Footer.
- Box-level navigation: When LibGuide authors choose to use the Side-Nav layout, they can choose whether to show box-level navigation on the page. The default color scheme used to display the box names is the same as used in the default footer text. The CSS styling for this issue can be added to the entire site, or directly in the Template Code for templates using Side-Nav layout. If you have multiple Side-Nav layout templates, it may be easier to add it in the Custom JS/CSS for the entire site.
- Profile Box's Email Me button: The default contrast on this button is not strong enough. There's no setting to change these colors in LibGuides, so you must add custom CSS to change them.

If you are a LibGuide CMS administrator, you can also decide if you want to allow your authors to customize the tab and box colors of their individual guides. If you do allow them to customize these features, you may want to recommend that they use a color contrast checker or you may want to periodically review individual guides.

Banner Images

You can set a banner image that appears on all LibGuides at the top of the page. If you set a banner image—Admin > Look & Feel > Header / Footer / Tabs / Boxes > Page Header—the default alternate text that LibGuides provides is only "Banner Image." WAVE flags this as suspicious alternate text, most likely since it contains the word *image*. There is no option to add alternate text for this banner image in the Page Header section. A work-around is to create a custom header in HTML, using the Display This HTML option instead of the Use This Image option.

Another issue that comes up via WAVE is duplicate links at the top of the page. This occurs because your banner image is automatically linked to your institution URL. The next link on the page in the default LibGuides setup is the beginning of the bread-crumb navigation shown in figure 10.5, which also links to your institution URL. A work-around is to customize your bread-crumb navigation using custom CSS, so that the first URL of the bread-crumb navigation doesn't match the banner URL. Another option would be to not display the bread-crumb navigation at all, again via custom CSS.

Library Home / **LibGuides** / Library Services for Distance Students / Home

Figure 10.5. Example of bread-crumb navigation. *WCU Libraries header courtesy of West Chester University Library*

Guidance for Authors

LibGuide administrators need to be concerned about accessibility issues during setup, but there are also many decisions that affect accessibility at the LibGuide author level. As administrator, you may want to provide an authoring guide that includes a section on accessibility as the University of Waterloo Library does (Szigeti 2015).

If you have LibGuides CMS, you could also consider implementing Publishing Workflow: Content > Publishing Workflow. This requires that all guides be reviewed by content reviewers (that you specify) before the guide can be published, or made public. This would allow you to have the content reviewers check the accessibility of the guide before it is published, as well as any other checks you decide upon. However, waiting for guides to be approved adds time to publication, which may frustrate your authors. It also increases the workload of the content reviewers. Deciding whether to implement Publishing Workflow is most likely part of a larger conversation regarding your LibGuides installation than just accessibility. However, if you have already implemented Publishing Workflow, adding accessibility checks to your review process is worthwhile.

ACCESSIBILITY FOR LIBGUIDES AUTHORS

Many of the decisions you make as you create or update your LibGuides impact the guides' accessibility. Here are some guidelines to keep in mind as you create or modify your guides. The first four guidelines match accessibility problems identified by screen reader users in a 2012 WebAIM survey (http://webaim.org/projects/screenreadersurvey4/). The guidelines are arranged in order from most often encountered to least encountered.

- Avoid confusing links.
- Provide alternate text for all images.

- Avoid confusing forms.
- Use headings to add structure.
- Consider the presentation order.
- Avoid color contrast issues.
- Provide captioning for embedded videos.

Avoid Confusing Links

Since screen readers can jump from link to link without reading the text around the link, the text of the link itself needs to provide some indication of where the link goes. If your links say only "click here" or "more," someone using a screen reader has no idea what content to expect when they follow the link. Similarly, if several links on the page say the same thing but go to different pages, then screen reader users may instead assume they all go to the same place.

For clarity, each link should give a short description of where it is going. For example, in figure 10.6 the link alone does not clearly describe where it goes; the reader needs the rest of the sentence to figure it out. If you wanted to make the link descriptive, one option is the phrasing used in figure 10.7. As described on the WebAIM "Links and Hypertext" page (http://webaim.org/techniques/hypertext/), most screen readers also announce that it is a link, so you shouldn't start the link text with "link to" since the word *link* would be repeated.

We are unable to get textbooks for current WCU courses through ILL; more info on your options.

Figure 10.6.   Vague descriptive link text.

We are unable to get textbooks for current WCU courses through ILL; options for getting textbooks.

Figure 10.7.   Link text that clearly describes the destination page.

Provide Alternate Text for All Images

When you insert an image in LibGuides, be sure to fill out the Alternative Text field on the Image Properties dialogue box as seen in figure 10.8. Every image needs to have alternative text provided. When writing alternative text, don't start with "image of" or "picture of" since the screen reader lets the user know that it is an image. Instead, focus on how you would quickly describe the image to someone else. Try to do it in ten words or less. As suggested on WebAIM's "Alternative Text" page (http://webaim.org/techniques/alttext/), a quick description won't do; you may need to either replace the image with written description or provide a link to a long description.

If you choose to use the Books from the Catalog feature, please be aware that no alternative text will be provided for the cover images (Magnuson 2015). If your institution follows strict accessibility guidelines, you may not want to use this feature. An alternative would be to use a list and provide the book's title and a description in

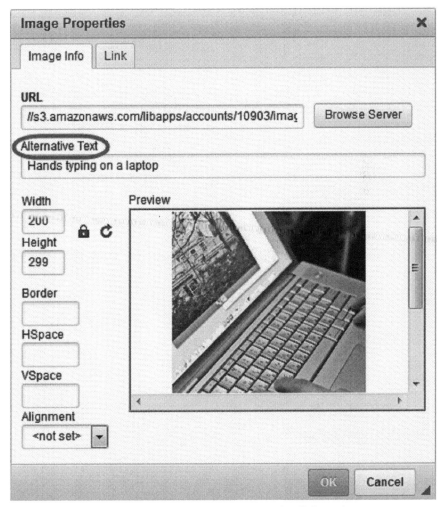

Figure 10.8. Alternate Text field on the Image Properties dialogue box.

it. The book's title could link to the catalog record. Another alternative would be to use a GoodReads custom widget, which displays a customized combination of book cover, title, author, and your review (which could include call number information that you enter). These widgets provide alternate text and are keyboard accessible.

Avoid Confusing Forms

For sighted readers, the label describing what a field is can be clearly associated with where the reader should select or enter his or her answer. However, someone using a screen reader can't depend on that visual association to know what a text entry box, checkbox, or radio button represents. As a result, <label> elements need to be used to describe what each entry field represents.

How does this affect you, the LibGuide author who is not manually coding their guides? The problem is that the Poll option displayed in figure 10.9 does not label the radio buttons in the code. According to Magnuson (2015) this problem has been reported but not yet fixed. You also cannot access the HTML editing view for the poll to edit the code yourself. As a result, polls are not fully accessible. As an alternative, you can insert a LibSurveys widget, as these widgets are keyboard accessible and pass a WAVE check. You will need to avoid using conditional logic in the survey that makes fields appear or disappear as this makes navigation difficult for screen reader users and isn't encouraged for accessibility. Another potential work-around is to use SurveyMonkey, which specifies that it conforms with a web accessibility standard (WCAG 2.0, AA) and also provides guidelines for creating accessible surveys (http://help.surveymonkey.com/articles/en_US/kb/508-Compliance).

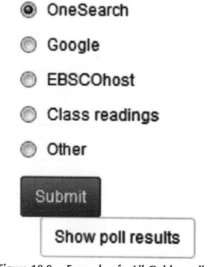

Figure 10.9.   Example of a LibGuides poll.

Use Headings to Add Structure

Screen readers can also jump directly from heading to heading within a document. If you use headings to break up the content within a box, you should use the Paragraph Format options in the editor, as shown in figure 10.10, to create headings instead of using bold or a larger font. Be sure to start the headings in each box with Heading 3, since Heading 1 is used for the guide title and Heading 2 is used for the box title. If you don't like how Heading 3 appears, you can add some styling to it in HTML code view or ask your LibGuide administrator to change it for all guides.

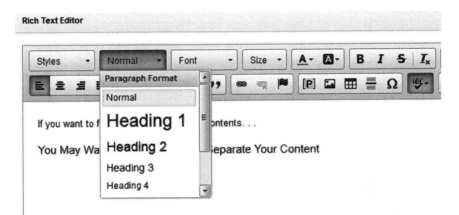

Figure 10.10. Paragraph format drop-down box displaying heading options.

LibGuides provides headings down to Heading 6 in the Paragraph Format box, so you can have four levels of headings within a LibGuides box.

Consider the Presentation Order

When you are ordering the boxes on your page, keep in mind that the order in which they are displayed to screen readers and those on mobile devices doesn't match how you might scan the page. The presentation order will start with the top left box and then work its way down the left most column; then it will move from top to bottom of the next column and so on across the page as shown in figure 10.11. If you

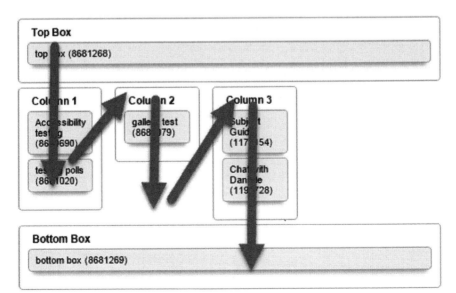

Figure 10.11. Presentation order of boxes when the display switches to a single column.

use a Top Box it will be displayed first. If you use a Bottom Box it will be displayed last. This is particularly important to keep in mind for those using Tab layout. If you use a three-column format and put the most important information in the center column, the information both mobile and screen reader users see first will not be the most important information.

If you are using Side-Nav layout, keep in mind that any boxes you put under the side navigation will be displayed before the content in the main column. If you are switching your content between Tabs layout and Side-Nav layout, the visual order of your boxes changes significantly. When you go from a three-column Tabs layout to a Side-Nav layout, all boxes move to the main column of the page, and the visual order of the boxes matches the presentation order that a mobile or screen reader user sees. When you go from a Side-Nav layout to Tabs layout, all of your boxes move to the left column, with the visual order once again matching the presentation order that a mobile or screen reader user sees.

Avoid Color Contrast Issues

In general, you should avoid changing the color of text in your LibGuides. Rely upon bold and italic styles for emphasis instead. If you are changing any colors within your LibGuide, whether it is font color change or a change to the box title color scheme, check that the color scheme you are using has a strong contrast so that it is readable. You can use a color contrast checker like the one provided by WebAIM (http://webaim.org/resources/contrastchecker/) to choose colors.

Several Springshare services—such as LibChat, LibCal appointment scheduler, and LibAnswers FAQs—have widgets that look like a button that you can add to LibGuides. If you are adding any button-format widgets, you can usually customize the color of the button. Figure 10.12 is an example of a customized LibChat button-format widget. Again, check the contrast of the button you create. Some button-format widgets open in a new window, which may cause a problem for some readers using older screen readers, but it is not enough to declare these widgets inaccessible, as described on the WebAIM "Links and Hypertext" page (http://webaim .org/techniques/hypertext/).

Other widgets open in an overlay as a light box. Both the overlays and light boxes are keyboard accessible. The LibAnswers overlay widget in figure 10.13 uses a default color scheme for the dates and topics listed that has low contrast. However, the widget has a space for custom CSS that you can use to change these colors. The Appointment Scheduler widget also has contrast issues, and CSS styling would have to be added within the widget code manually (no custom CSS field on the widget creation page). The light box and overlays depend on scripting, which involves more complex accessibility checks, so you may want to check with the campus office that works with students for disabilities to be sure that these widgets are fully accessible to your readers.

Another area where contrast is a concern is in Gallery boxes. The default color scheme for the gallery image labels and captions (white) and the lack of a back-

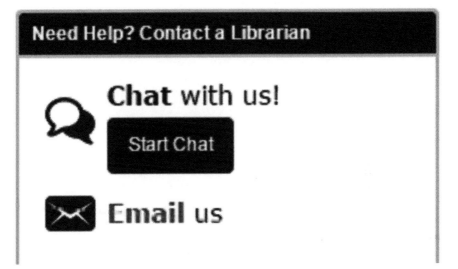

Figure 10.12.   Example of LibChat button-format widget.

ground for this text causes contrast problems. The gallery images also have default alternate text of Gallery Image 1, Gallery Image 2, and so on. The default Gallery box is not accessible for this reason. You can work with your LibGuides administrator to customize the CSS to change the color scheme and change where the text is displayed to improve the accessibility. See figure 10.14 for a Gallery box with custom CSS to create stronger contrast. Figure 10.15 shows the code used to change the Gallery box.

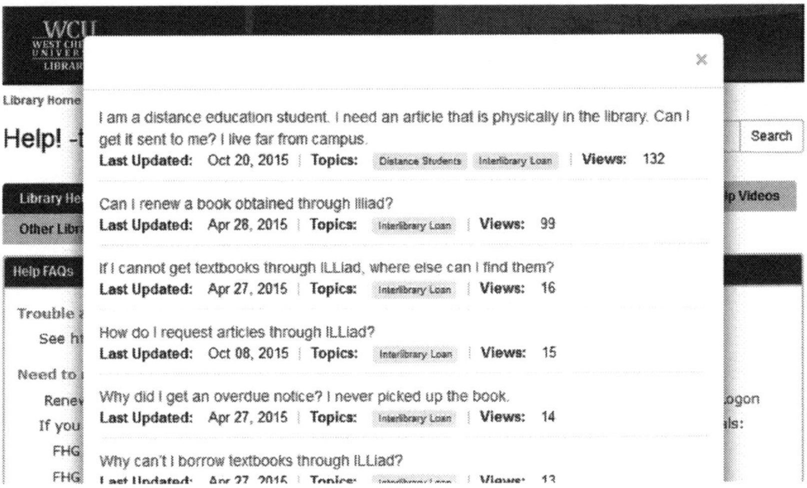

Figure 10.13.   Example of a widget that opens into an overlay. *WCU Libraries header courtesy of West Chester University Library*

Figure 10.14. Gallery box modified via custom CSS to improve the display of captions. *Robin Hood Clutch image courtesy of West Chester University Library*

```
<style>
.carousel-caption { /* Text caption for image */
  position: static;  /*center */
  padding-top: 0px;  /* remove white space */
  padding-bottom: 0px;
}
.carousel-indicators{ /* Remove slide show "dots" */
  display: none;
}
.carousel-inner>.item>img{ /* Slide show image */
margin: auto; /* Center */
}
.carousel-inner>.item>a>img{ /* Center image if hyperlink */
margin: auto;
}
.s-lib-box-content{ /* remove white space */
padding-bottom: 0px;
}
</style>
```

Figure 10.15. Custom CSS modifying Gallery box to have stronger contrast.

Provide Captioning for Embedded Videos

If you are embedding videos that have audio content on your LibGuide, the video should have captions. Captions can be open or closed as described on the WebAIM "Captions, Transcripts, and Audio Descriptions" page (http://webaim.org/techniques/captions/). If you are embedding someone else's video and can't add captioning to the video itself, you can provide a transcript of the video to meet accessibility guidelines. The transcript should be linked immediately after the video as in figure 10.16, and in HTML format if possible.

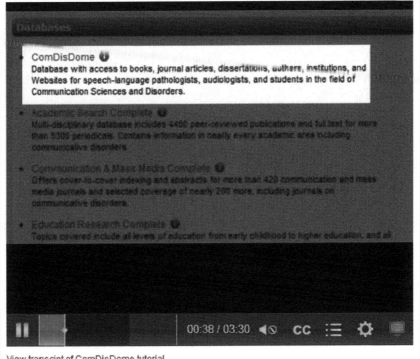

View transcipt of ComDisDome tutorial.

Figure 10.16.   Video transcript provided immediately after embedded video.

CONCLUSION

Make sure your LibGuides are accessible to the widest possible audience by keeping in mind the needs of three groups of readers: those using screen readers and/or keyboard navigation, those with color blindness or low vision, and those with hearing impairments. Other readers, like your mobile users, will also benefit from the work you do for these three groups.

For LibGuides administrators, this means addressing accessibility issues in the design of your LibGuides installation. You'll need to ensure that your color scheme has a strong contrast and is readable. Doing this for your high level navigation (Tabs or Side-Nav layout) and box headings is done using LibGuides-provided options. For the footer text, Side-Nav layout box listing, and Email Me buttons in all profile boxes, you'll need to add custom CSS to improve the contrast of the default color scheme. You'll also need to create a custom LibGuides header using the Display This HTML option instead of uploading a banner image to ensure that the header has useful alternate text. You may also want to alter the bread-crumb navigation via custom CSS to remove the duplicate link caused by the header image and initial link of the bread-crumb navigation both going to your institution's URL. Finally, you should probably provide some guidance on accessibility to your LibGuides authors, either through a guide or by adding accessibility checks to your review process in Publishing Workflow.

LibGuides authors should incorporate accessibility throughout their creation process. When designing the content of your guide, think about how the boxes you create will be presented to mobile users and screen reader users. Use headings to break up content within boxes, instead of bold. When you insert links and images, make sure the link text describes where it goes, and don't forget to fill out the alternate text field in the Image Properties. When you design images or add color to your LibGuide, make sure there's a strong contrast and that information is conveyed in more ways than just color. Adding a video? Makes sure the image is captioned or be sure to provide a transcript for it. Finally, while adding widgets to your LibGuide is a great way to add interesting content or link to other services, it's important to consider the accessibility of the widgets you're adding.

There are many different points to remember as you get started with accessibility. Fortunately, there are several web accessibility checkers you can use to double-check your work. Keep in mind that your campus office that provides services to students with disabilities may also be able to help you test the accessibility of your guides and any widgets you want to add.

RECOMMENDED RESOURCES

- WAVE web accessibility tool (http://wave.webaim.org/): This tool checks your site and generates a report. The errors it finds will definitely cause accessibility problems, while alerts aren't guaranteed to cause a problem but should be checked. Includes a check for contrast problems.
- Browser plug-ins that emulate screen readers:

  - Fangs Screen Reader Emulator (https://addons.mozilla.org/en-US/firefox/addon/fangs-screen-reader-emulator/)
  - ChromeShades (https://chrome.google.com/webstore/detail/chromeshades/hlklboladblmgfpkenhlgbhoojdlfoao)

- Color Contrast Checker (http://webaim.org/resources/contrastchecker/): This resource from WebAIM lets you enter colors in hexadecimal code to see if they provide enough contrast and is helpful when setting up your default color scheme
- Vischeck (http://www.vischeck.com/vischeck/vischeckImage.php): Upload images or download plug-ins for Photoshop (Mac and Windows) to see how your images would appear for various types of color blindness.
- WebAIM (http://webaim.org/): This website serves as a comprehensive reference on web accessibility issues; it includes short informative articles with examples.
- Web Accessibility for Designers (http://webaim.org/resources/designers): This page has an infographic from WebAIM that serves as an excellent quick reference to help you keep accessibility in mind.
- Riley-Huff, Debra A. 2012. "Web Accessibility and Universal Design." *Library Technology Reports* 48 (7): 29–35. This article provides an excellent introduction to various standards that enhance the accessibility of your content as well as advice on writing accessible web content.

REFERENCES

Magnuson, Lauren. 2015. "Accessibility Testing LibGuides 2.0." *ACRL TechConnect* (blog). Accessed October 10, 2015. http://acrl.ala.org/techconnect/post/accessibility-testing-libguides-2-0.

Szigeti, Kathy. 2015. "1a. Formatting for Accessibility & Usability." *Waterloo LibGuides for Guide Authors*. Accessed October 10, 2015. http://subjectguides.uwaterloo.ca/content.php?pid=80053&sid=613089.

11

LibGuides

Creating Accessible User Experiences

Melissa Fortson Green, the University of Alabama

Libraries should provide accessible web content to ensure equal access and opportunity, limit barriers to access and engagement, and make sure information and services are available to the widest possible audience. Everyone can benefit from accessible web content, not just people with disabilities. Accessible sites are generally easier to use and steps taken to make web content more accessible also improve discoverability and the experience of mobile device users. Finally, in many cases, accessibility is the law. Libraries should ensure their online resources are accessible to comply with federal, state, and other requirements to avoid legal action and financial consequences. Thousands of libraries worldwide use some combination of LibApps to manage content, provide online reference services, facilitate staffing and events, and analyze data. Libraries rely on Springhare products to deliver essential information and services, but inaccessible guides and other content limit access for users with disabilities.

This chapter discusses how readers can create more accessible user experiences and content for users with accessibility needs. The chapter will make the case, and outline the benefits of, accessibility to all while addressing accessibility laws, requirements, standards, and guidelines. Common challenges and solutions will be shared, along with specific considerations for guides, pages, boxes, assets, and images, and recommendations for administrators. As content added to LibGuides must also be accessible, instructions for creating accessible audio, video, documents, and files will be shared. Strategies for evaluating accessibility of the LibGuides platform and LibGuide content will be offered, including Voluntary Product Accessibility Templates (VPATs) and automated accessibility evaluation tools. As automated evaluation is not an adequate substitute for user testing, the chapter will conclude with best practices for usability and accessibility testing with users with disabilities.

While people-first language is used in this chapter, it is important to note that some prefer identity-first language, including many autistic self-advocates and members of the deaf community. A good rule of thumb: Avoid referring to a person's disability unless it's relevant. If it is relevant, ask and use the person's preferred terms.

WHY ACCESSIBILITY MATTERS

The power of the Web is in its universality. Access by everyone regardless of disability is an essential aspect. (Berners-Lee 1997)

Why should we, library and information professionals, care about accessibility? The Library Bill of Rights, the American Library Association's statement on library users' rights to intellectual freedom and its expectations of libraries to support those rights, has been interpreted for a number of specific library practices, including services to persons with disabilities. The interpretation asserts that the library is responsible for providing materials for all members of the community the library serves and that all information resources provided should be equally accessible to all users (ALA Council 2015). The key word here: all. While the Library Bill of Rights isn't a legal document and following its principles isn't a requirement, it is an aspirational statement of the basic principles that should govern the service of all libraries. It also reflects the belief that access to information—including for people with disabilities—is a core value of librarianship.

Access to information is also a basic human right. Article 9 of the United Nations Convention on the Rights of Persons with Disabilities directs states' parties to the convention to provide equal access to information and communications, and information and communication systems, to enable people with disabilities to live independently and fully participate in all aspects of life (United Nations 2006). The United Nations Treaty Collection website lists 160 signatories and 159 parties for this international human rights treaty including Canada, Mexico, and the European Union (United Nations 2015). The United States has not ratified the treaty as of this writing (2015).

Who We Are Leaving Out

Just who are we talking about when we talk about "people with disabilities"? Who are we leaving out when we fail to ensure our technologies are accessible? The World Health Organization's (2015, 1) 2014 figures indicate that about 15 percent of the world's population has some form of disability. Estimates from the United States Census Bureau's 2013 American Community Survey indicate that about 12.6 percent of the U.S. population reported a disability (Erickson, Lee, and von Schrader 2015, 1). Many LibGuides users work in a higher education environment; in the latest available data, 11 percent of undergraduates at U.S. degree-granting postsecondary institutions reported having a disability (United States Department of Education 2013, 1). Additional data may be available from state, local, and university offices.

These numbers must be taken with a grain of salt—they rely on self-reporting, and definitions of disability vary across measurements, making it difficult to make comparisons. More importantly, the disability experience is diverse and deeply personal and can't be accounted for by looking at numbers. However, statistics can give us an idea of just how many people we leave out when we fail to design for accessibility. In short, it is too many.

Designing for Accessibility Benefits Everyone

Designing websites for accessibility benefits everyone, not just people with disabilities. There is a significant overlap between making digital materials accessible for mobile device users and people with disabilities, and accessible web content is generally more usable. Someone using a mobile phone in bright sunlight and someone who is color-blind may both have difficulty perceiving color; both the smartphone owner attempting to watch a video in a noisy environment and the deaf or hard of hearing user may be unable to hear the audio track. While accessibility and usability aren't the same thing, everyone can benefit from intuitive and consistent interactions and elements (W3C 2013; W3C 2015a).

Accessibility also increases findability and search engine optimization (SEO). Proper heading structure and descriptive link text are a boon to both accessibility and SEO, and accessibility techniques such as alternative text for images and transcripts and captions for multimedia expose online content to search engines. In fact, Google uses alternative text to help determine the subject of an image and therefore the best image search results to return.

The relationship between accessibility, mobile friendliness, and discoverability became even more pronounced in February 2015 when Google announced changes to help users discover more mobile-friendly content (https://googlewebmastercentral. blogspot.com/2015/02/finding-more-mobile-friendly-search.html). This change, which went into effect on April 21, 2015—popularly referred to as "Mobilegeddon Day"—adjusted the search engine's algorithm to give higher ranking to mobile-friendly sites that avoid Flash and other software not common on mobile devices, use text that is readable without zooming, size content to the screen, and provide enough space between links for the correct one to be easily tapped (https://plus. google.com/s/%23mobilegeddon).

Applicable Laws and Requirements

In many cases, accessibility is required by law. If you live in the United States, applicable laws include the Americans with Disabilities Act (ADA) and the Rehabilitation Act of 1973 (Section 504 and Section 508). The ADA is comprehensive civil rights legislation that protects people with disabilities from discrimination in public services, programs, and activities. While the ADA doesn't explicitly address web accessibility, it does require that state and local governments, businesses, and nonprofit organizations that serve the public communicate with people with disabilities as effectively as they communicate with others. This originally meant providing sign language interpreters, Braille materials, and other aids and services to make information accessible to people who have speech, hearing, or vision impairments. Increasingly, websites are being reviewed to determine whether they comply with the ADA's effective communications requirements.

The Rehabilitation Act prohibits discrimination on the basis of disability in federal employment and in programs conducted by federal agencies or receiving federal money. The portions of the act relevant to accessibility are Section 504, which states that programs or activities receiving federal money must not discriminate on the basis of disability, and Section 508, which requires information technology procured or used by the federal government to be accessible to people with disabilities. This includes employees and members of the public.

Additional laws and requirements apply in college and university settings. In June 2010, the U.S. Departments of Justice and Education issued a "Dear Colleague" letter reminding colleges and universities of their responsibility to ensure students have equal access to electronic book readers and other technologies used for teaching and learning (Perez and Ali 2010). Universities are now charged with planning for accessible technology tools, services, and information. According to the Departments of Justice and Education, public education institutions must provide accessible programs and services, have a plan to make technology resources accessible, demonstrate progress toward fulfilling obligations, and keep lines of communication obvious and open (Thompson 2015).

Many other countries have recognized the need to ensure the web is accessible to people with disabilities. Introducing their collection of world accessibility laws and requirements, WebAIM, a nonprofit organization based at Utah State University's Center for Persons with Disabilities, notes that each nation seems to take a slightly different approach to the issue of access, some with human or civil rights laws and others with technology procurement requirements. A fairly common approach is to adopt version 2.0 of the Web Content Accessibility Guidelines (http://webaim.org/standards/wcag/).

STANDARDS AND GUIDELINES

Two sets of standards and guidelines are most commonly used to define what makes web content accessible. The Web Content Accessibility Guidelines are developed by the World Wide Web Consortium (W3C), an international body that develops standards for the web. Guidelines in Section 508 of the Rehabilitation Act apply to electronic and information technology developed, procured, maintained, or used by federal agencies.

Version 2.0 of the Web Content Accessibility Guidelines (WCAG 2.0) outlines four principles for accessible web content. According to WCAG 2.0, in order for individuals with disabilities to access web content, that content must be perceivable, operable, understandable, and robust (POUR) (W3C 2008). POUR (http://webaim.org/articles/pour/) can be summarized as follows:

- Perceivable: Available to the senses through the browser or assistive technologies. Individuals who do not have full use of their vision can make sense of the information without the ability to read text or view images or use assistive technology to convert the information into another format (speech to text, for example). Captions and transcripts make information available to people who can't hear it. Information can be transformed from one form to another: text into audio and Braille, audio into text (preferably before it reaches the user).
- Operable: Users can interact with all controls and elements with a mouse, keyboard, or assistive device. Content should be accessible to the keyboard and devices that emulate its functionality, and users should be able to locate, navigate, and interact with content.
- Understandable: Content is clear, limiting confusion and ambiguity. Language should be simple and concise, functionality should be understandable, and navigation should be consistent.
- Robust: A wide range of technologies can access the content. Users can choose their own technologies, including operating systems, browsers, and browser versions, and customize them to meet their accessibility needs.

There are three levels of WCAG 2.0 conformance: Level A (least stringent), Level AA (more stringent), and Level AAA (most stringent). The "double A" level of conformance has been widely adopted as the desired standard for web accessibility, and the update to Section 508 being considered at the time of this writing proposes to apply the WCAG 2.0 AA success criteria to not only the web but also electronic documents and software (Yanchulis 2015).

Section 508 defines *web accessibility* with sixteen standards (United States Access Board 2015). The following are most relevant to LibGuide authors:

- Text equivalents should be provided for all non-text elements, including images and embedded media.
- Videos should have synchronized captions and, when appropriate, audio descriptions.
- Important information should not be conveyed through color alone, and content should be organized with appropriate markup, not just visual styles.
- Table rows and columns are identified, and data is associated with them correctly. LibGuides authors can apply these standards, along with the POUR principles, to guide options, pages, boxes, and assets.

DESIGNING FOR ACCESSIBILITY

Applying these following key principles of accessible design to their LibGuides, guide authors can easily create more accessible user experiences.

Link Responsibly

LibGuides typically include lots of links, and this content isn't limited to the Link asset type. Database assets created in the central repository, embedded media and widgets, books from the catalog, lists of guides—all of these content types, as well as some others, function as links or incorporate link functionality. While the practice is discouraged, the Rich Text/HTML asset type can also be used to add links or linked content. As screen readers and other assistive technologies essentially "see" online content as a series of links and lists, LibGuides' heavy reliance on hyperlinks presents many opportunities to enhance or diminish accessibility. LibGuide authors can enhance guide accessibility by following these suggestions:

- When creating a new link asset, authors should provide a descriptive title in the Link Name field, avoiding ambiguous titles like Resources, More Information, and Contact Us. Sufficient details about the link should be provided in the Description field: enough information for users to know why the link is there and where they will end up if they select it. Can you read the title and description out of context and understand it? If the URL were to break, would users be able to locate the resource with the information provided in the link title and description? If the answer to these questions is yes, it's likely that the link is fairly accessible and usable.
- When adding a link to a Rich Text/HTML asset, it is not necessary to use the HTML title attribute to duplicate the link text; for those users who have their screen readers configured to read text and title, hearing the same information twice can be annoying and possibly confusing.
- It's especially important to inform the user when a link leads to a non-HTML resource like a PDF, Word, or PowerPoint file. This can be accomplished by indicating the format of the content you're linking to in parentheses at the end of the link name. When using the HTML editor to add a link, make sure the (PDF) or (PowerPoint) is part of the actual link, not just unlinked text immediately following it.
- When adding link assets, don't force links to open in a new window with the Open in New Window option. When adding a link to a Rich Text/HTML asset via the rich text editor, choose Target <not set>; when adding a link via the HTML editor, don't append the <a target="_blank"> attribute. Forcing links to open in a new window is problematic for many reasons, among them that screen readers may not tell the user that a new window has been opened. Sighted users may see the new window but not understand what has hap-

pened; this is of particular concern for users with cognitive disabilities, but such confusion negatively impacts usability for all. Whenever possible, let the user control how links are opened with their browser settings: in a new tab, in a new window, or in the current window. If you must force a link to open in a new window—maybe you're moving from a secure site to an insecure one, for example—be sure to warn the user about what's about to happen. For example, include (opens in a new window) in parentheses at the end of the link text.

- The Database, Link, Book from the Catalog, and Document/File asset types offer the following options for how an item description will be displayed: beneath the item title, upon hover over the item title, upon hover over an icon, or hidden entirely. Description Display options for the RSS asset type are "Display beneath item title" and "Hover over item title." To make the description available to the largest number of users, authors should choose to display the description beneath the item title when adding these asset types.

In addition to providing context for links and not forcing links to open in a new window, there are few more link-related considerations:

- Using the minimum number of links in your guides and breaking lists of links into manageable sections will make your guides easier to use, as will setting friendly URLs for guides and pages.
- Reusing links as much as possible will minimize the number of broken links and help maintain consistency in link names, descriptions, and display settings.
- To avoid misleading visual cues, don't emphasize text by underlining, as users expect underlined text to function as a link.
- Along the same lines, use consistent link styling throughout your guides; for non-administrator authors, this usually means not using visual formatting to change the appearance of links in Rich Text/HTML assets and not using Guide Custom JS/CSS (LibGuides CMS only) to alter how links appear within individual guides.

Provide Appropriate Text Equivalents

High-quality images relevant to a guide's purpose and audience make content more engaging and easier to understand, particularly for those with cognitive and learning disabilities. Screenshots, diagrams, photos, and illustrations supplement text and links, often conveying information or ideas less easily understood in a narrative format. However, images can create major barriers when they are not accessible. By using alternative text and contextual descriptions to provide text equivalents for images, guide authors can ensure access for a wider audience.

Alternative text (alt text) for images provides a textual alternative to non-text content. Alt text is read by screen readers in place of an image, conveying the image's content and functionality to those with visual or certain cognitive disabilities. Alt text offers benefits to other users, too, as it displayed in place of an image if the image file is not loaded in a browser and can be indexed by search engines. LibGuide authors have the ability to provide alt text for images when adding them to Rich Text/HTML content items. Here are a few things to keep in mind when adding alt text:

- After selecting an image from a personal or shared library or uploading a new image to the Image Manager, the author is prompted to supply several properties for the image, including alt text. Text entered into the Alternative Text field of the Image Properties box will be added to the alt attribute of the "img" element.
- Authors may also add alternative text to images already present in their guides by double-clicking the image in the rich text editor or selecting the image in the rich text editor, then selecting the image icon in the editor's toolbar.
- Alternative text can also be added via the HTML editor with the <img alt="text"> syntax. See the WebAIM "Alternative Text" (http://webaim.org/techniques/alttext/) article for tips on determining appropriate alternative text for images.
- Every image should have an alt attribute. The recommended practice for decorative images is to give an empty or null alt attribute (alt="").
- Make sure your image file names are short, descriptive, and otherwise fit for public consumption. When an alt attribute is missing, screen readers may read the image file name or, when an image is the only item being linked to, the URL of the image.

Image descriptions can also be provided in text adjacent to the image or within the page containing the image. If you describe the image in the surrounding text, it's not necessary to duplicate that description in the actual alt text field.

Finally, don't overdo it with annotation and animation. Limiting the number of screenshot callouts minimizes distraction while emphasizing only the most important aspects of the image; this benefits all users, but especially those with cognitive and learning disabilities. Strobing, flickering, or flashing GIFs and other animations can trigger seizures, migraines, nausea, and dizziness for some users and should be avoided.

Offer Transcripts, Captions, and Audio Descriptions

Tutorials, podcasts, and other audio and video content make great additions to LibGuides. Audio and video can be used to introduce new concepts, illustrate complex processes and ideas, enhance learning by providing multiple means of representation, and meet patrons at their point of need, anytime, anywhere. Springshare makes it easy to embed media and widgets in a LibGuide, but it's up to the guide author to ensure the content is accessible. This can be accomplished by providing transcripts, captions, and audio descriptions.

Transcripts can be formatted in a number of different ways but are typically text documents without time information. They contain a text version of the audio: spoken words, important sound effects, and, sometimes, descriptions of other audio content. Transcripts are usually the easiest and fastest way to provide basic accessibility for audio and video content. They are essential to people who are unable to hear or have difficulty hearing audio and those who are unable to see or have difficulty seeing video. But others can also benefit, including people who prefer reading to watching or listening or who have difficulty processing auditory information, users who aren't proficient in the language of the audio or video file, users who can't hear audio in noisy environments or don't wish to disturb others by playing audio in quiet environments, and individuals unable to download large audio or video files. Transcripts can also be indexed by search engines (WebAIM 2015).

In addition to transcripts, captions should also be provided for all video with audio. Captions also provide text versions of audio, but they are synchronized with the media; the text content appears on the screen at the same time as the audio. Captions can be created from a transcript by breaking the text up into small segments (caption frames) and synchronizing them with the media. There are two primary types of captions: open and closed. Open captions are part of the video and can't be turned off. Closed captions exist in a separate track that can be turned on and off. Most web players, including YouTube and Vimeo, support closed captions (WebAIM 2015). Generally speaking, closed captions offer the better experience for LibGuides users because they can be hidden or enabled by the viewer as desired. If the closed captioned video embedded in a LibGuide is hosted on YouTube, viewers also have access to auto-translated captions.

Audio descriptions make video accessible for people who are blind or visually impaired by providing short, audible descriptions of what is visible on the screen. They are necessary when the video presents key content that viewers with visual disabilities can't see, but they don't have to be included if that content is described in the regular audio track. Video creators can often eliminate the need for audio descriptions by reading or describing everything shown on the screen (WebAIM 2015).

LibGuides authors can embed audio and video content using the Media/Widget or Rich Text/HTML asset types. Regardless of how the content is added, guide authors should

- Provide transcripts by uploading accessible files as Document/File assets or linking to accessible files hosted externally. Pasting the text into a Rich Text/HTML asset below or beside the embedded audio or video is also an option, but be sure to format the Rich Text/HTML correctly. It's also good practice to include the transcript text or a link to a transcript file where the media is hosted, such as in the YouTube, Vimeo, or Soundcloud description field.
- Embed videos that are already captioned or use captioning features in video creation tools such as TechSmith Camtasia and Adobe Captivate to add captions to uncaptioned videos you own.

- To add captions to uncaptioned videos you don't own, use tools such as Amara or Overstream to add them and generate embed codes. While accessibility generally trumps copyright, this is preferable to downloading, captioning, and republishing the video on your own website (3Play Media 2015).
- Provide direct links to embedded media. You can edit the embed code to include the direct link or add the direct link as a Link asset or Rich Text/HTML asset before or after the embedded video.
- If you are hosting the embedded media on your own site, make sure the player you provide is keyboard accessible and gives viewers the ability to stop, pause, mute, toggle captions on and off, and otherwise control the playback experience.

Use Color Thoughtfully

Whether it's by changing Tab/Box colors (if not locked down at the system level), customizing box background or text styles, or adding images, LibGuide authors have many options for using color. With great power comes great responsibility, though. Ensure access to the widest range of users. LibGuide authors should use color thoughtfully and with accessibility in mind.

Don't use color alone to convey meaning. When working with color, regardless of the medium, make sure color isn't your only method of conveying important information. When using color, a good question to ask yourself is "Could someone understand this content with the color removed?" This is primarily to ensure your content is accessible to people who are color-blind, but it's also a principle of universal design for learning: by using more than just color to convey information, you're providing multiple means of representation. You are also ensuring that users who print pages of your guide in black and white or grayscale can still access all of the information.

In addition to not using color alone to convey meaning, it's essential to provide sufficient color contrast. In order to be perceivable, your foreground color needs to be significantly different from the background color. There are several tools you can use to check for sufficient contrast. One of my favorites is the WebAIM Color Contrast Checker (http://webaim.org/resources/contrastchecker/), which not only lets you check to see if your color choices meet the contrast ratios specified by WCAG 2.0 (one ratio for normal text and another for large text), but also helps you pick color combinations that provide sufficient contrast. To use the checker, you enter the hexadecimal codes for the background and foreground colors. If your color combination fails to pass the test, you can use WebAIM's lighten and darken options to modify the colors by slight degrees until you get a result that has sufficient contrast. There's also a very low-tech way to see if color contrast is sufficient: print the content in question in grayscale.

Images of text are often problematic because they lack text equivalents and sufficient color contrast. When text is presented as an image, users are unable to override the fonts and background colors. Some people with low vision make text on the screen easier to see by using their device or browser settings to heighten color contrast or invert colors. Presenting text as a graphic, rather than actual text, limits the ability to make these accessibility-enhancing changes.

Structure Content with Headings and Lists

Headings and lists add structure and meaning to web pages and documents by labeling each content part and indicating the order and relative importance of those parts. In order for documents and web content to be accessible, it's important to use headings and lists appropriately. The following information applies to Rich Text/HTML assets in the LibGuides system as well as documents created externally and added as Document/File assets or linked to from a guide.

Someone who does not have full use of their vision can't see larger or bold font but can "see" appropriate markup and use it to navigate through a document or page with a screen reader or other assistive technology. When content creators are working with word processing programs, that means using true styles—Title, Heading 1, Heading 2, and so on—rather than simply changing the font, enlarging the font size, and using bold, underlining, or italics to identify the text that you want to be perceived as a title or a heading. The same goes for LibGuides: Don't use visual formatting to add headings to your content. Instead, select headings from the rich text editor's Paragraph Format options or add heading tags to the HTML. As Heading 1 is used for the Guide Name and Heading 2 is used for the Box Name by default, any additional headings added by guide authors should begin with Heading 3.

Another common mistake is using headings to achieve visual results only: marking something that isn't actually a heading as a heading because you like the look of it or using the various heading levels out of order because you prefer how they appear. If you want your Heading 4 to look more like a Heading 3, talk with your LibGuides administrator about accomplishing this with CSS classes.

Lists also convey content order and structure and have rules regarding their use. Choosing which type of list to use is not a matter of aesthetics. Unordered lists—which usually appear as bullets—should be used when there is no order of sequence or importance. Ordered lists—which are usually enumerated with numbers or letters—should be used to imply or emphasize a progression or sequence. When adding a list to a document, use the word processing program's options for creating a bulleted or numbered list rather than simply inserting symbols or typing numbers. When adding Rich Text/HTML lists to a LibGuide, use the Insert/Remove Numbered List or Insert/Remove Bulleted List options in the rich text editor or use the <ol> and <ul> tags in the HTML editor.

Tables

Accessible tables require appropriate markup just like headings and lists. When using tables to present data, guide authors should

- Use the simplest table possible. This will make the content easier to perceive, understand, and navigate. If a lot of tabular data needs to be presented, consider using multiple simple tables rather than a single large, complex table.
- Indicate row and column headers. Sighted users can quickly scan a table, associating data with headers for each row and column. In order for assistive technology to "see" the relationships between the various cells, LibGuide authors should use the rich text editor's Table Properties to indicate which rows and columns contain headers. Alternately, <th> and <scope> tags can be added via the HTML editor (W3C 2015b).
- Describe the table's structure and content.

  ○ Text added to the Table Properties' Summary field should explain how data is organized in the table or how to navigate it. Text added to this field is assigned the summary attribute of the <table> tag. It is not displayed visually. The summary attribute can also be added via the HTML editor.
  ○ Text added to the Table Properties' Caption field should tell users what information they can expect to find in the table. The caption should be succinct, just enough information for someone to find the table and decide if he wants to read it. Text added to this field becomes associated with the table with the <caption> element and is displayed visually. The <caption> element can also be added via the HTML editor.

Book from the Catalog Assets

As of this writing, there are some accessibility issues presented by the Book from the Catalog asset type. Cover images appear to lack alt attributes. Some might argue that the images are decorative and don't require description. However, since both the cover image and the book title function as links, have the same destination, and are located next to each other, alt text might help differentiate between the two, as suggested by Magnuson (2015). While her post is not official product documentation, it presents the most current and complete assessment of the accessibility of the LibGuides version 2 (LGv2) platform available at the time of this writing. Springshare Lounge is another place to find posts by LibGuides users, discussing problems with particular asset types as well as other accessibility concerns.

Gallery Boxes

Guide authors may use the Gallery Box to create a box of rotating images uploaded to the Image Manager or found online, essentially creating an image carousel. However, Gallery Boxes are problematic for accessibility and should be avoided. Animations can be distracting, transitions between images too fast, and keyboard navigation lacking. Eggert and Abou-Zahra recommend when using carousels that designers, developers, and content creators provide appropriate markup for the carousel and its items; allow users to pause, stop, hide, or otherwise control the movement of the carousel; and ensure all carousel functions are keyboard operable. At this time, Springshare's Gallery Box does not meet all of these requirements. Additionally, there is not sufficient contrast between the default foreground label and caption text and the background color, and the non-administrator author is unable to specify other colors.

For Administrators

In addition to following the accessible design principles outlined earlier, LibGuides and LibGuides CMS administrators can do the following to enhance the accessibility of all published guides in the system:

- When setting site-wide settings and properties, choose a user-friendly system name and institution reference, avoiding acronyms and abbreviations. Provide proxy URLs that can be added to proxy enabled links, and don't force links to open in a new window.
- In the Look & Feel area, choose settings that allow the widest possible access when styling pages, navigation tabs, and boxes. Upload header images with sufficient color contrast between the foreground text and background. Include appropriate heading levels, descriptive link titles, and alt text for images in Page Header HTML and Guide/Page Footer HTML. When styling tabs and boxes, use a color contrast checker to choose font and background colors with sufficient contrast. Under Design Settings, choose Lock All Guides with This Design and Override Any Individual Guide Design Settings.
- If you add Custom JS/CSS Code, be sure it's accessible, especially if you modify the function or appearance of search or other buttons, forms, and input boxes.
- Help ensure consistent navigation by forcing all guides (existing and new) to use the same template. If you create custom guide templates, ensure those templates are accessible.
- Keep your subjects, tags, and URLs clear and concise, and, to ensure consistency in tagging, consider pre-populating the system with tags and/or establishing and enforce guidelines for the creation of new tags. Use and encourage authors to use friendly URLs wherever possible for guides, guide pages, profiles, groups, subjects, databases, redirects, and so on. Check author-created friendly URLs and edit as necessary.
- Encourage the reuse of assets by pre-populating as many of them as possible. If you give your link assets good titles and descriptions and specify the appropriate display and target behavior, those accessible design choices can be carried over when authors reuse your links. The same goes for images in the Shared Library, Media/Widget assets, and other reusable content.
- LibGuides CMS features "fully customizable individual guides—everything from headers/footers to full templates. But, admins can lock down this feature if they want a uniform look in the system." Locking it down will decrease the likelihood that individual guide authors will introduce inaccessible code.

EVALUATING LIBGUIDE ACCESSIBILITY

LibGuides authors can create more accessible user experiences by applying the principles of accessible design outlined in the previous section. While the accessibility standards and guidelines on which the principles are based should hold up as browsers and assistive technologies change, LibGuides are evolving organisms. The accessibility of the base LibGuides platform and LibGuides CMS will change as the code base is developed and features are introduced and removed. Custom CSS, JavaScript, and other Look & Feel options specified at the system level can increase or decrease accessibility, as can content, formatting, and style changes made by individual guide authors. For all of these reasons, and because each LibGuide has its own purpose and audience, it's better to conduct ongoing evaluation of your own guides and guide systems than to rely on someone else's assessment that may not apply to your LibGuide environment or may no longer be accurate by the time you read these words. This section discusses some of the tools and strategies LibGuide administrators and authors can use to assess the accessibility of their guides.

Voluntary Product Accessibility Templates

The Voluntary Product Accessibility Template, or VPAT, is a standard industry tool used to document a commercial electronic or information technology product's accessibility according to the Section 508 standards. By completing the official VPAT document available from the Information Technology Industry Council, vendors indicate to what degree their products comply with each accessibility criterion (Information Technology Industry Council 2015). VPATs for Springshare products, including LibGuides and LibGuides CMS, can be obtained upon request from Springshare.

VPATs are important tools in assessing the accessibility of technology products, with a few caveats. VPATs are vendor supplied, and their completeness and accuracy vary depending on the product knowledge and familiarity with accessibility standards of the person who completes them. A product that meets all of the criteria outlined in the VPAT may not be fully accessible or usable, just as a product that does not fully meet all of the criteria may fairly accessible and usable for many.

Product Updates

While Springshare offers quite a bit of accessibility information in its LibGuides version 1 (LGv1) accessibility guide and several accessibility-related FAQ entries, there is less accessibility-related documentation in the LGv2 guides available to LibGuides authors through the Help link in the command bar. Much of the information in the LGv1 guide is still applicable to LGv2. However, the LGv1 guide does not include some of the accessibility enhancements that have come with LGv2, nor does it provide updates on ongoing accessibility-related work.

Several accessibility-related product updates have been announced via the Lib-Guides 2—Known Issues/Latest Code Update guide, the Springshare blog, and the *SpringyNews* newsletter. The Springshare Lounge includes many posts providing crowdsourced information about the accessibility of the platform and accessibility tips for guide administrators and authors.

Automated Accessibility Evaluation Tools

No automated check can tell you if your LibGuide and its content are accessible; human testing is required. For example, while an automated checker can determine if alt text is present, it can't tell if the content is meaningful or appropriate for the context in which it appears. However, you can use web accessibility evaluation tools and the accessibility features built into Microsoft Word, Adobe Acrobat, and other authoring programs to do an initial check of your work and get it ready for user testing.

All web accessibility evaluation tools perform automated checks for accessibility issues, but the features they offer vary and they target different audiences. The W3C's Web Accessibility Evaluation Tools List (2014) outlines dozens of software programs and online services that can help determine if web content meets accessibility guidelines, and the list is filterable to help users find ones that match their particular needs.

A favorite set of tools for LibGuide administrators and authors is the WAVE online web service and Chrome browser extension. WAVE stands for Web Accessibility Evaluation Tool, and it provides guide authors with visual feedback about the accessibility of their guides by displaying icons and indicators on the page that is being evaluated. WAVE is easy to use. To evaluate a page, you simply enter its address on the WAVE website or click on the WAVE icon in the Chrome browser extension. WAVE reloads the page, now with embedded icons and indicators. Each icon, box, and piece of information added by WAVE presents some information about the accessibility of the page. You can view a brief overview of what each icon or indicator means by clicking it and viewing its documentation or by accessing the documentation panel on the left. Additional features and options are described on the WAVE site. WAVE is a very user-friendly tool that both the novice and the experienced user can easily incorporate into their work (http://wave.webaim.org/).

Like spell-check, which alerts authors to possible spelling errors, Accessibility Checker in Word, Excel, and PowerPoint alerts authors about possible accessibility issues in Office files. To test accessibility of your content, you should go to File > Info > Check for Issues > Check Accessibility. The Accessibility Checker task pane will appear next to your file, showing the inspection results and why and how to fix any errors (Microsoft Corporation 2015).

Adobe Acrobat Pro offers two tools to assist content authors in creating accessible PDFs: the Accessibility Checker (Full Check) and the Make Accessible Action Wizard. The Make Accessible Action Wizard walks users through the steps required to make a PDF accessible. It looks for common elements that need further action, such as scanned text, form fields, tables, and images without alternative text, and prompts authors to make any necessary changes. The Accessibility Full Check can be run as the final step in the Make Accessible Action Wizard or on its own to perform a thorough check for many characteristics of accessible PDFs (Adobe Systems 2015).

Accessibility checking and repair features are available in many other document and media creation tools. Check your product documentation or support site for information about the available options, keeping in mind that these tools can't ensure your content is accessible or usable; only humans can.

User Testing

Content can meet accessibility guidelines and still be unusable; design and content can simultaneously reflect user-centered practices and be inaccessible, especially for assistive technology users. After reviewing their guides to check for and fix any obvious accessibility problems, guide authors should consider conducting usability tests to better understand how real users with accessibility needs experience their guides. These are some of the practices for conducting user testing with users with disabilities recommended by web accessibility software and service providers (Deque Systems, Inc., 2014).

- Remember that users with disabilities are also like other users. In addition to addressing disability-related concerns in testing, also consider addressing general usability issues that impact users of all abilities.
- Recognize the great amount of variability within each category of disability. Five categories of disability are typically considered when evaluating accessibility: visual, hearing/auditory, cognitive, motor/ambulatory, and seizure or other disorders triggered by flashing, flickering, and strobing content. Within each of these categories, user abilities and needs vary greatly. Users may also have multiple disabilities across multiple categories. Don't assume that one participant represents all users with disabilities, or even all users within the same category of disability.
- Keep the accessibility of your testing environment in mind when choosing a testing location. If participants would typically use their own assistive technologies to access your content, consider allowing them to use those technologies during testing. When conducting tests in a lab environment, make sure you know what kinds of devices and software your participants will need to use and plan accordingly.

From the code base to system settings and individual guide content, LibGuides are subject to change. Authors can continually evaluate the accessibility of their guides by keeping up with product documentation, using automated accessibility evaluation tools, and conducting usability and accessibility testing with users with disabilities.

CONCLUSION

Each major category of disability should be considered when developing LibGuides and LibGuide content; better yet, LibGuides should be universally designed to anticipate and meet the needs of users of all abilities. Libraries should ensure their online resources are accessible to ensure equal access and opportunity, make their information and services easier to find and use, and comply with legal and other requirements.

LibGuide authors and administrators should follow the web accessibility guidelines and standards as well as the suggestions outlined for guides, pages, boxes, assets, images, and administrative settings. As external content added to LibGuides must also be accessible, audio, video, documents, and files should be created with accessibility in mind. VPATs, automated accessibility evaluation tools, and usability testing with users with disabilities should be used to continuously gauge guide and system accessibility. By following these principles, LibGuide authors and administrators can ensure their guides are accessible to users with disabilities, their guides provide more accessible user experiences, and their guide content is accessible to the widest possible audience.

REFERENCES

Adobe Systems. 2015. "Create and Verify PDF Accessibility (Acrobat Pro DC)." Adobe Help. Last modified December 9. Accessed November December 10, 2015. https://helpx.adobe .com/acrobat/using/create-verify-pdf-accessibility.html.

ALA Council. 2015. "Services to Persons with Disabilities: An Interpretation of the Library Bill of Rights." American Library Association. Accessed November 10, 2015. http://www.ala.org/ advocacy/intfreedom/librarybill/interpretations/servicespeopledisabilities.

Berners-Lee, Tim. 1997. "World Wide Web Consortium Launches International Program Office for Web Accessibility Initiative." World Wide Web Consortium (W3C), October 22. Accessed November 10, 2015. http://www.w3.org/Press/IPO-announce.

Deque Systems, Inc. 2014. "How to Incorporate Users with Disabilities in UX Testing." *Accessibility Matters—Deque Blog*, November 18. Accessed February 29, 2016. http://www.deque. com/blog/incorporate-users-disabilities-ux-testing/.

Eggert, Eric, and Shadi Abou-Zahra. 2015. "Carousels Tutorial." Web Accessibility Initiative. Last modified February 27. Accessed October 19, 2015. http://www.w3.org/WAI/tutorials/ carousels/.

Erickson, W., C. Lee, and S. von Schrader. 2015. "Disability Statistics from the 2013 American Community Survey." Cornell University Employment and Disability Institute (EDI). Accessed October 19, 2015. http://www.disabilitystatistics.org/reports/acs.cfm.

Information Technology Industry Council. 2015. "Accessibility." Accessed November 10, 2015. https://www.itic.org/policy/accessibility/.

Magnuson, Lauren. 2015. "Accessibility Testing LibGuides 2.0" *ACRL TechConnect Blog*, September 28. Accessed February 29, 2016. http://acrl.ala.org/techconnect/post/accessibility -testing-libguides-2-0.

Microsoft Corporation. 2015. "Check for Accessibility Issues." 2015. Office Support. Accessed November 10, 2015. https://support.office.com/en-us/article/Check-for-accessibility-issues-a16f6de0-2f39-4a2b-8bd8-5ad801426c7f.

Perez, Thomas E., and Russlynn Ali. 2010. "Joint 'Dear Colleague' Letter: Electronic Book Readers." U.S. Department of Education Office for Civil Rights, June 29. Accessed February 29, 2016. http://www2.ed.gov/about/offices/list/ocr/letters/colleague-20100629.html.

Thompson, Rachel. 2015. "Carrots and Sticks: Making the Case for Accessibility." Presented at HighEdWeb Alabama, Tuscaloosa, AL, June 29–30, 2015.

3Play Media. 2015. "Captioning 101." Accessed October 19, 2015. http://www.3playmedia.com/faq-category/captioning-101/.

United Nations. 2006. "Convention on the Rights of Persons with Disabilities." Last modified August 9. Accessed November 10, 2015. http://www.un.org/disabilities/convention/conventionfull.shtml.

United Nations. 2015. "Convention on the Rights of Persons with Disabilities status as at: 09–11–2015 06:53:37 EDT." United Nations Treaty Collection. Accessed November 10, 2015. https://treaties.un.org/pages/ViewDetails.aspx?src=TREATY&mtdsg_no=IV-15&chapter=4&lang=en.

United States Access Board. 2015. "Section 508 Standards for Electronic and Information Technology." Accessed October 19, 2015. http://www.access-board.gov/guidelines-and-standards/communications-and-it/about-the-section-508-standards/section-508-standards.

United States Department of Education. 2013. "Digest of Education Statistics, 2013 (NCES 2015–011), Table 311.10." National Center for Education Statistics (NCES). Last modified May 7. Accessed February 29, 2016. http://nces.ed.gov/programs/digest/d13/tables/dt13_311.10.asp.

WebAIM. 2015. "Captions, Transcripts, and Audio Descriptions." WebAIM. Accessed October 19, 2015. http://webaim.org/techniques/captions/.

World Health Organization. 2015. "Disability and Health." Accessed November 10, 2015. http://www.who.int/mediacentre/factsheets/fs352/en/.

W3C. 2008. "Web Content Accessibility Guidelines (WCAG) 2.0." World Wide Web Consortium (W3C). Last modified December 11. Accessed October 19, 2015. http://www.w3.org/TR/WCAG20/.

W3C. 2013. "Shared Web Experiences: Barriers Common to Mobile Device Users and People with Disabilities." Web Accessibility Initiative. Last modified January 22. Accessed October 19, 2015. http://www.w3.org/WAI/mobile/experiences.

W3C. 2014. "Web Accessibility Evaluation Tools List." Web Accessibility Initiative. Last modified December 19. Accessed October 19, 2015. http://www.w3.org/WAI/ER/tools/.

W3C. 2015a. "Financial Factors in Developing a Web Accessibility Business Case for Your Organization." Web Accessibility Initiative. Accessed October 1, 2015. http://www.w3.org/WAI/bcase/fin.html.

W3C. 2015b. "Tables Tutorial." Web Accessibility Initiative. Last modified March 2. Accessed October 19, 2015. http://www.w3.org/WAI/tutorials/tables/.

Yanchulis, Dave. 2015. "Overview of the Proposed Rule." United States Access Board. Accessed October 19, 2015. http://www.access-board.gov/guidelines-and-standards/communications-and-it/about-the-ict-refresh/overview-of-the-proposed-rule.

IV

PEDAGOGY AND INSTRUCTION WITH LIBGUIDES

12

Infusing Pedagogy into LibGuides

Elizabeth German, Texas A&M
Stephanie Graves, Texas A&M

Web developer is not a label that many librarians are comfortable owning. Librarians more closely identify themselves as information specialists, reference librarians, curators, and teachers. Nevertheless, when librarians start developing content on the web through a blog, content management system, or LibGuides, they enter the vast web development community. Like any specialized profession, the web development community includes a variety of professionals with unique skills. Good web development includes roles for graphic designers, coding programmers, content strategists, copywriters, user interface designers, and information architects.

When librarians create a LibGuide, they take on many of these roles. For example, librarians become content strategists when they need to prioritize the most important information to display to users. They become designers as they determine the layout and style of a page, and they use the same skills as a copywriter as they write the text for a guide. Librarians, however, are not always prepared to take on these roles when they become LibGuide creators. They might lack the special training, education in web theory, and design skills that web developers spend time establishing. We believe that, despite not having formal web development training, librarians possess many skills as educators that can be transferred into web development skills through reflective application of pedagogy practices in the online environment.

The art and science of teaching is something that many librarians practice as a part of their duties, typically through one-shot classes that still dominate library instruction programs. However, the one-shot library class limits the amount of instruction that librarians can offer. In response, the library community has embraced pedagogical methods to ensure that their library instruction has maximum impact for students. Librarians have also looked for technologies to help support learning both in and outside of the traditional classroom environment. Due to this, LibGuides have become a pervasive instruction tool. In fact, many LibGuides are created as "class guides" and used to supplement library instruction sessions. In order to be successful instructional tools, they need to be designed with good pedagogy in mind. The following three pedagogical concepts are common in library instruction:

1. Learning outcomes, statements that specify what the learner should be able to do or know after a learning activity (Association of College and Research Libraries [ACRL] 2000).
2. Lesson plans, a road map for the class session (American Association of School Librarians 2013).
3. Differentiated instruction, the framework for developing instruction for multiple avenues for learning (Tomlinson 1999).

These concepts will be partnered with analogous web development concepts to illustrate how pedagogy can be translated into LibGuide design. First, learning outcomes and their relationship to user stories in web design will be explored. Examples will show how learning outcomes can be used to make a user story that will inform LibGuides design principles. Next, the theory of lesson plans will be paired with web content outlines. Content outlines help librarians focus on developing guides that are clutter free and easy to use. Finally, there will be a discussion on how an understanding of differentiated instruction translates to Universal Design principles for website creation. Multimodal teaching principles will be highlighted as a method of creating guides that are accessible to a wider variety of learners.

Pairing teaching principles with web concepts will help instruction librarians translate their knowledge of teaching into better LibGuides for their learners. Additionally, exploring the intersections of the two disciplines creates a shared language and a common understanding that librarians and web designers can use to work with each other. By adopting principles from both fields, librarians will be able to create better guides using principles that they can apply in both the classroom and the web.

LEARNING OUTCOMES TO USER STORIES

Learning outcomes are statements that specify what learners should be able to do or know after a learning activity (ACRL 2000). Instructors use outcomes to express a measureable change in student skills, behavior, and/or knowledge. Note that the focus of learning outcomes is the student, not the teacher. Outcomes-based education flips the focus of traditional instruction from *what content will the teacher cover* to *what new skills or knowledge will the students possess after learning*. These measurable changes in student behavior form the basis for learning assessment (ACRL 2010).

Outcomes-based education has exploded in recent decades as a response to calls for accountability in education. Librarians responded by developing learning outcomes for information literacy education. The *Information Literacy Competency Standards for Higher Education* (ACRL 2000) provide five standards, twenty-two performance indicators, and over eight-four suggested learning outcomes. These outcomes have been widely adopted, measured, and used to demonstrate student learning in library instruction sessions.

Building from the standards, the *Framework for Information Literacy for Higher Education* (ACRL 2015a) has been adopted to embrace and extend educational reforms that emphasize a more nuanced and complex set of ideas. There are six "frames" that incorporate and express various dimensions of learning, covering context, process, value, inquiry, scholarship, and exploration.

Library instruction sessions at Texas A&M typically have three to seven different learning outcomes from the ACRL standards. The number of learning outcomes can vary depending upon the goals, complexity, and length of the instruction. For each learning outcome the librarian must think about how they are going to present it, what type of learning activity is needed (e.g., lecture, video, reading, etc.), and how will they assess if the learner achieved the outcome. The learning outcome drives the instructional planning process and ensures that there is intentional alignment between the learning activities and the desired outcomes.

Learning outcomes describe what the learner will be able to do or know after the learning activity. User stories describe what the user should be able to do with the software or website. Table 12.1 shows examples of learning outcomes and related user stories.

Table 12.1. Two learning outcomes and their analogous user stories.

Learning Outcome	User Story
As a result of library instruction, students will be able to explain the rationale for citing in order to evaluate the consequences for not citing appropriately.	As a student, I don't want to get in trouble for not citing correctly.
As a result of library instruction, students will be able to identify material formats in order to select appropriate resources for their research need.	As a student, I want to find a book chapter so that I can cite it in my paper.

While there are many different ways and personal preferences to writing learning outcomes or user stories, using a structured formulaic model will be useful for comparing the two. Each statement describes a singular behavior that can be designed for and assessed either in a classroom or on the web. These formulas help teachers and web designers quickly create concise statements.

- Structure of a Learning Outcome

  ◦ As a result of [learning experience or class] students will be able to [action verb] in order to [reason why they need to do the behavior].

- Structure of a User Story

  ◦ As a [type of user], I want [some goal] so that [some reason].

Notice the similarities between the elements of a learning outcome and the elements of a user story. Each identifies a "who" or central character. In learning outcomes, the "who" is always the student. In user stories, the "who" is always the user of the software or application. Since class guides are learning objects, the central character of both the learning outcomes and the user story is the student using the guides. The next element in both statements indicates the intended action of the student. Learning outcomes use action verbs to describe what a student should do, while user stories use the concepts of goals to describe the task that a student needs to accomplish. In both cases, this element expresses the measureable object of the learning. It answers the question of "What is the student doing?" Finally, both statements end with a reason, or "why" element. The "why" element is important because it articulates the motivation for learning something or completing a task. Through stating the motivation, this element explicitly illuminates for the teacher or web developer the importance of why the outcome or user story is necessary for successful instruction or product. Through review of the "why" within learning outcomes and user stories, it is easy to verify if the instruction or product will meet the needs of the student or user. To move from learning outcomes to user stories, librarians can start by asking themselves clarifying questions based on the learning outcomes they have already developed for the class.

- What should students be able to do or know as a result of the library instruction? Why?
- Does the class guide support the classroom learning outcomes?
- Does the class guide supplement the classroom outcomes with additional learning outcomes?

Once the learning outcomes for both the class and the guide are defined, librarians should translate those outcomes into user stories following the preceding formula. The aim is to define how students will use the class guide to accomplish specific tasks related to the learning outcomes. Create these user stories, and LibGuides transforms from a seemingly random list of resources into useful learning tools.

Learning outcomes and user stories share many commonalities. They both focus on the learner or user and not the instructor or the website. They are explicit about what tasks need to be accomplished by the student. They set paths for how to prioritize content for designers. They indicate what success would look like by defining measurable goals. By using learning outcomes to create user stories for LibGuides, library guides will become more useful for learners.

LESSON PLANS TO CONTENT OUTLINES

Once instructors have developed learning outcomes, the next step in instructional planning is creating a lesson plan. The lesson plan is a detailed road map for the class session, including instructional content, learning activities, and assessments. Numerous examples of lessons exist within the library community, such as the *Library Instruction Cookbook* (Sittler and Cook 2009) and *PRIMO Peer-Reviewed Instructional Materials Online* (ACRL 2015b). K–12 librarians may be more familiar with lesson planning. The American Association of School Librarians hosts an archive of lesson plans from *Standards for the 21st-Century Learner Lesson Plan Database* (AASL 2015). Lesson planning is a vital part of the instructional planning process. It defines the scope of instruction, making sure that all elements of the class structure are intentionally designed for the best learning experience.

As instructors create lesson plans, they will consider issues of cognitive load. Even if the name is unfamiliar to librarians, they will be familiar with the concept. Cognitive load theory posits that the brain can only handle a finite amount of information during a given time frame (Plass, Moreno, and Brünken 2010). Miller (1956) introduced the idea that working memory has limited capacity, suggested that humans could hold no more than seven units of information (five plus or minus two units), and that memory is better utilized by "chunking" information into smaller memorable groups. Since Miller's seminal work, others have suggested that the number of units may be smaller, around three to five units of information (Cowan 2010). Undoubtedly, chunking is evident in daily life. Examples of chunking include the way in which phone numbers and social security numbers are grouped into sets of three to four numbers in order to remember long strings of information. The process helps increase both short-term and long-term memory recall.

Using chunking to address cognitive load has become a ubiquitous part of pedagogical practice. Instructional designers use chunking to talk about designing memorable curricula, creating scaffolded lesson plans, and making scalable online learning objects. Classroom instructors use chunking to group related content into modules followed by learning activities and checks for understanding. Chunking is a valuable practice that allows the learner to process a learning activity before moving on to the next idea. The adage "less is more" sums up the basic concept of cognitive load. Present learners with too much information all at once, and they won't remember any of it.

Librarians can use their lesson planning skills to inform LibGuides design. In web development, the concepts implicit in cognitive load theory can be addressed using web content outlines. Content outlines are organized lists of content needed to meet the user stories for the site. They provide an overarching architectural plan for the design and navigation of a web page. Content outlines can take on any number of forms. They can look similar to writing outlines, or they can be more visual in nature, such as a skeleton drawing of what will be on a LibGuide. Content outlines are lesson plans for the web. Lesson plans outline the basic elements of an instructional plan and content outlines provide a framework for a LibGuide.

In a content outline for a LibGuide, chunking can be translated as creating an appropriate amount of tabs or pages. A guide with fifteen tabs or pages would be too many for a user to process given the limits of working memory. Similarly, if each box of content on a LibGuide is considered a chunk, using Miller's initial supposition, the maximum number of boxes on a page would be between five and nine.

Content outlines can take different forms depending on the type of information that needs to be communicated. Textbox 12.1 illustrates the content outline using a writing model that is useful when trying to describe a hierarchical relationship between content. Figure 12.1 illustrates using a visualization that is useful when the content has a more complex relationship than a linear hierarchy.

Lesson plans often do not provide a word-by-word script for instruction. Librarians can ad lib and improvise, as the class moves through the lesson, by reacting to students dynamically. However, when developing for the web, there is no such luxury. Every word that will be communicated is written out. Additionally, writing for print or scholarly communications is different from writing for the web. When writing for the web, it is a best practice to place content into digestible blocks for

---

TEXTBOX 12.1. CONTENT OUTLINE FOR A LIBGUIDE

Page 1: Home

    Box 1 (standard): Welcome
    Box 2 (tabbed): Top Resources

        Tab 1: Databases
        Tab 2: Journals
        Tab 2: Course Reserves

Page 2: Developing Keywords

    Box 1 (standard): Developing Keywords

    Sub Heading: What are keywords?

        Content: Video Tutorial

    How do I choose keywords?

        Content: Link to handout

Page 3: Your Assignment

    Box 1: Part 1
    Box 2: Part 2
    Box 3: Part 3

Page 4: Creating a Bibliography

    Box 1: Citation Style Chicago
    Box 2: Citation Management Software

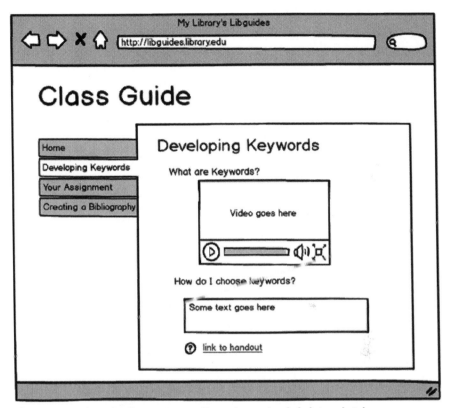

Figure 12.1. Sample of a content outline using a visual skeleton sketch.

the user. More specifically, writing for the web factors in the way in which humans digest information in the web environment (Nielsen 1997).

Humans read differently on the Internet than they do in print. Readers on the web skim the content of a page. They look for the chunks of a website, the headers, bold text, and bulleted lists to orient themselves quickly to relevant content. If the content outline includes more chunks than a user can digest, consider using progressive disclosure. Progressive disclosure is the process of chunking advanced content or features into headings, subheadings, or even subsequent pages so that all users can scan web pages quickly before making decisions on where they might want more information (Nielsen 2005). Chunking and progressive disclosure reduce clutter, allowing users to focus their attention on the needed information or task.

Generally, librarians tend to overload their guides with more information than the human brain can process efficiently. Baker (2014, 110) calls attention to this "kitchen sink" approach, stating, "As satisfying and efficient it may seem to us librarians to centralize resources in an organized framework, the subject guides can be too broad in scope or provide so much information that students become frustrated and confused." She argues that tutorial-type LibGuides that focus on specific assignment tasks will reduce cognitive load and allow for deeper learning (111).

When creating LibGuides, librarians should consider that learners are coming to the guide to accomplish a task. If they are overburdened with too many options, they will not make good choices and will not learn what the librarian had hoped they would by viewing the guide. Content outlines can help address this issue using the same practices used in chunking lesson plans.

DIFFERENTIATED INSTRUCTION TO UNIVERSAL DESIGN

Differentiated instruction (DI) is the practice of adapting instruction in order to better address the needs of different learners (Tomlinson 1999). Tomlinson identifies three areas of possible differentiation among students: readiness, interests, and/or learning profiles. DI encourages instructors to respond to learners by creating a variety of learning activities. For example, students with different learning styles may process information differently. Some students may respond well to participatory class discussions, while others need more individual reflection activities in order to participate. Students also come with a variety of educational experiences. Some students may be academically talented at certain tasks or subjects, while other are academically underprepared in those same areas. Additionally, student interests in a subject or task may affect motivation and engagement in the learning process.

Instruction librarians are well acquainted with the variety of student interests and skills that can be present in a classroom. Learners come to the library classroom with a wide variety of research experiences, information needs, and library knowledge. Strategies used in DI can help bridge the gaps. Some examples used in library instruction include

- Allowing visual learners to create concept maps of keywords.
- Using reflective research journals for introverted learners.
- Grouping students with shared interests or research experiences.
- Providing activities for auditory learners to talk about their research processes.
- Creating hands-on activities for kinesthetic learners.

Librarians' dedication to meeting learners where they are in their learning process shouldn't stop in the classroom. The majority of our library users will never see a library instructor. They will come to the library's website looking to meet their information needs. In the web environment, DI is similar to the concept of Universal Design (UD). Like differentiation, UD aims to improve instruction and access through inclusivity. UD is the value, theory, and practice that design for all types of users benefits any user. It has grown out of the accessibility movement, but has broadened the scope from disability compliance to practicing good design features. UD has grown from addressing specific physical limitations such as visual impairments to exploring a wide range of individuals and how they access information.

Understanding UD principles can improve LibGuides for library users just as using DI can improve in-class instruction. One easily addressed area of improvement is the headings within guides. Headings and chunking are very important for the understandability of a page. They are also necessary to make a website accessible to the visually impaired. When users are utilizing screen readers they navigate a website using the headers. The page title will be the first heading or in HTML, <H1> with subheadings as <H2> or <H3>. A book would be a good metaphor where <H1> is the book, <H2> a chapter, and <H3> a sentence. It would be incorrect to have a sentence that did not belong within a chapter. When reading the page it would be confusing for a user if the page was not in an order hierarchy of headings.

Illustrating this, textbox 12.2 shows how HTML code explicitly tells the screen reader how to identify the headers on the page independent of the style. On the left

TEXTBOX 12.2. COMPARISON BETWEEN HTML AND WYSIWYG CODING IN LIBGUIDES' HEADERS

Proper HTML	WYSIWYG HTML
<H1>Page Title</H1>	<p style="font-size:20px; font-weight:bold;">Page Title</p>
<H2>Introduction</H2>	<p style="font-size:16px; font-weight:bold;">Introduction</p>
<p>This is text for my introduction. Everything underneath the H2 header for introduction would be related to the introduction.</p>	<p>This is text for my introduction. Everything underneath the H2 header for introduction would be related to the introduction.</p>
<H2>Second Chunk</H2>	<p style="font-size:16px; font-weight:bold">Second Chunk</p>
<H3>Example 1</H3>	<p style="font-size:12px; font-weight:bold">Example 1</p>
<p> This H3 is a sub-header. Everything under Example 1 would be about Example 1. But it also would be related to the H2 "Second Chunk". </p>	<p> This H3 is a sub-header. Everything under Example 1 would be about Example 1. But it also would be related to the H2 "Second Chunk". </p>
<H3>Example 2</H3>	<p style="font-size:12px; font-weight:bold">Example 2</p>
<p>Everything under Example 2 would be about Example 2. It would also be about the Second Chunk. But it is different than Example 1. </p>	<p>Everything under Example 2 would be about Example 2. It would also be about the Second Chunk. But it is different than Example 1. </p>

side, the HTML code for page headers is used correctly. On the right side, headers were created using style elements from the LibGuides' "what you see is what you get" WYSIWYG (pronounced wiz-e-wig) editor.

If a screen reader were reading a page aloud, the code sample on the left side would be easier for users to make sense of the page. It also follows the same chunking idea described earlier. Making pages more accessible for visually impaired users improves design for all users.

A word of warning about headers in LibGuides: The current LibGuides WYSIWYG text editor allows librarians to select <H1> and <H2> headers. However, these headers are incorporated into the LibGuides style at the page (<H1>) or a box (<H2>) level. Therefore, content inside LibGuides boxes should only select <H3>, <H4>, <H5>, or <H6> headers. This ensures structured headings across a LibGuides page that work appropriately with screen readers for the visually impaired.

Other concepts in UD include considerations for nonnative speakers, multiple generations of users, and cultural differences. Instructors and web designers should practice care when using metaphors, cultural references, or jargon. For instance, referencing the card catalog may not be useful to younger students who may never have seen a card catalog. Including links to the OPAC in our guide may not translate to nonnative speakers. Just as in teaching, use clear and precise language in the text of your guide, avoid extraneous descriptions, and give consideration to the domain knowledge the user is expected to have prior to viewing the content.

BETTER LIBGUIDES LEAD TO A BETTER LIBRARY WEBSITE

LibGuides are a foundational tool for providing access to library content. Librarians can create a better user experience in LibGuides by translating instructional principles into their web development practices. Efforts to create more meaningful guides will be minimized, however, unless there is widespread recognition that LibGuides do not exist in isolation. They are part of the libraries' web ecosystem, and how they are integrated into it affects the user experience.

Traditionally, access to LibGuides is constructed similarly to archival finding aids, grouped by collection or subject on a LibGuides menu page. The user must first know to look for LibGuides on the library website, making the choice to use a guide instead of the library search box. Guides are rarely integrated into searching functions, such as discovery layers, where users are typically directed. No matter how well designed the LibGuide system, if the library website has not "bought into" the usefulness of LibGuides and provided integrated search capabilities, LibGuides will remain unconnected to their objective.

This issue may be compounded by organization structures. LibGuide administrators are typically from public services while website administrators are usually from an information technology unit. This silo effect can cause friction and mismatched intents when designing a library's holistic web ecosystem. This friction comes through to the user in very real ways. Users experience mismatched designs, conflicting color schemes, language differences, and redundant services. In an ideal environment, LibGuides would factor into the overall strategy of resource access and resource access would factor in the overall strategy of the teaching mission of the libraries.

Improving LibGuides is only a first step in creating a more meaningful conversation about the role of library websites as educational tools. Access to materials has historically been the focus of developing web systems such as the Online Public Access Catalog (OPAC), LibGuides, and more recently discovery services. However, a singular focus on access to collections overlooks the clear teaching mission of libraries. Libraries are institutions of learning; we would be remiss not to address the centrality of pedagogy for the library web ecosystem. While in recent years, greater attention has been paid to improving the user experience of library systems such as discovery layers, repositories, and catalogs, the focus of these systems as an instruction tool has been ignored.

Excluding the libraries' web ecosystem as a medium for library instruction is shortsighted. Instead of simply providing access to materials, librarians and web professionals should move toward finding a solution to the question "How can library systems teach the information seeking skills while users access material?" This move would contribute to the educational success of our students, facilitating the learner's transition from one state of knowledge to a new state of knowledge. Librarians can model this new paradigm through the reflective application of pedagogy in their LibGuides design. Their efforts and advocacy can open up new conversations with web professionals, librarians, and database vendors about design for learning.

Pedagogy skills and web skills can be transferable. In order for LibGuides to be successful tools, they need to be developed with web development skills. Likewise, for our library websites to fulfill the educational goals of the library, all library websites need to be developed with learning in mind.

REFERENCES

American Association of School Librarians. 2013. "Standards for the 21st-Century Learner Lesson Plan Database." Accessed October 29, 2015. http://www.ala.org/aasl/standards -guidelines/lesson-plan.

Association of College and Research Libraries. 2000. *Information Literacy Competency Standards for Higher Education.*" Accessed October 29, 2015. http://www.ala.org/acrl/sites/ala .org.acrl/files/content/standards/standards.pdf.

Association of College and Research Libraries. 2015a. *Framework for Information Literacy for Higher Education.*" Accessed October 29, 15. http://www.ala.org/acrl/sites/ala.org.acrl/files/ content/issues/infolit/Framework_ILHE.pdf.

Association of College and Research Libraries. 2015b. *PRIMO: Peer-Reviewed Instructional Materials Online.* Accessed October 29, 2015. http://primodb.org/.

Baker, Ruth L. 2014. "Designing LibGuides as Instructional Tools for Critical Thinking and Effective Online Learning." *Journal of Library & Information Services in Distance Learning* 8 (3–4): 107–117.

Cowan, Nelson. 2010. "The Magical Mystery Four: How Is Working Memory Capacity Limited, and Why?" *Current Directions in Psychological Science* 19 (1): 51–57. http://doi .org/10.1177/0963721409359277

Miller, George A. 1956. "The Magical Number Seven, Plus or Minus Two: Some Limits on Our Capacity for Processing Information." *Psychological Review* 63 (2): 81–97. http:// dx.doi.org/10.1037/h0043158

Nielsen, Jacob. 1997. "How Users Read on the Web." *Nielsen/Norman Group* (blog), October 1. Accessed October 29, 2015. http://www.nngroup.com/articles/how-users-read-on-the-web/.

Nielsen, Jacob. 2005. "Progressive Disclosure." *Nielsen/Norman Group* (blog). Accessed October 29, 2015. http://www.nngroup.com/articles/progressive-disclosure/.

Plass, Jan L., Roxana Moreno, and Roland Brünken. 2010. *Cognitive Load Theory*. New York: Cambridge University Press.

Sittler, Ryan L., and Douglas Cook. 2009. *The Library Instruction Cookbook*. Chicago: Association of College and Research Libraries.

Tomlinson, Carol Ann. 1999. *The Differentiated Classroom: Responding to the Needs of All Learners*. Alexandria, VA: Association for Supervision and Curriculum Development.

13

Access and Universal Design for Learning in LibGuides 2.0

Kimberly Shotick, Northeastern Illinois University

The days of LibGuides used solely as pathfinders are long gone. LibGuides have evolved to serve a variety of purposes on library websites and, as learning takes place increasingly online, can be considered learning environments. Like any learning environment, there are barriers we must overcome that may limit the usefulness of our LibGuides. Students with visual disabilities and learning disabilities and those who have different learning preferences may be at a disadvantage when it comes to traditional LibGuides built for the fictional student who learns without any barriers. Using the principles of Universal Design for Learning (UDL) we can ensure that our LibGuides are not only accessible, but also effective learning aids for students of all abilities and inclinations.

Web environments are prime arenas to apply UDL principles given the ease of incorporating multimedia and elements that work well with assistive technology. By combining traditional web accessibility standards with principles from UDL, LibGuides can be accessible for all learners. Additionally, librarians can coordinate accessibility efforts with teaching and staff training in order to become more effective with information literacy efforts both on and offline.

UNIVERSAL DESIGN FOR LEARNING

Universal Design (UD) roots are in architecture. The idea is simple: construct a building for those in the margins, and everyone benefits (Meyer and Rose 2005). The idea originated with North Carolina State University researchers, from a variety of disciplines, who argued that both products and environments should be designed so that they are inherently usable by everyone (Connell et al. 1997). For example, an elevator provides access to people with physical disabilities, but it may also benefit older adults, women who are pregnant, families with strollers, or someone who is carrying a heavy load. Everyone benefits from accessible features without requiring special accommodations.

The applicability of UD doesn't stop with physical structures. Signage should also be accessible to the greatest number of people. Designers accomplish this by considering who may have trouble reading or seeing signs and considering design elements that can make it easier for them, such as sans-serif and high-contrast text and backgrounds. This same accessibility translates to virtual environments, which can carry unique obstacles hidden behind HTML. Despite efforts to make websites more accessible by the international organization World Wide Web Consortium (W3C), postsecondary websites remain widely inaccessible due to webmaster and administrator ignorance of accessibility issues and legal obligations (Burgstahler 2008).

UD was applied to learning environments by Meyer, Rose, and Gordon of the Center for Applied Special Technology (CAST), who shared a desire to reach diverse learners and used the term *Universal Design for Learning* to describe the application of UD to instructional design. Advances in neural sciences and technology enabled the application of UD to learning and instruction (Rose and Meyer 2002). Just as an architect would consider how people may best access all areas of a building, an instructional designer should consider the accessibility of information and instruction when designing learning objects in order to deliver accessible instruction to learners with varied learning preferences and abilities. Meyer, Rose, and Gordon (2014) investigated barriers to learning that existed in a print-based world and discovered that students who were once enthusiastic about learning became stigmatized by learning environments that were inaccessible. UDL seeks to eliminate barriers at the design phase of instruction so that, like with UD in architecture, students won't be stigmatized by an environment that forces them to ask for special accommodations. Designing accessible instruction is a simple, yet radical way of looking at instruction which has historically been inaccessible to many learners.

The three key principles of UDL are to provide multiple modes of representation, multiple means of expression, and multiple means of engagement (Hall, Meyer, and Rose 2012). These principles can be applied to the design of any instructional setting. However, when applied to online environments, the nature of the online experience presents potential challenges to addressing some principles while it offers an advantage over others. UDL principles can be effectively utilized in LibGuides design by taking advantage of features specific to the system while avoiding potential pitfalls that make its content inaccessible to some learners.

PRINCIPLES OF UDL IN LIBGUIDES

First Principle: Multiple Modes of Representation

By offering alternatives to instruction delivery, librarians can provide the learner options that may best suit her learning preferences and/or accessibility needs. In the example of a traditional classroom session this may mean sending students an accessible PDF copy of lecture slides that contain multiple representations of the same information, such as text, bullet points, and graphics.

The LibGuides environment presents more opportunities for application of this principle than obstacles. Content aimed at achieving a learning outcome should be available in different formats, which is easy to do. For example, if there is an important concept conveyed in a video, offer a text alternative. *The Introduction to Research at the NEIU Library* LibGuides from Northeastern Illinois University in figure 13.1 contains multiple video tutorials along with PDF versions of the tutorial concepts (Ronald Williams Library 2015). The concepts from the conceptual animated tutorials are echoed in the point-and-click video tutorials, PDFs, and box text. PDFs can be made accessible by avoiding using scanned files, inserting alt text when an image contains information unique to the rest of the document, and inserting the proper metadata in the file properties. Adobe Acrobat Pro has a feature called Accessibility Checker that will identify potential accessibility issues in PDFs.

An advantage to echoing content in various formats is that it not only makes them more accessible to individuals with disabilities, but it also accounts for the multiple

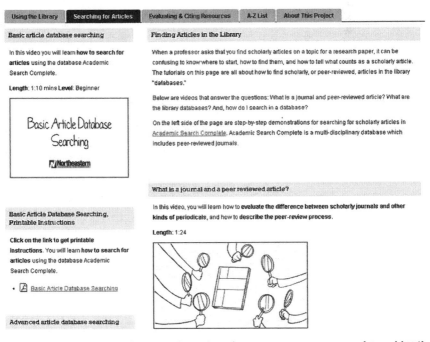

Figure 13.1. Instructional content in various formats. *Image courtesy of Ronald Williams Library 2015*

learning preferences that students bring to the situation. This is the power of UDL in action—small considerations can eliminate barriers for many.

There are also potential obstacles in offering multiple modes of representation in the LibGuides environment. Too much visual information on a LibGuides page can produce information overload, which can present a significant obstacle for learning. Approaching each page as a single lesson can lead to logical break points in the content. Tabs help maintain a balance of learning objectives and visual layout.

Begin LibGuides design with the question "What do I want my students to be able to do/know after interacting with this page?" If students are expected to accomplish too many outcomes, the LibGuides will be overloaded even before providing multiple modes of representation. Limiting the lesson plan to a few learning outcomes will make achieving UDL principles more likely and without information overload. The "tabbed" and "gallery" box features available in LibGuides version 2 allow for more content without taking up more real estate on the guide. These box types can be a good tool for providing multiple modes of disseminating the same content in one box.

Second Principle: Multiple Means of Expression

This principle asks us to provide flexibility in how individuals learn and express what they know. In the traditional classroom, for example, students may be given a quiz to test their knowledge. Alternative assessments, in that context, would give them the option to express their understanding of content through mediums that best suit them as individual learners, whether that is through a quiz, essay, or creative work. The LibGuides environment presents opportunities to offer users multiple means of expression. The concept of incorporating *multiple* means for user expression in LibGuides is novel. However, in teaching, LibGuides may be used in combination with in-classroom or virtual instruction. Virtual instruction, in particular, presents opportunities for allowing users to express their knowledge in a variety of ways, such as through a text, video, or graphic posts on a virtual discussion board. For example, a LibGuide on constructing a literature review may be a resource that students use in conjunction with discussion or group work that allows them to express their understanding of the LibGuides content. Additionally, LibGuides offer opportunities for virtual modes of user expression such as polling, widgets, LibSurveys, or embedded Google forms.

The example in figure 13.2 asks students to answer several questions that review concepts taught in the guide content. This form was created with Google forms and is embedded directly into LibGuides to provide instant feedback. Students can use this to assess their own learning, or it can be used in conjunction with instruction. The form could be calibrated to collect student information for grading purposes, or it could be used anonymously as formative assessment during library instruction.

There are some obstacles to offering multiple means of expression in the LibGuides environment. The current polling feature is limited and the more complex

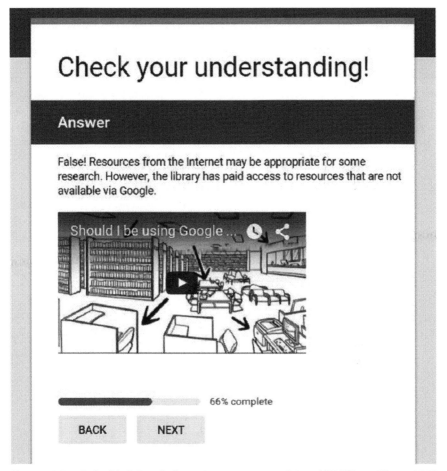

Figure 13.2.   Embedded Google form. *Image courtesy of Ronald Williams Library 2015*

Google forms have a steep learning curve. The larger obstacle could be the ideo-logical shift for some librarians who are accustomed to guides as static pathfinders. Despite the limits of the polling feature, it is an easy way to add an interactive ele-ment to an otherwise static page. Enlist colleagues with technical expertise to create a general Google form that can easily be adapted for multiple applications.

Third Principle: Multiple Means of Engagement

The third principle focuses on the student's internal motivation and is often the least explored (Hall, Meyer, and Rose 2012). We need to foster learners who can regulate their own learning in order to cultivate motivation in learning. Stu-dents may approach learning with myriad distractions. Eliminating distractions and allowing students a chance to reflect on their learning can sustain motivation throughout a learning experience.

The LibGuides environment presents opportunities to offer users multiple means of engagement. One strategy that is often used in teaching is the reflective paper. After a lesson, the students are asked to reflect on the most difficult concepts or on what they learned. This is often called a "minute paper" and is a popular assessment technique used in instruction (Angelo and Cross 1993). The same strategy can be applied to a LibGuide or can be used in coordination with a LibGuide and instruction. For example, a LibGuide about academic honesty could include an open-ended question for the learner to respond to either in the guide itself (via LibSurveys or an embedded Google form) or on a discussion forum in the learning management system. The opportunity to reflect reinforces the content and allows the student to contextualize the lesson as it relates to the student's experiences.

Online environments present unique obstacles for user engagement. Motivation, in particular, can be difficult for some learners in this environment. The goal of engaging a student should be an affective goal that relates to that student's mood and other motivating factors (Rose and Meyer 2002). Distracted, tired, or confused learners may approach a LibGuide, but it cannot realistically be altered in real time to suit their particular motivating factors. Instead, LibGuides can be designed with limited distractions, explicit learning outcomes, and a light or fun tone that may help alleviate students' stress while learning.

SECTION 508 STANDARDS AND WCAG 2.0

In 2000 the U.S. Access Board published *The Standards for Electronic and Information Technology*, also known as Section 508 of the Rehabilitation Act of 1973, requiring that federally funded entities make electronically presented information available to people with disabilities (Waddell 2006). Under these standards, federally funded entities are legally liable if they have inaccessible websites. While there is some debate about its applicability to Universities, many have taken these standards as "best practices" for their websites (Waddell 2006). Many Section 508 standards mesh with the application of UDL on websites. Application of UDL principles in web design naturally satisfies many Section 508 standards. However, UDL is more conceptual and tied to theory, whereas Section 508 is technically prescriptive.

As of this writing, Section 508 is currently undergoing a refresh that will include incorporation of Web Content Accessibility Guidelines (WCAG) 2.0 aimed at making all technologies accessible (United States Access Board 2015). These guidelines state that web content should be perceivable, operable, understandable, and robust (Caldwell et. al 2008). While the guidelines themselves are not testable, each contains criteria that are relevant to LibGuides. *Perceivable* LibGuides have text alternatives for non-text items and utilize color schemas that do not interfere with reading (e.g., a white background with black text). *Operable* LibGuides have clear titles with logically organized boxes that are labeled informatively. *Understandable* LibGuides provide definitions for jargon. *Robust* LibGuides do not contain HTML errors or broken links and can be read by a screen reader.

Since LibGuides are not built by the user most of the criteria from the WCGA 2.0 guidelines have already been met by existing formatting in LibGuides. Users and admins only have control over the general look and feel of the guides and the box content. The simplest controllable element in LibGuides, to be compliant with Section 508, is supplying text descriptions for images (alt text). If you are using an image in LibGuides, be sure to fill out the alt text section of the image properties with the following information, as is appropriate to the qualities of the image: a brief description of the information contained within the image, a note that the image is decorative, or a description of the link text. For example, if inserting a picture of a stack of books, enter "stack of books" as the alt text. The information in the alt text should be as brief as possible while still conveying all of the information in the image.

Another simple way of complying with Section 508, while following UDL best practices, is to have captioning for videos embedded in or linked from LibGuides. Videos without captions should be replaced by more accessible videos. For users uploading their own videos, YouTube has an option that will automatically caption uploaded videos. However, it can be embarrassingly inaccurate. It is rather simple to upload a text transcript and sync captions for uploaded videos in the Video Manager section of YouTube. One advantage of using YouTube captions, rather than adding captions in a video editing application, is that their captions can be translated, resized, moved around, and otherwise altered by the viewer to suit his or her preferences. A step further than captioning would be to provide the user with a printed handout of instructions available in video form. Not only do print versions make video tutorials more accessible for the visually disabled, but they may be preferred by print learners, as in the earlier example.

EVALUATION

The next step after designing and assembling a LibGuide is to test its accessibility. The Web Accessibility Evaluation Tool (WAVE) is an online tool that tests accessibility features of websites. The website (http://wave.webaim.org/) allows users to enter a URL and identify various accessibility roadblocks, features, and errors that may be buried in the HTML. For instance, WAVE will identify when images are used without alt text. It also identifies when two adjacent links point to the same URL (for example, a banner and home page link that both point to a library's home page). While this redundancy can be desirable from a usability standpoint, too much redundancy can be cumbersome to someone using a screen reader.

Those with sight disabilities primarily use screen readers to access web content. JAWS and NVDA are two programs that read on-screen text and help users navigate web content. NVDA is an open source program and can be downloaded for free.

LibGuides designers can download the program on their machines to evaluate the accessibility of their LibGuides and interact with them from a perspective that may be different from their own.

Finally, working with a disabilities office or local disabilities resources can help improve accessibility of LibGuides and library websites. This serves not only to improve their accessibility, but also to promote those resources with disabilities office professionals who have direct contact with students. At the very least, the effort will identify the library as an ally, improving future relationships that can lead to collaboration and resource sharing.

IMPLEMENTATION

The appeal of LibGuides is that they make website building easy. Librarians with little HTML knowledge can build interactive learning objects that integrate with library websites, catalogs, chat services, and more (Ahmed 2013). Rose and Meyer (2002, 132) saw learning tools with built-in flexibility as "the future of curriculum design" over ten years ago. In order to be flexible learning tools, LibGuides content and designs need to be intentionally accessible. Instead of being a repository of links and lists, they can be learning platforms with embedded modules, quizzes, instructional videos, and more. Taking UDL and accessibility into consideration, LibGuides can be dynamic learning tools. Such tools are designed with sensitivity to the diversity of learners.

Librarians at East Carolina University (ECU) incorporated UDL elements into existing LibGuides making them a dynamic and accessible teaching tool for information literacy concepts (Webb and Hoover 2015a). Their design takes into account the multiple learning preferences that students arrive with as well as the potential accessibility roadblocks they may encounter online. ECU librarians utilized a UDL mapping technique in order to incorporate content that was geared to diverse learning styles (Webb and Hoover 2015b). The resulting LibGuides incorporate audio clips, visual cartoons, and kinesthetic activities.

The CSE Citation page, shown in figure 13.3, includes kinesthetic activities that allow students to interact with the content through clicking along with visual and textual representations of information. The guide also meets the WCAG 2.0 guidelines; the text is highly contrasted with the background, making the guide perceivable. Boxes are labeled clearly, and a header box identifies the guide layout, making it operable. Additional tutorials are linked to help make the guide understandable. Finally, the guide is robust enough to be accessed with a screen reader.

UDL principles are more easily applied to LibGuides that are learning tools and may not be appropriate for guides that serve as pathfinders. However, general accessibility issues are easily identifiable through evaluative tools, such as the WAVE website. For those LibGuides that serve a more instructive purpose, LibGuides designers can implement UDL principles just by adding multimedia to their guides

Figure 13.3.   Biology: CSE Citation page. *Webb and Hoover 2015a*

and complying with Section 508 standards. Librarians should be having conversations about accessibility, and UDL should be a part of those conversations.

Librarians wishing to increase the accessibility of their LibGuides can run an audit with the following checklist:

1. Alt text is used to describe non-decorative images.
2. Captions or transcripts are available for videos and/or audio.
3. Color schemes do not interfere with reading.
4. Assistive technology can be used to navigate guide content.

For LibGuides that are intended to be used as *learning tools*, as opposed to *pathfinders*, consider these additional elements:

1. Content is presented in multiple formats (e.g., video and text).
2. Concepts are echoed in multiple formats.
3. Guide content offers some level of interaction (e.g., polling or quizzing).

By auditing existing guides and applying the checklist to newly created content, librarians can begin conversations about accessibility that extend beyond LibGuides and to other library-operated websites, facilities, and instruction efforts. Institutional change can be difficult in higher education, but partnerships with accessibility advocates, such as student and faculty support units (e.g., centers for teaching and learning and student tutoring centers), can shift accessibility efforts from *reactive* to *proactive*. Virginia Commonwealth University (VCU) and Virginia Tech undertook collaborative accessibility training and outreach efforts on their respective campuses that resulted in increased faculty awareness of accessibility issues and strategies (Finn et al. 2008). Librarians can be leaders in similar collaborations at their institutions by initiating conversations and contributing to faculty training. First, however, the library can start its own internal UDL initiative by educating library colleagues and applying UDL to instruction in all formats, including LibGuides.

CONCLUSION

As academic librarianship evolves, so must our practices as educators. The LibGuides platform has developed to allow for more customization and can be used to create a dynamic learning environment. As educators, we have the responsibility to use that customization to ensure that our LibGuides are fully accessible. Luckily, there are tools and design principles intended to help educators do just that: create accessible learning objects.

Following the principles of UDL, LibGuides should offer multiple means of representation. In practice, LibGuides content should be echoed in various formats (graphics and text conveying the concept of Boolean logic, for example). LibGuides should also offer multiple means of expression and engagement, allowing learners to interact with guide content but not *requiring* them to do so. For example, the ECU Libraries Biology LibGuide (2015) invites users to navigate the guide by clicking hyperlinked arrows to the various tabs in the guide in a linear fashion. However, the user is free to navigate the guide out of sequence by clicking on the various guide tabs. While these considerations may seem trite, the user who learns best by thinking through concepts in a linear fashion and the user who just needs to review one concept from a single LibGuides tab are both served by the addition of the navigational arrows. These small design considerations greatly improve accessibility.

In addition to considering the three principles of UDL, we must ensure we meet Section 508 requirements. Free evaluative tools, such as WAVE, exist to identify accessibility issues, and fixes are often as easy as adding a few words of descriptive text for images. Evaluation can also involve using assistive technology, such as a free screen reading program, to navigate the LibGuides and identify areas that are inaccessible or clunky for individuals with visual disabilities. Finally, an improved or new partnership with accessibility advocates is another low-effort way to increase accessibility efforts while having the potential additional benefits down the road that often come with partnerships, such as collaborative grants or projects.

Build for those in the margins and everyone benefits—that is the simple idea behind UD. When applied to learning in the online environment, UDL goes beyond best practices for website accessibility to include all learners. Application of the three principles of UDL—to provide multiple means of representation, expression, and engagement—not only satisfies Section 508 and our legal requirement to provide accessible learning environments, but it transforms LibGuides into dynamic learning tools that are accessible to all. This is important in the LibGuides environment where our goal as librarians is to make information accessible. If we are making curated lists of resources and online learning tools available only to the able-sighted or those who prefer text-based learning, then we are simply not doing our jobs.

REFERENCES

Ahmed, Nedda H. 2013. "Design: Why It Is Important and How to Get it Right." In *Using LibGuides to Enhance Library Services*, edited by Aaron W. Dobbs, Ryan L. Sittler, and Douglas Cook, 103–120. Chicago: ALA TechSource.

Angelo, Thomas A., and Patricia K. Cross. 1993. *Classroom Assessment Techniques: A Handbook for College Teachers*. 2nd ed. San Francisco: Jossey-Bass.

Burgstahler, Sheryl E. 2008. "Universal Design of Technological Environments: From Principles to Practice." In *Universal Design in Higher Education*, edited by Sheryl E. Burgstahler, 213–224. Cambridge, MA: Harvard Education Press.

Caldwell, Ben, Michael Cooper, Loretta Guarino Reid, and Gregg Vanderheiden. 2008. *WebContent Accessibility Guidelines 2.0*. Accessed November 8, 2015. http://www.w3.org/TR/WCAG20/.

Connell, Bettye Rose, Mike Jones, Ron Mace, Jim Mueller, Abir Mullick, Elaine Ostroff, Jon Sanford, Ed Steinfeld, Molly Story, and Gregg Vanderheiden. 1997. "The Principles of Universal Design." NC State University, the Center for Universal Design. Last modified April 1. Accessed February 29, 2016. http://www.ncsu.edu/ncsu/design/cud/about_ud/udprinciplestext.htm.

ECU Libraries. 2015. "Biology: CSE Citation." Accessed December 3, 2015. http://libguides.ecu.edu/c.php?g=17257&p=98185.

Finn, Donald E., Elizabeth Evans Getzel, Susan B. Asselin, and Virginia Reilly. 2008. "Implementing Universal Design: Collaborations across Campus." In *Universal Design in Higher Education*, edited by Sheryl E. Burgstahler, 267–277. Cambridge, MA: Harvard Education Press.

Hall, Tracy E., Anne Meyer, and David H. Rose, eds. 2012. *Universal Design for Learning in the Classroom: Practical Applications*. New York: Guilford Press.

Meyer, Anne, and David H. Rose. 2005. "The Future Is in the Margins: The Role of Technology and Disability in Educational Reform." In *The Universally Designed Classroom: Accessible Curriculum and Digital Technologies*, edited by David H. Rose, Anne Meyer, and Chuck Hitchcock, 13–35. Cambridge, MA: Harvard Education Press.

Meyer, Anne, David H. Rose, and David Gordon. 2014. *Universal Design for Learning: Theory and Practice*. Wakefield, MA: CAST.

Ronald Williams Library. 2016. "Introduction to Research at the NEIU Library: Searching for Articles." Northeastern Illinois University, July 28. Accessed August 16, 2016. http://libguides.neiu.edu/tutorials/howtosearchforarticles.

Rose, David H., and Anne Meyer. 2002. *Teaching Every Student in the Digital Age: Universal Design for Learning*. Alexandria, VA: Association for Supervision and Curriculum Development.

United States Access Board. 2015. "About the ICT Refresh." Accessed November 08, 2015. http://www.access-board.gov/guidelines-and-standards/communications-and-it/about-the-ict-refresh.

Waddell, Cynthia D. 2006. "Overview of Law and Guidelines." In *Web Accessibility: Web Standards and Regulatory Compliance*, edited by Chris Mills, 54–67. New York: Springer Verlag.

Webb, Katy Kavanagh, and Jeanne Hoover. 2015a. "CSE Citation." BIOL 1051/1101: Biology Information Literacy Tutorial. Last modified October 28. Accessed October 30, 2015. http://libguides.ecu.edu/c.php?g=17255&p=96307.

Webb, Katy Kavanagh, and Jeanne Hoover. 2015b. "Universal Design for Learning (UDL) in the Academic Library: A Methodology for Mapping Multiple Means of Representation in Library Tutorials." *College & Research Libraries* 76 (4): 537–553.

14

LibGuides Two Ways

Teaching Information Literacy
In and Out of the Classroom

Lucinda Rush, MLIS, MME, Old Dominion University

Librarians at Old Dominion University (ODU) Libraries use the LibGuides platform in a creative way to meet immediate, practical needs. Traditionally, we have offered two types of information literacy tutorials. The first is a lengthy, module-based tutorial and is used in our information literacy–designated courses to cover skills in-depth and which students must complete over the course of a semester. The second is a short tutorial designed to give students an introduction or a refresher covering basic research skills, information literacy concepts, and library services.

Prior to migrating to a new web platform, ODU Libraries hosted short click-through tutorials on our local website. When ODU Libraries migrated to our new web platform we lost the ability to locally host tutorials. We turned to LibGuides and created a new and improved interactive guide to introduce our students to basic research skills and reach out to students at their points of need.

USING LIBGUIDES FOR TEACHING

We believe the traditional pathfinder, or provider of links to resources, is no longer needed by college students today as finding information becomes easier and easier. LibGuides and similar tools should be considered instructional tools that can be used in a formal setting and at the point of user need. LibGuides enables librarians to easily create guides in a timely manner that target specific user groups (Leibiger and Aldrich 2013).

The LibGuides platform has interactive elements built-in, such as polls, quizzes, the ability to embed videos and social media links that allow students to engage with the content (Beck 2009). Beck suggests using free software such as Jing to create videos to demonstrate use of databases to embed into LibGuides. Bielat, Befus, and Arnold

(2013) highlight that the usability of the LibGuides platform allows librarians to focus on crafting content rather than on the mechanics of tutorial design.

General Academic Environment

Mokia and Rolen (2012) identified academic libraries that use LibGuides for information literacy tutorials. They found that LibGuides can be an excellent tool for information literacy tutorials due to its ease of use and flexibility.

Librarians at the College at Brockport collaborated with their faculty colleagues to create a LibGuide supporting both students and faculty throughout the research process (Little et al. 2010). The tabs were labeled in the order of the research process and designed to allow users to select the relevant tab at their point of need. The LibGuide contents, while presented in a particular order, did not necessarily require users to review the guide in order. Little et al. found that the LibGuides platform allowed for continuous updates based on user feedback.

Librarians at the University of Texas Libraries used LibGuides to create an information literacy tutorial. Their goal was to create a guide that could be accessed by anyone at the point of need (Yelinek et al. 2010). They adapted James Madison University's "Go for the Gold" content for their LibGuide and embedded quizzes using SurveyGizmo and reported their experience that the tutorial was well received by both faculty and students.

Medical Library Environment

Stankus and Parker (2012) indicate that LibGuides are regularly used in medicine and health sciences, and librarians in these areas have utilized point of need, assignment, and subject-based approaches for their design. They also found that chat widgets were embedded into about half of the LibGuides that they examined.

Librarians at Dalhousie University created LibGuides for medical students targeted to each year of their program (Neves and Dooley 2013). Librarians embedded their online chat into the LibGuides to provide point of need interaction for the students and to reinforce the belief that librarians are partners in students' research processes. The librarians also encouraged students to view themselves as content contributors by providing students a box in which they could suggest additional resources to be added to the guide. Librarians also included their own content-related webcasts on the guide.

Pedagogy

LibGuides boxes allow for easy chunking of information, which allows students to grasp concepts at a pace that is comfortable and to easily pick out the particular information that they need. Chunking is an approach to teaching that breaks up large pieces of information into smaller pieces to facilitate better recall and understanding.

Baker (2014) recommends use of LibGuides because of the ease of chunking information in the box format provided. Chunking can be easily incorporated into any type of LibGuide, whether it is subject or course specific, or as in this case a more general research guide.

Scaffolding is another teaching technique that we used in "Research Fundamentals" that can be easily implemented with LibGuides. Scaffolding provides support to users at each level and allows them to incorporate more elements into their knowledge base when they are ready or at the point of need (Axford, Harders, and Wise 2009). As with chunking, the design of the LibGuides platform easily enables scaffolding; this technique can be used with subject-specific and course guides that may be used throughout the course of a semester or completion of an assignment. LibGuides themselves can also be scaffolded, such as the guides created for the medical students at Dalhousie University, which were organized by the students' year in the program (Neves and Dooley 2013).

It is well documented (Baker 2014; Hintz et al. 2010), that incorporating active learning strategies into teaching is beneficial for students. Engaging students in active learning via an online learning tool such as LibGuides can help to engage students in what could otherwise be a very passive learning environment. Baker (2014) argues that online guides that are interactive and scaffolded are more engaging for students than pathfinder-type guides that are used solely for the purpose of providing links to resources.

Georgia Southern University librarians compared a group of students using a pathfinder-style LibGuide to a group of students using a tutorial-style LibGuide for the same assignment (Baker 2014). The students who used the tutorial-style guide were more successful and reported that they had a better experience than those who used the stand-alone pathfinder-style guide. Hintz et al. (2010) surveyed students to determine their preferences in subject guide design, and embedded instruction was ranked fourth in their list of top ten student priorities for subject guide design.

THE "RESEARCH FUNDAMENTALS" LIBGUIDE AT ODU LIBRARIES

The "Research Fundamentals" LibGuide at ODU Libraries was created during the summer of 2014 as a means of providing instruction on basic research skills and library services. Its purpose is twofold. First, it was designed for faculty who want their students to have a brief introduction or refresher in research skills and library services. Faculty can require their students to go through each section of the guide and complete a quiz at the end of the guide. Second, it serves as a stand-alone guide for users who need help with getting started with research or learning about library resources and services. While the ODU Libraries provides an in-depth series of information tutorials that most students complete during their information literacy general education course, the LibGuides platform offers a flexible space for librarians to create and provide a less intense tutorial to reach students outside of the information literacy class.

The "Research Fundamentals" LibGuide also serves as a stand-alone point-of-need guide, the sections of the guide can be browsed, selected, or completed in the order that they appear. The home page of the guide provides information about the ODU Libraries and includes a One Minute Tips video created by ODU librarians about the information cycle. ODU Libraries' One Minute Tips videos are designed with undergraduates in mind, and provide step-by-step information along with elements of humor in one minute (Rush and Stott 2014). The home page of the guide is designed to give students an overview of the physical ODU Libraries and to introduce them to how information is created and how they might use different types of resources.

"Research Fundamentals" includes interactive elements in each section, including short videos or Prezi presentations to provide extra reinforcement for learners if they choose to use them. For example, the Discovery Tool tab in figure 14.1 includes a one-minute video that explains how to search using our discovery layer, a search box so users can practice searching, and text boxes that explain what the Discovery Tool finds and basic searching tips.

In the "Research Fundamentals" guide, the chunking technique is used throughout the guide. For example, the section title Books includes boxes that provide information about how to search for books in the online catalog, where books are located, how books may be used in research, how to find and access e-books, and a list of recommended books for first-year students, as depicted in figure 14.2. If users are trying to figure out how to search for books, they will immediately be drawn to

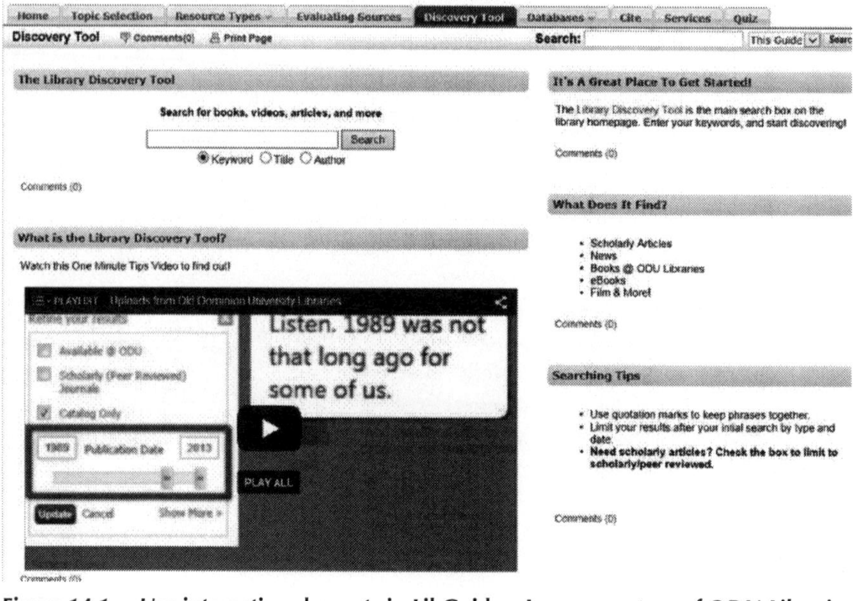

Figure 14.1.   Use interactive elements in LibGuides. *Image courtesy of ODU Libraries*

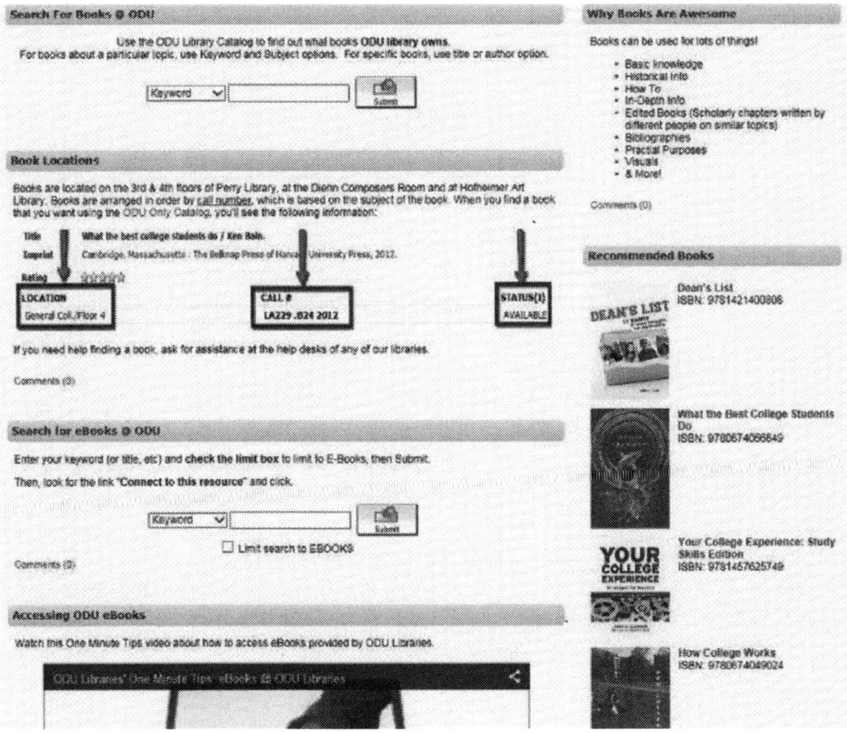

Figure 14.2. Example of chunking technique used in the "Research Fundamentals" LibGuide. *Image courtesy of ODU Libraries*

the box labeled Search for Books @ ODU. Users who are completing the guide as a tutorial may be more interested in why they would use books rather than the logistics of finding books, which they may not need to do at that moment.

The "Research Fundamentals" tabs are placed in a strategic order that models the scaffolding that we employ in our instruction program at ODU Libraries. In our lower-level general education classes, we introduce the Libraries' discovery layer, showing students how to find resources for general research topics. In our upper-level classes we focus on subject-specific research, and students use databases within their disciplines. "Research Fundamentals" introduces our discovery layer, and the next tab introduces subject-specific databases, allowing students to absorb the information in the order that they will use it during their studies, or to select the tab that contains the information that they need.

FORMATIVE ASSESSMENT

We used Qualtrics to facilitate the online quiz that students take after navigating through the "Research Fundamentals" tutorial. We had unlimited access and support for Qualtrics through our campus license, otherwise we would have explored LibSurveys for our quizzes. We used elements of formative assessment in designing the quiz that users complete after navigating through the "Research Fundamentals" LibGuide. Formative assessment provides students with ongoing feedback throughout the assessment process, and the student can use that feedback to improve and enhance learning (Sadler 1998).

The quiz is designed so that users are required to answer a question correctly prior to moving on to the next question. Users are given feedback after each question. For example, the first question assesses user knowledge of a developed research question. If the users answer the question correctly, they receive a message that states "Good job! This topic is broad enough to find a lot of resources for, but specific enough to focus your writing. Please go on to the next question!" If they get the question wrong, they are told why and asked to try again, as depicted in figure 14.3. Providing feedback after each response, even if users select the correct answer, provides reinforcement and helps to facilitate more in-depth learning, as shown in figure 14.4.

We used green font for feedback for correct answers and red for incorrect answers, as an old-school play on green light, red light that we hoped most users would intuitively internalize. This method helps to address the problem of students going directly to the quiz and attempting to complete it without navigating through the pages of the guide. Our rationale is that students are still provided with feedback and are learning even while completing the assessment. The quiz opens in a new window, so students can easily navigate from the quiz to the guide if they need additional reinforcement or need to double check their answers.

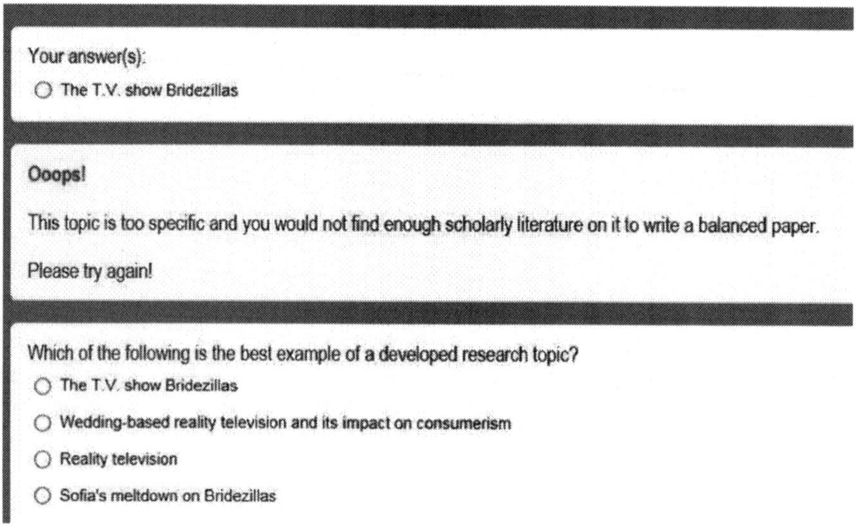

Your answer(s):
○ The T.V. show Bridezillas

Ooops!

This topic is too specific and you would not find enough scholarly literature on it to write a balanced paper.

Please try again!

Which of the following is the best example of a developed research topic?
○ The T.V. show Bridezillas
○ Wedding-based reality television and its impact on consumerism
○ Reality television
○ Sofia's meltdown on Bridezillas

Figure 14.3. Incorrect question, "Research Fundamentals" quiz. *Image courtesy of ODU Libraries*

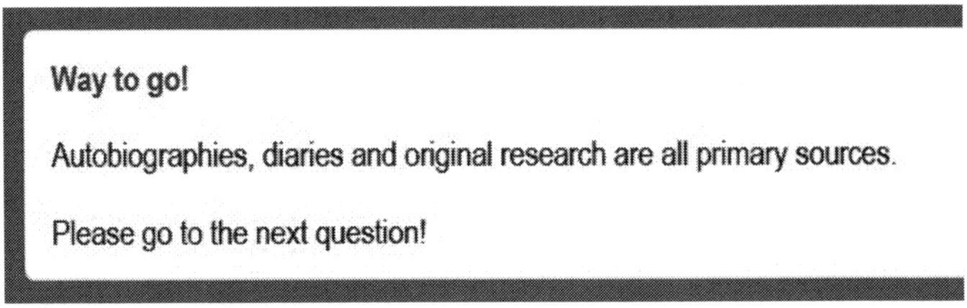

Way to go!

Autobiographies, diaries and original research are all primary sources.

Please go to the next question!

Figure 14.4. Feedback after correctly answered quiz question. *Image courtesy of ODU Libraries*

The quiz page was the second-most accessed in "Research Fundamentals"; it had 1,080 clicks. Content-page use is lower. The Topic Selection page received the most use with 993 clicks. This indicates that most users do not navigate through the entirety of the guide. Instead, they seem to attempt to complete the quiz without going through the tutorial. We feel that the guide is still very useful to our students despite this. We believe this because the quiz is designed so that users are required to answer a question correctly prior to moving on to the next one, and they are provided with feedback when the get a question wrong. Additionally, those who are required to complete the process for a class are also learning about the guide as a result. They may visit it later when then need help.

PROMOTION AND USE OF THE "RESEARCH FUNDAMENTALS" GUIDE

As with all library resources and services, they are only useful if faculty and students know about them and use them. We took several steps after "Research Fundamentals" was completed to promote it to faculty and students, and continue to promote it to our primary users. Twenty-seven instructors have signed up for their classes to complete the quiz since the implementation of the guide and a total of 1,078 students have successfully completed the quiz thus far.

Faculty Outreach

At ODU Libraries, we found contacting faculty directly to be the most successful way to promote the use of the guide. In promoting it to faculty initially, librarians contacted faculty members who had previously used our STARQuest guide—an online tutorial with similar content to our new solution. We let them know about the new guide and the phasing out of the STARQuest tutorial and gave them the opportunity to sign up for their students to complete the new guide and quiz. We also placed information about the guide in the daily email announcements that faculty receive via email and promoted it to instructors of lower-level courses by sending them targeted, individual emails.

Outreach to new faculty is another way that we have been successful in adding new users to the guide. New faculty contact the library fairly regularly desiring information about library tours. We use these inquiries as an opportunity to encourage faculty to make use of "Research Fundamentals" with their classes. While a physical tour is useful, what faculty usually want is an introduction to library resources and services. Since we prefer our one-shot instruction sessions to be assignment-based and do not generally give what traditionally was thought of as a library orientation, LibGuides has offered us a flexible and accessible way to offer faculty another more stable option. Another way that we encourage use of the guide, as well as other LibGuides, is to remind faculty to include links to the guides on their LMS and in their syllabus.

In promoting the guide to students, we have found the most success in providing it to them at their point of information need. "Research Fundamentals" is a quick and easy way to point users to introductory-level information during chat and in-person reference questions. When users need help in understanding what a primary resource is, or how to find a primary research article, the link to the Primary Resources section of the guide can be easily and quickly retrieved to share with the user. If users are unaware of what the discovery layer search on our website searches, the link to the page about that topic can be easily shared for the user to explore.

Social Media

Reaching students at their point of informational need may sometimes mean posting a link to the LibGuide on the library's social media channels at relevant points in the semester. For example, students typically need citation help six to eight weeks into the semester, when their first papers are due. We post about "Research Fundamentals" and link to our "Citation: It's Important" Prezi during this high-demand time. Sharing pieces of the guide with students at their point of need not only helps them solve an immediate problem; it also plants the seed that the guides are there as something that they can seek out in the future for help with other problems.

Students can also be introduced to "Research Fundamentals" during library instruction sessions. The flexible design of the guide allows it to facilitate various in-class activities during library instruction. For research assignments that are non-subject specific, for example, an English Composition class that consists of students from a variety of majors, pieces of the guide can be used to teach students how to get started with their research. Using a general guide such as this encourages students to use it for other classes as well, as opposed to creating a guide for a specific class, for one specific assignment, that students will only use one time.

CONCLUSION

While the "Research Fundamentals" LibGuide was originally intended as a "quick fix" to a problem, we have found it to be extremely valuable and now plan to maintain, market, and use it as a teaching tool in the foreseeable future. The LibGuides platform has provided us with a tool to create a tutorial-style guide that also serves as a point-of-need guide. Users can navigate through the entire guide and take the quiz at the end to learn the basics of research and services provided specifically at ODU Libraries, or they can select the page that is most pertinent to their information need. The guide is easy to maintain and adapt as our user needs and information changes and can be implemented in many teaching situations, including formal instruction and informal reference interactions both online and in person. The ability to incorporate active elements including videos, user feedback boxes, and quizzes make it an effective teaching tool as a tutorial, for in-class use, and for individual use. LibGuides also allows for easy scaffolding and chunking of information to aid in student learning by providing a boxed and tabbed layout that makes it easy for users to pick out the information that they need.

Reaching out to specific faculty members has been the most successful way for librarians at ODU to promote use of the guide. Gone are the days when simply providing a list of links to resources for users was enough. Finding information is easy for entry-level students, but knowing what the information is, how to cite it, and how to evaluate and synthesize effectively is challenging for undergraduate students today. Our online learning tools should not only provide resources, but also aid students in learning the foundations of information literacy concepts and applying them to each research situation that they encounter.

REFERENCES

Axford, Beverly, Pamela Harders, and Fay Wise. 2009. *Scaffolding Literacy: An Integrated and Sequential Approach to Teaching Reading, Spelling, and Writing.* Camberwell, Victoria: Australian Council for Education Research.

Baker, Ruth L. 2014. "Designing LibGuides as Instructional Tools for Critical Thinking and Effective Online Learning." *Journal of Library & Information Services in Distance Learning* 8 (3–4): 107–117. doi: 10.1080/1533290X.2014.944423

Beck, Bernd W. 2009. "Electronic Roundup: Subject Guides 2.0: A Look at LibGuides and Jing." *Behavioral and Social Sciences Librarian* 28: 206–209. doi: 10.1090/01639269093280763

Bielat, Veronica, Rebeca Befus, and Judith Arnold. 2013. "Integrating LibGuides into the Teaching-Learning Process." In *Using LibGuides to Enhance Library Services: A LITA Guide*, edited by Aaron W. Dobbs, Ryan L. Sittler, and Douglas Cook, 121–142. Chicago: ALA TechSource.

Hintz, Kimberly, Paula Farrar, Shirin Eshghi, Barbara Sobol, Jo-Anne Naslund, Teresa Lee, Tara Stephens, and Aleha McCauley. 2010. "Letting Students Take the Lead: A User-Centred Approach to Evaluating Subject Guides." *Evidence Based Library & Information Practice* 5 (4): 39–52.

Leibiger, Carol A., and Alan W. Aldrich. 2013. "The Mother of All LibGuides: Applying Principles of Communication and Network Theory in LibGuide Design." In *Proceedings of the Association of College and Research Libraries*, Indianapolis, IN, 429–441.

Little, J. J., M. Fallon, J. Dauenhauer, B. Balzano, and D. Halquist. 2010. "Interdisciplinary Collaboration: A Faculty Learning Community Creates a Comprehensive LibGuide." *Reference Services Review* 38 (3): 431–444. doi: 10.1108/00907321011070919.

Mokia, Rosemary, and Rhonda Rolen. 2012. "LibGuides: Improving Student and Faculty Access to Information Literacy." *Codex: The Journal of the Louisiana Chapter of the ACRL* 1 (4): 37–45.

Neves, Karen M., and Sarah Jane Dooley. 2013. "Using LibGuides to offer Library Service to Undergraduate Medical Students Based on the Case-Oriented Problem Solving Method." *Journal of the Medical Library Association* 99 (1): 94–97. doi: 10.3163/1536–5050.99.1.017.

Rush, Lucinda, and Rachel Stott. 2014. "Minute to Learn it: Integrating One-Minute Videos into Information Literacy Programming." *Internet Reference Services Quarterly* 15 (2): 219–232. doi: 10.1090/10875301.2014.97829.

Sadler, Royce D. 1998. "Formative Assessment: Revisiting the Territory." *Assessment in Education: Principles, Policy & Practice* 5 (1): 77–84. doi: 10.1080/0969595980050104.

Stankus, Tony, and Martha A. Parker. 2012. "The Anatomy of Nursing LibGuides." *Sciences & Technology Libraries* 31: 242–255. doi: 10.1080/0194262X.2012.678222.

Yelinek, Kathryn, Linda Neyer, Darla Bressler, Michael Coffta, and David Magolis. 2010. "Using LibGuides for an Information Literacy Tutorial: Tutorial 2.0." *College & Research Libraries News* 71 (7): 352–355.

15

Redesigning LibGuides as Online Learning Modules

Melissa Gomis, University of Michigan

As knowledge creators and consumers we understand that people want customized information at their point of need. As library instructors and consultants we also understand that our students learn better when they are actively engaged in their learning environments. One way to achieve this type of engagement is through a flipped classroom. The general idea of a flipped classroom environment is that students will learn outside of the classroom, usually through videos and other online content, and spend in-person time discussing questions, working through problems, and interacting with each other (Educause Learning Initiative 2012). A flipped classroom environment can empower students to take ownership and control over their own learning by focusing more attention on the sections of a topic or lesson they are struggling with rather than having to go through content at the exact same pace as their classmates.

The LibGuides platform allowed us to take the flipped classroom model and apply it to open workshops and consultations around technology and design concepts. A well-designed LibGuide can guide users through content typically covered in a general, open (anyone can attend) technology workshop; allow users to work and learn at their own pace; and allow users to work on their own projects. In-person, one-on-one, or group instruction sessions can be used for more advanced questions to discuss main points and/or provide clarification to students.

I conducted focus groups and usability tests to understand how our users learn new technologies, what they like about the resources they use to learn, and what they don't like in order to successfully create a flipped classroom model for open workshops. User data was compiled to create and implement several recommendations regarding guide and content layout and video creation. Our technology guides have successfully flipped the classroom. They continue to see significant yearly increases in use, which have been directly tied to a decrease in open workshops. Demand continues for in-person and small-group technology consultations though our users do consult our LibGuides prior to these meetings.

BACKGROUND

The Knowledge Navigation Center (KNC) at the University of Michigan (UM) is a technology facility, open to all members of the campus community, which encourages and enables the creation of digital scholarship. The KNC provides one-on-one consultations, access and support for video editing and digitization equipment, and workshops on required skills and supported software programs. Supported topics include formatting dissertations, designing professional portfolios, designing conference posters, image editing and manipulation, citation management, digitization, video editing, and more. Since its inception, the KNC staff has maintained print handouts and documentation for all KNC workshop content. These handouts were comprised of text and screenshots giving detailed step-by-step descriptions of topics covered in the sessions. They generally ranged in length from ten to twenty pages, and new versions were created for each Mac and PC software release.

When the UM Libraries adopted LibGuides in 2008, the KNC initially uploaded these print handouts to LibGuides using the PDF upload tool, added KNC contact information to the guides, and promoted in-person workshops as our main resource for people wanting to learn a new software tool. We didn't fully utilize LibGuides functionality, opting instead to maintain print handouts as our users were still requesting them. The UM Libraries implementation of LibGuides does not include a customized print layout CSS stylesheet, so instead we continued to develop styled and accessible PDF documentation. KNC staff wanted to transition fully into the LibGuides environment to decrease print and online redundancies and better serve our users.

We wanted to create useful resources and be thoughtful in our approach to content. Creating and updating quality technology LibGuides poses unique challenges because there is usually more than one way to accomplish a task. Likewise, updates, new versions, and new programs consistently enter the market. Core users may have different software versions, and there are so many operating systems each with their own subversions. All these things need to be taken into consideration.

Another challenge in creating these guides is that online technology resources have increased in volume and quality through the years. Our core users have access to resources like Lynda.com, YouTube, and custom software company videos and instructions. In addition to taking into consideration software versions, operating systems, and existing resources technology, LibGuides may encounter publicity and findability issues. Our library website and LibGuides implementation are organized by subject area and technology guides are not tied to a specific course, curriculum, or subject area. Users across the humanities, social sciences, and STEM fields can often benefit from tailored LibGuides addressing specific tasks, programs, or technologies.

Creating campus-wide resources introduces findability concerns and potential publicity challenges because we rely on subject specialists and staff at our reference desks among others to promote our resources.

We conducted focus groups and usability testing with our four main user groups—faculty, graduate students, undergraduate students, and staff—to better understand their needs and learning styles. We wanted to determine how our users learn new technologies and troubleshoot problems, as well as learn their preferences regarding the resources used to learn new technologies. We also solicited feedback about our print handouts such as perceptions about design, layout, and content. We based our content and design decisions on their feedback. Additionally, we incorporated best practices for accessibility and universal design into our decision making. We relied heavily on universal design principles both for our web content and for our visual design when creating our content.

As a result, we saw a steady and dramatic increase in the usage statistics for our guides over a four-year period and a decrease in attendance at our general drop-in workshops during that same time frame. Our guides now serve as the first point of entry to our services and consultations for a lot of users and enable just-in-time modular learning. We also still receive requests for one-on-one consultations for more in-depth questions.

Our guides have "flipped" the consultation, which has allowed us to focus our time with users on tackling difficult problems, brainstorming creative solutions, and discussing pros/cons of various tools and workflows rather than focusing on the basics of how to use a particular tool. Most people comfortable with technology can learn the basics of a tool on their own either through trial and error or using online resources or a combination of both. We continue to offer a few general overview workshops for people wanting a guided introduction and for those less comfortable with technology.

The instructional technology librarian at the University of Michigan conducted focus groups and usability tests to determine user needs and processes in learning new technologies and information-seeking behaviors. The findings from the focus groups and usability tests confirmed previously held beliefs around information-seeking behavior of our users. We created video content, based on the survey feedback that fit specific criteria, such as improving guide content, layout, and video content. As a result our in-person consultations have decreased in number. LibGuides can be used as an effective teaching platform when content is well written and findable. LibGuides authors create unique, meaningful, and useful content while leveraging quality existing resources when appropriate.

FOCUS GROUPS

The goals of the focus groups were to understand the ways users engage with our workshop handouts, understand information-seeking behaviors for learning new technologies, and get feedback on ideal handout formats and layouts. We conducted four focus groups: faculty, graduate students, undergraduate students, and staff. Participants were limited to people who had either registered or attended one of our workshops in the past. Participants included five faculty members, five graduate students, seven undergraduate students, and ten staff members. Participants varied in age, gender, and web and technological expertise. These numbers are fairly representative of the patron groups that attend our workshops and use our services. Graduate students and staff are the two biggest user groups taking advantage of our in-person services, which is slightly different from the focus group attendees. Participants received lunch in exchange for their time, and each focus group was asked the same series of questions.

Focus group questions:

1. Think of the last time you had to use software or other technology tools that you knew little or nothing about. Where did you begin? Did you encounter any questions or problems, and how did you resolve them?
2. What do you like most about the resources you use to learn about technology? What do you like least?
3. [Give them a workshop handout] Think about the layout of the handout. What would you change? What works well for you (font, organization, length)? What doesn't work well for you? How would you prefer to access this information?
4. Which handout(s) have you used? Which part or parts were most important to your work?

Summary of Findings

1. Think of the last time you had to use software or other technology tools that you knew little or nothing about. Where did you begin? Did you encounter any questions or problems, and how did you resolve them?

Not surprisingly the majority of participants in the focus groups first turn to Google, software company websites, trial and error, and other people (colleagues and friends) when they are trying to learn a new technology or troubleshoot a technology question. Graduate and undergraduate students were more likely to turn to other people as their first entry to a software program in the form of online communities and resources, such as online manuals and forums. They were also more likely to turn to colleagues and friends as they were starting out with a new technology or thinking about technology options.

Faculty and staff members were more likely to engage in self-exploration and discovery using materials and trial and error as their first point of entry for a technology. They also said they attend workshops to gain an overview of a software program;

however, our attendance numbers indicate graduate students and staff are the most likely user groups to attend an open workshop. Specifically, the staff focus group mentioned having issues with knowing the correct terminology to use when searching Help features or Google and issues with identifying which resources will be the best or most effective as a barrier to fully utilizing online resources.

2. What do you like most about the resources you use to learn about technology? What do you like least?

Every participant in the focus groups stated they prefer online materials because of the ease of access, speed, and visuals that are available. They also like attending open workshops because they appreciate the interactivity, the guided instruction and ability to follow along, and the supplementary handout materials. Graduate students mentioned a difference between tools they were learning for personal use versus tools for scholarship. They were satisfied with online resources when they were learning tools for their personal life and expressed a desire to interact face-to-face with a professional when they planned to use a tool for scholarship.

Other benefits to face-to-face interaction that came up in all the groups were efficiency and accuracy. As a graduate student stated, "I'll give up if I don't have the time. I knew something was possible but didn't have the time to go through five layers of figuring it out." A second graduate student echoed those sentiments: "I did it the same way I knew how even though there were better ways to do this. I tried new technologies and methods [video], but eventually gave up and just did audio." Having access to experts who not only know the available tools, but also know best practices and have an understanding of how people in other disciplines use tools is seen as an important resource and point of connection.

Despite the desire for in-person connections and expertise, attendance at our open workshops has been steadily declining. Participants in the focus groups cited barriers to attending open workshop sessions, including registering for workshop sessions, sessions being full, lack of clarity on exactly what will be covered, and the possibility of workshop attendees slowing down the session. Our users want online resources and expertise. We need to find a way to provide these types of services.

3. [Give them a workshop handout] Think about the layout of the handout. What would you change? What works well for you (font, organization, length)? What doesn't work well for you? What would you like that isn't here?

People in all of the focus groups mentioned liking the table of contents in the print handouts. It provides an overview or index of the content covered and helps people quickly jump to their section(s) of interest. The visuals in the form of screenshots, bolded text to highlight keywords or information, and step-by-step instructions were well-liked features within the handouts across all groups.

In response to what doesn't work well, participants in all groups mentioned that the amount of text in the handout was overwhelming. Several people, across groups, indicated the amount of content (ranging from ten to twenty pages) was good for someone familiar with the software program, but not for someone just starting out. An alternative suggestion was to create a one- to two-page starter handout in addition to the longer document. This would meet the needs of someone just looking for a basic overview, and the longer documentation helps the user who needs to use the software for their scholarship. In response to features they would like to see in our resources, participants mentioned videos, definitions of unclear terms, tasks to practice with and/or follow while learning the software, and bulleted text for easier scanning of content.

4. Which handout(s) have you used? Which part or parts were most important to your work?

Participants mentioned having used a range of our handouts covering topics, including image editing, presentation creation, web design, dissertation formatting, and citation management. Little to no additional information was gained from this question that hadn't already been captured.

USABILITY TESTING

LibGuides usability tests have been conducted on how users navigate the LibGuides structure as a whole and within individual guides. Previous usability tests (Beaton et al. 2009; Tawatao et al. 2010) have discovered that users recognize tabs in guides and understand that they lead to other pages with additional content. Building on existing knowledge our usability test was created and conducted to determine how tab labels affect guide usability. We also wanted to determine a name for our collection of Technology guides. Technology is a vague word and holds various meaning for different people. We wanted to better understand what the name Technology Guides meant to current users and figure out if there was a more meaningful term to describe the content.

Research has indicated that the name Research Guides is confusing to users and this finding encouraged us to explore the overall name for technology specific guides (Beaton et al. 2009). To further aid our understanding of how users engage with our LibGuides, five usability tests were conducted with graduate students and staff. None of the participants were familiar with our research guides on the LibGuides platform. The questions in the usability test were open-ended and task based. The task-based questions were used to determine if the tab labels matched the expectation users had for the information they would find on that page. Task-based questions were specifically designed to contain core information for our users but without using language that was immediately obvious based on the tab label.

Usability test questions:

1. I am going to show you three printouts of web pages. Please take a few minutes to look them over. If you had to describe them as a group to someone else, how would you describe them? What would you call them?
2. [Show participant guide name without the description] What information do you expect to be on the guide? [Show participant guide description] Do you find the description of the resource useful? If yes, what is useful? Do you find the tagging feature useful?
3. [Show them the guide tabs for Zotero, Creating Posters, and RefWorks] Which tabs do you think hold the most relevant information? Specify top three.

    a. Where do you think you would find information on using Zotero with Word?
    b. Where do you think you would find information on how to move data from RefWorks to Zotero or EndNote?
    c. Where do you think you would find information on using the UM poster templates?

4. Are there elements of the guide you would like to see added or changed?

Summary of Findings

1. I am going to show you three printouts of web pages. Please take a few minutes to look them over. If you had to describe them as a group to someone else, how would you describe them? What would you call them?

Currently our LibGuides implementation is titled Research Guides and the section for our guides is under the Technology category. Participants were unable to group the content in the technology guides together by name in a meaningful way. Most of the participants couldn't think of a name to collectively call the guides and the ones who did suggested Technology Guides, Software Guides, and Research Guides. This may indicate that even though Technology Guides is a vague term, it is meaningful enough to our users and will work as a category name.

2. [Show participant guide name without the description] What information do you expect to be on the guide? [Show participant guide description] Do you find the description of the resource useful? If yes, what is useful? Do you find the tagging feature useful?

The descriptions of the guides were found to be useful to a certain extent. The information contained in the description assists with providing access to guides in search results and can provide a generic overview to users though it may not be as helpful to users who are novices to a topic and/or for topics that have more than one guide. None of the usability test participants found the tagging feature helpful. In fact, they didn't even notice the tags until they were pointed out to them. Instead of enabling discovery and access, they only served to clutter up the description text of the guide.

3. [Show them the guide tabs for Zotero, Creating Posters, and RefWorks] Which tabs do you think hold the most relevant information? Specify top three.

   a. Where do you think you would find information on using Zotero with Word?
   b. Where do you think you would find information on how to move data from RefWorks to Zotero or EndNote?
   c. Where do you think you would find information on using the UM poster templates?

Users performed well on the task-based questions. This was a strong indication that our tab labels were meaningful to our users, and they were able to accurately determine which tab contained the information needed to complete each task. This was the most important part of the usability test, because it provided a glimpse into how users think about information or tasks they are trying to complete. Finding the information they need in our guides should not be the challenging part of their work.

4. Are there elements of the guide you would like to see added or changed?

Through discussing elements of the guide people would want to change, we found that inconsistent layout and naming conventions confused users. They wanted each guide to start with a Home or Getting Started tab, and they wanted guides under one topic (e.g., citation management) to contain information that was consistently labeled and ordered across all guides on that same topic.

GUIDE REDESIGN

Based on our findings we decided to implement several ideas, generated from our focus group discussions and usability tests, into our guides. We started small by focusing on our *Microsoft Word 2010 and 2013 for Dissertations* guide. This was selected because it has a built in audience, which enables targeted promotion and teaches our users how to conduct specific tasks in Microsoft Word rather than providing a general overview of the entire program.

We incorporated multiple ways of navigating the guide by creating a table of contents in addition to tab-based navigation. Each section of the guide contains step-by-step instructions written for the web, and overall the content provided visuals in the form of screenshots and videos. A few academic libraries also added table of contents in addition to tabbed navigation for their LibGuides after conducting usability testing. The addition at MIT and EMU of guide content boxes was to aid users who don't always see the tabs (Pittsley and Memmott 2012). Our main purposes for the guide table of contents were to aid in navigation and to reveal all of our content up-front, including subpages and important items within a page. The table of contents that we created includes "chapter" sections and subsections in addition to main section headings.

The scope of the tabs and instructions on the guide was restricted to content regarding required formatting for dissertations at the University of Michigan. Formatting that is optional rather than required and/or alternate and less efficient ways of completing tasks was left out of the guide documentation to reduce clutter. This less important information is still detailed in the PDF handout, for example, how to manually create a table of contents in Word, for those interested in that content. Creating a difference between the guide and the PDF content also provided more of a focus for each.

Video Content

Since a lot of high quality video tutorials on how to use Microsoft Word already exist, we wanted to leverage this existing content and fill in the gaps as needed with our own videos. The first step was to decide how to determine which content would benefit from a video tutorial and then how to scope it. We created a series of questions that would take both areas into consideration. Content that is available in videos is also available in text and screenshots on the guide to provide multiple means of learning and to ensure all people can access the information.

Video Creation Worksheet

Each of these items will need to be considered when thinking about creating a new video and taken holistically rather than having one question determine whether a video is created. Incorporating videos and hosting them on YouTube has helped to increase traffic to our guides. Creating, editing, and maintaining quality instructional videos require skill and a lot of time. We created a series of questions to help with scoping content.

Who is the audience?   Content that has an excessively narrow focus and/or content whose primary audience does not include faculty and/or students should be rethought.

What need are we trying to address or what problem are we trying to solve?   Content that doesn't directly address a problem but is more generally informative should be reframed. We are operating under the assumption that people watching our videos are trying to accomplish a specific task.

Is this the only/best way to meet these needs?   Can this information be conveyed through text and screenshots, or is a video really the best way to clearly show everything that needs to be shown? Videos take much more time to create and edit once they are out of date.

How much time and energy will be needed to create and then maintain this content?   Content that exceeds a four-minute video and/or content that requires a lot of graphic design to be informative may require too much time and energy. This depends on other factors, for example, if the video will be used for course sessions that may balance the amount of work it will take to create.

Does similar or related content already exist elsewhere?   We don't want to create redundant or duplicate content. If usable or reusable content already exists, then use it. Creative commons licensed content may be best for people looking to make some edits to existing content. Additionally, some vendors allow their documentation to be reused and edited. For example, ProQuest allows customers to reuse and edit their RefWorks LibGuide. Occasionally there is a need to create slightly redundant content when there is a gap and a large group of people who need the content. For example, we created a video on adding multiple styles of page numbers to one Word document. This information does exist on the Microsoft website; however, the steps for a dissertation are specific and the need for that information is ongoing. The video we created has received nearly 200,000 hits, which is a strong indication of need.

How long is the content likely to be relevant?   If the content will quickly become out of date, then a video may not be the best method for sharing that information.

How often will it need to be updated?   If the video will need to be updated frequently, this may not be the best method for sharing that particular information. If you do have a video that needs to be updated frequently, make sure you organize and keep all final drafts of the media assets and other documentation (e.g., scripts, graphics, quizzes, etc.) in one place. If you relied on a colleague or someone outside the library to create your video content, make sure they give you access to the files and instructions on how to edit them. Depending on the tool and the content either longer video sections or shorter sections may be easier to edit. You will want to determine this before you create the video.

How will users be made aware of this content?   If the content is created for a specific class or organization, then pushing it out to the intended audience is easy, but for content that is created for a larger and possibly unknown group of people (e.g., everyone at UM formatting a dissertation), one will need to be strategic about how content is distributed. Our guides with videos, which are embedded into guide boxes and hosted on YouTube, have become extremely popular locally, nationally, and internationally. The popularity continues to increase each year, and so far we haven't had to do any major content updates. A lot of our users comment and interact with each other in the YouTube commenting feature. They also get to ask questions that can be answered by other viewers or library employees. Our "Word for Dissertations" guide, which provides access to some of our most unique content, continues to see yearly increases in views by 60 percent or more with the largest yearly increase being 187 percent. These large increases were seen in all of our Microsoft Office software guides, which are providing content that is findable and useful to the UM campus and beyond.

Analysis of the yearly guide statistics, individual page view statistics, and YouTube statistics and comments indicate the majority of people reach our content through Google searching. The Home or Getting Started front page is usually the seventh to tenth most viewed page and despite being in the middle of the page ranking still draws strong usage. This information indicates that more than half of our users are entering via direct links rather than from the main URL. This data is different from what others have reported about their LibGuides. Pittsley and Memmott (2012) report that in the fall of 2010 the first page of each guide was the most heavily used. One reason most of our users are finding our content through Google and other means may be because they aren't affiliated with the University of Michigan.

Web Content

We know that people don't read information online. They hunt, they scan, and they skim. The percentage varies a bit depending on the source, but generally users read one-third or less of content on a web page (Nielsen 2008). Librarians love to distribute information, but people seeking information on the web just want to find what they need and move on. We must write our content for the medium we are using. Since we know users aren't reading all of our content, we should pare it down to essential information that inspires action on the part of our users and meets their needs. We prepared our content for the web by utilizing several universal principles of design: chunking, visual hierarchy, and accessibility.

Chunking

One way we improved our content for the web was by chunking. We chose this as both a visual and instructional design technique to aid working memory. As Lidwell et al. (2010) remind us, by putting a small number of units of information together into a "chunk," we enable users to better remember content. Displaying smaller units of information in one group also reduces clutter on a web page, which improves visual design. This technique allows people to recall and retain information, which is what we are hoping to accomplish with our guides. Some types of LibGuides are meant to be a resource for a specific topic that people can return to over and over. Our technology guides are meant to teach people how to accomplish a task so they can move on with their work.

We organized our guide content by task with each being constrained to one tab. For example, adding page numbers is a tab on our "Word for Dissertations" guide. That tab covers adding page numbers and using sections to control page number styles within a dissertation. Users never have to scroll through a long page of content and can easily jump around to content within the guide as needed. Each tab is a concrete lesson that covers everything users would need to know about a particular aspect of formatting their dissertation.

Visual Hierarchy

Visual hierarchy is a simple structure for organizing and demonstrating information hierarchy. We utilized this concept in our guides so that users can easily scan content and understand general sections within a guide page without having to read all of the content (Lidwell et al. 2010). Each tab represents a chunk of information on our guides and the information in each guide is presented with a hierarchy.

There are a couple of ways hierarchies can be achieved in LibGuides. One is to create a single content box and use Headings to format text within it, which creates a hierarchy. Another way is to create a separate box for each section of text. We chose to create separate boxes for our content because it was easier for us to edit and allowed for reuse on other guides as necessary.

Accessibility

The third design principle we heavily relied on is accessibility, which refers to the idea that a space should be usable by as many people as possible and preferably without modification (Lidwell et al. 2010). We present our information with text, images, videos, and PDF files. Content available in one format is available in at least one other format. Some people like to learn by reading online with text and images, some people like to use videos, and some people prefer to interact with print content. All of our images contain alt text for people using screen readers, and our videos are fully accessible with captioning.

CONCLUSION

Technology and design LibGuides can be used as effective teaching tools if creators are thoughtful about the content. People turn to Google to locate resources but still want to be able to meet in person with an expert when needed. LibGuides can be the connection between the two. Guide content for technology should provide general overviews of how to accomplish the most popular tasks for research and teaching. Guide creators can provide contact information on the guide to allow users to contact creators for follow-up on more in-depth, complex, or unusual questions.

In order to allow users to find our high-quality content, among competing information sources, it is important to increase discoverability. Creating and embedding YouTube-hosted video content and providing well-named and described content is an easy way to increase findability in Google. Users want consistently labeled tabs across guides that contain similar content (e.g., guides related to citation and PDF management), and they want multiple methods of navigation, which we accomplished through the use of tabs and a table of contents on the Home tab.

The decision to include video components into LibGuides should be carefully considered and follow a checklist or series of questions, as described earlier, to assist in scoping video content. Using a checklist or evaluation criteria early on will help immensely when the desire for video content increases. Further, sometimes there is a need for slightly redundant video content as evidenced by our videos on formatting page numbers for dissertations. While Microsoft contains documentation on adding page numbers, there is a lack in documentation on how to easily have separate numbered styles for different sections of a dissertation or other Word documents.

There is a connection between aesthetic design and usability that plays out in following universal design principles in constructing LibGuides, such as chunking information, establishing a visual hierarchy, and being mindful of accessibility considerations. Following best practices for writing for the web and for accessibility will allow your content to be used by people with a variety of learning styles and abilities. Ultimately, doing all of these things will result in better services for our users.

REFERENCES

Beaton, Barbara, Jennifer Bonnet, Suzanne Chapman, Bill Deuber, Shevon Desai, Kat Hagedorn, Julie Piacentine, Karen Reiman-Sendi, and Ken Varnum. 2009. *LibGuides Usability Task Force Guerrilla Testing*. Accessed October 29, 2015. http://www.lib.umich.edu/files/services/usability/libguides_rept_final.pdf.

Educause Learning Initiative. 2012. "Flipped Classroom." In *7 Things You Should Know About*. Accessed October 1, 2015. https://net.educause.edu/ir/library/pdf/ELI7081.pdf.

Lidwell, William, Kritina Holden, Jill Butler, and Kimberly Elam. 2010. *Universal Principles of Design: 125 Ways to Enhance Usability, Influence Perception, Increase Appeal, Make Better Design Decisions, and Teach Through Design*. Beverly, MA: Rockport Publishers.

Nielsen, Jakob. 2008. "How Little Do Users Read?" *Nielsen Norman Group* (blog), May 6. Accessed October 1, 2015. https://www.nngroup.com/articles/how-little-do-users-read/.

Pittsley, Kate, and Sara Memmott. 2012. "Improving Independent Student Navigation of Complex Educational Web Sites: An Analysis of Two Navigation Design Changes in Libguides." *Information Technology and Libraries* 31 (3): 12.

Tawatao, Christine, Rachel Hungerford, Lauren Ray, and Jennifer Ward. 2010. "LibGuides Usability Testing: Customizing a Product to Work for Your Users." University of Washington Research Works Archive. Accessed October 29, 2015. http://hdl.handle.net/1773/17101.

Index

accessible design, 162–69, 222; accessibility checkers, 142–43; accessible content, 85; of banner images, 144; best practices, 145–53; and bread-crumb navigation, 144–45; captioning embedded videos, 153; for color blindness and low vision, 142; color choices, 85, 98, 112, 116, 122–23, 142–44, 150, 166; compliance with law, 85, 157–60; contrast issues, 143–44, 150; CynthiaSays validator, 142; evaluating for accessible design, 157–59, 170–72; for hearing impairment, 142, 153; in higher education, 160; keyboard navigation for visual impairment, 139–41; and LibGuides CMS options, 144, 145; and mobile-friendly design, 159; screen reader emulators, 140; screen readers for visual impairment, 139–41; Skip Navigation link, 141; standards, 160–61; training on accessibility, 88; and Universal Design for Learning (UDL), 194–96; Voluntary Product Accessibility Templates, 157; W3C Markup Validator, 143; WAVE web accessibility tool, 88; Web Content Accessibility Guidelines (W3C), 160

AChecker accessibility checker, 96

administration. *See* LibGuides administration

Ajax (Asynchronous JavaScript and XML). *See* JavaScript (JS)

ALA. *See* American Library Association

American Library Association (ALA), ii

Americans with Disabilities Act, compliance, 85, 159

APIs (Application Programming Interfaces). *See* LibGuides APIs

A-Z Database List (asset manager, LibGuides version 2), 10, 30; benefits, 35; choosing nonproprietary resources, 36; custom descriptions, 37; functionality and design, 36–38; implementation, 35–38

Best Bets (LibGuides version 2), 30, 32–35, 38, 84–85

Bootstrap CSS Library. *See* Cascading Style Sheets (CSS)

Bootstrap open-source framework, 43–56, 112; breakpoint, 49–50; column and row layout and nesting, 44–48; as foundation for LibGuides CMS, 44–45; grid layout, 44–46; helper classes, 54–55; mobile-first design, 44–46; NavBar options, 49–51; NavBar

About the Editors and Contributors

Aaron W. Dobbs is an associate professor and scholarly communication and electronic resources librarian at Shippensburg University of Pennsylvania. Aaron manages the library website, fully managed in LibGuides, and lives in the future as often as possible. His previous publication and presentation topics include LibGuides, web design, future planning, and library assessment. His current research areas include library assessment and anticipating future users' research skills, needs, and background assumptions. Aaron can be contacted via email at aaron@thelibrarian. org and via Twitter: @awd.

Ryan L. Sittler, PhD, is an associate professor and instructional technology/information literacy librarian at California University of Pennsylvania. He holds a PhD in communications media and instructional technology from Indiana University of Pennsylvania, and his research interests are in information literacy and educational media design for learning and performance improvement. Previous publication topics include instructional technology as it applies to librarians, information literacy teaching and learning, and LibGuides utilization. Ryan can be contacted via email at sittler@calu.edu or via Twitter: @ryanlsittler.

*   *   *

Jennifer W. Bazeley has a BM and an MM in viola performance from the Eastman School of Music and an MLIS from Dominican University in Illinois. She has worked in technical services at the library in the Field Museum in Chicago, the Mason Public Library in Ohio, and the library at the Cincinnati Art Museum. She began working in the Miami University Library in Oxford, Ohio, in November 2009 and is currently interim head of technical services.

Jonathan Bradley, PhD, is the web learning environments application developer at Virginia Tech's Newman Library. Jonathan creates educational technologies and trains faculty and staff in their use, both inside and outside of the library. He is the technical admin for Virginia Tech's LibGuides instance, and most of his previous research has surrounded pedagogy at the university level.

Jaleh Fazelian, MA, MLS, is the head of research, learning, and information at John Carroll University. She received her bachelor and master degrees in historical studies from Southern Illinois University in Edwardsville and her master of library science from Indiana University. Jaleh is an active member and the current president of the Middle East Librarians Association. Her research interests include social media and the Arab Spring, navigating middle management and peer relationships, and using social media for professional development and networking. Jaleh and Melissa Vetter were co-administrators of the Washington University Libraries' LibGuides system from 2008 to 2014.

Elizabeth German is the instructional design librarian at Texas A&M University Libraries in College Station, Texas, where she works to create high quality learning experiences for the Texas A&M community. She previously has been the web services coordinator at the University of Houston and visiting e-scholarship librarian at the University of Illinois. Her previous publication and presentation topics include web design, user analysis, discovery systems, and team development in libraries. Her current research focus is around the idea of the libraries website as a learning system and the relationship between user experience and project management.

Melissa Gomis is the instructional technology librarian at the University of Michigan. She manages an instructional technology facility, which is a consulting and teaching center for faculty, students, and staff across all disciplines. Her work focuses on consulting and teaching citation management and organization, digitizing materials, developing online exhibits, designing and managing web projects, and visual communication and design.

Brighid M. Gonzales is the technology librarian at Our Lady of the Lake University in San Antonio where she manages the library website, electronic databases, and various library systems and technologies, including LibGuides. Her professional interests include web services, library UX, electronic resources, metadata, and digital libraries. Brighid received her BS in communication from the University of Evansville and her MLIS from San Jose State University.

Stephanie Graves is the coordinator for learning and outreach at Texas A&M University Libraries in College Station, Texas. She received her MLIS from the University of Illinois Urbana Champaign. She is active in the American Library Association and the Reference and Users Services Association. Stephanie's research explores the intersection of information literacy, user experience, and emerging technologies. Her publications have appeared in journals such as *Reference Services Review, Journal of Academic Librarianship*, and *Reference and User Services Quarterly*. She is passionate about the library's role in the educational mission of universities.

Melissa Fortson Green is the academic technologies instruction librarian for the University of Alabama Libraries. A librarian, teacher, and technology enthusiast, Melissa provides instructional support for the use of the Libraries' academic software packages. Melissa worked in the disability community before becoming a librarian and embraces technology's potential to foster access and inclusion for all.

Emily Marie King, MSLS, is the digital services librarian at the College of Southern Nevada. She oversees all aspects of the web presence for the College of Southern Nevada's Library Services, including defining web content strategy and administering LibGuides. She has been involved with the initial setup of many content management systems and has transitioned two LibGuides systems from version 1 to version 2. She is passionate about creating positive and intuitive user experiences for all patrons using the library online. Her research interests include content management strategy, creating new learning models that take advantage of emerging technologies, and best practices in designing online environments.

Stefanie Metko, MLIS, is the online learning and education librarian at Virginia Tech University Libraries, which serves both the Blacksburg, Virginia, campus and all extended campus locations across the state. Currently, she coordinates the online learning team at the libraries to include responsibility for scheduling training workshops for LibGuides and collaborating with librarians on the design aspects of LibGuides and other online learning platforms. Her professional interests include program development, online pedagogy, universal design, and creation of digital objects for online learning.

Jennifer J. Natale has an MLIS from Rutgers University, an MS in counseling from Springfield College, and a BS in psychology from the University of Connecticut. She has a background in student affairs and nonprofit administration. She began working at Miami University Libraries in November 2013 and is currently a public services librarian.

Lauren Pressley is the director of the University of Washington Tacoma Library and an associate dean of the UW Libraries. Her professional interests include strategic planning, formal and informal learning, the evolving information environment, and the future of libraries, which has led to her involvement in LibGuides projects at every library she has worked in. Her current research focuses on organizational change, person-centered leadership, and the use of learning theory across the organization.

Lucinda Rush, MLIS, MME, is the education reference librarian at Old Dominion University in Norfolk, Virginia. Prior to becoming a librarian, Lucinda taught music to middle school students for ten years. Her previous publications and presentation topics include incorporating games into teaching and learning, bridging the gap between SNS and education, and best practices for creating and incorporating videos into information literacy programming.

Kimberly Shotick is the eLearning librarian and reference coordinator at Northeastern Illinois University (NEIU) in Chicago. Kimberly's research interests include online learning, critical information literacy, and community informatics. She holds an MLIS from the University of Illinois Urbana–Champaign and her MA from NEIU. She presented at the Association of College and Research Libraries 2015 conference, along with other NEIU librarians, on creating a suite of sustainable information literacy tutorials.

Danielle Skaggs is the eLearning and outreach librarian at West Chester University of Pennsylvania. She manages the library website and LibGuides, which are separate (for now). Beyond improving the library's online presence, Danielle is interested in social media, the research needs of distance students, and improving her graphic design skills.

Aida Marissa Smith, MLIS, has served as the LibGuides site administrator at the American Public University System Library, an online academic library, for more than six years. She has worked with library management and librarians, in a completely virtual setting, to implement LibGuides v1, upgrade to LibGuides CMS, migrate to LibGuides v2, and implement a LibGuides content management strategy. Smith is also the library liaison to the university's nursing, health information management, and sociology programs.

Elizabeth Sullivan has an MLS from State University of New York at Buffalo with a BA in psychology and a BA in theology, both from Quincy University in Illinois. She has worked in public and corporate libraries prior to joining Miami University Libraries in November 2008 as the psychology librarian.

Paul Thompson is the web development specialist for University Libraries at the University of Akron in sunny/warm/cold/snowy/rainy Akron, Ohio. He manages the library's web presence, integrating several systems including LibGuides and LibCal, dotCMS, and WordPress. He fully embraces his inner geek and loves to read and write science fiction in his spare time. Paul and his wife live in space graciously on loan from their two dogs, Lucy and Linus.

Christine Tobias, MLIS, is the head of user experience at Michigan State University Libraries. In addition to managing and participating in user experience and assessment projects, Christine is also an administrator of LibGuides and works with campus partners on wayfinding solutions. Her previous publication and presentation topics include LibGuides (LGv1), virtual reference, distance library services, organizational management, and library assessment. Her research interests include library assessment, wayfinding, and space studies with a focus on user behavior in intentional, informal learning spaces.

Melissa Vetter, MSLIS, is head of research services and psychology subject librarian at Washington University in St. Louis. She received her Master of Library Science degree from the University of Illinois at Urbana–Champaign. Melissa has been an administrator of her institution's LibGuides system since all library subject and course guides were moved onto the new platform in 2008. Her research interests included a focus on library services to graduate students, structuring a new model to guide the services and functions of subject librarians, and ways in which libraries can engage undergraduates and meet their needs for community building. Melissa and Jaleh Hazelian were co-administrators of the Washington University Libraries' LibGuides system from 2008 to 2014.

Joshua Welker, MISLT, is the information technology librarian at the University of Central Missouri. He administers the library's online platforms like LibGuides and databases. Additionally, he manages the library's technology infrastructure.